INTRODUCTION

TO THE

STUDY and PRACTICE OF LAW

IN A NUTSHELL

FOURTH EDITION

By

KENNEY F. HEGLAND
James E. Rogers Professor of Law
University of Arizona

THOMSON
™
WEST

Mat # 40149443

West Group has created this publication to provide you with accurate and authoritative information concerning the subject matter covered. However, this publication was not necessarily prepared by persons licensed to practice law in a particular jurisdiction. West Group is not engaged in rendering legal or other professional advice, and this publication is not a substitute for the advice of an attorney. If you require legal or other expert advice, you should seek the services of a competent attorney or other professional.

TEXT IS PRINTED ON 10% POST CONSUMER RECYCLED PAPER

To lawyers:

In good times, great jokes;
In bad times, great friends.

*

PREFACE

This book is in its fourth edition; it's gotta be pretty good by now. Over the years it has introduced thousands of law students to the mysteries and joys of law school; it has made them better students and hence, down the road, better lawyers. I'm thrilled and I'm humbled.

Now it's your turn. About to embark on a great journey, you'll have hopes, dreams, and fears.

"Is law school right for me? How will I do? Will I be happy? Do I have to read the *whole* book?"

No matter how lofty our dreams we live in the present moment. No, you don't have to read the whole book, at least not now. A crib sheet follows.

Even if you are not committed to a life in law, this book might be of interest. Law affects our lives as no other institution. It reflects the great philosophical questions concerning the nature of justice, the allocation of power, and the ability of language to capture our thoughts and control our actions. This book will give you an insider's view of the training of lawyers and the operation of the common law. You will get a sense of how lawyers argue appeals and how they try lawsuits. You will grapple with some of the ethical problems lawyers face and learn something of what they do all day. In short you will end with a working knowledge of law and of the profession.

This isn't a kick-back, underline and nod-off kind of book. You'll throw pots. I'll give you cases to analyze, exams to take, writing exercises to do, and law memos to critique. Resist the temptation to skip these activities. They will put you in good stead in your legal studies. You won't get much feedback in law school. Often the first thing you turn in is the final exam. Get muddy now. While you won't get individual feedback, my discussion of common mistakes and suggestions for improvement will come close to it.

Here's the crib sheet.

The first *eighty-six* pages are essential. Read them, even reread them, as soon as you can. You will get a good sense of legal analysis and the goals and methods of legal education. Your next priority will be chapters Seven through Fourteen; they offer valuable insights into studying law. Next I recommend reading the chapters on legal writing and oral argument (Part Four) as they will deepen your appreciation of legal analysis and of legal expression. Part Three, walking you through a jury trial, and Part Five, on career options, can wait until later in the first semester.

Eighty-six pages are not too much to begin a career. No excuses.

Now a more detailed overview of the book.

Prologue: The best of schools, the worst of schools

What are the goals of legal education? How do the methods of legal education relate to what lawyers actually do? It is fair to say that generations of law students have graduated without a clue. I did. You don't have to.

Part One: Legal Analysis Made Simple

This is the heart of the entire matter. Working on your very first case, you will learn how our common law system works and you will begin "thinking like a lawyer." You will be able to hit the street running.

Part Two: Study Skills

Legal study is unlike other kinds of academic study. It stresses application over memorization. Here you will learn how to read appellate cases, how to brief them, and how to take law exams. There are examples and exercises. Of course, law school is stressful. This part closes with a chapter on "Fear and Loathing in the First Year."

Part Three: Litigation

This Part is kick-back and read. It walks you through a typical lawsuit, from late night television advertising to closing argument. You'll see a Complaint, read parts of a deposition, hear jury instructions, and finally visualize yourself waxing poetic, bringing tears from the jurors and a knowing nod from the judge. This will help you better understand your first year course on Civil Procedure, and, seeing how legal doctrine plays out in trial, it will deepen your understanding of law.

This Part gives you a good understanding of how courts, as opposed to philosophers and scientists, attempt to answer the question, *"What is the truth?"*

Part Four: Legal Writing and Oral Advocacy

Become a student of legal expression. Lawyers write letters, memos, and briefs. They make oral arguments. The chapters on legal writing can supplement your writing course and the chapters on oral argument will help in Moot Court. However, independent of those activities, read chapters 19 through 22 on writing and chapter 24 on oral argument. They are important.

Part Five: Finishing School and Beginning a Career

Many come to law school without a clear idea of what they will do after graduation. That is probably a good thing as even the best of plans change. The last two chapters of this book, which should be read sometime during your first year, will introduce you to the vast range of available options and give you some ideas on things to do during law school to see which might be right for you. One chapter describes the options in terms of variables such as working with people versus working with ideas, contentiousness and *esprit de corps*. The next is a series of short pieces by lawyers doing various kinds of law jobs. Of course, before you begin your career, you will need to get by the last two years of law school. The first chapter of this part tells you how to get the most out of those years and includes a short history of American legal education.

———

Over the years this book has gone through countless drafts, edits, and discussions. I have been lucky enough to know so many insightful people who have generously shared their time, their questions, and their good ideas.

First my students, at Arizona, Harvard and U.C.L.A. Their tough questions (and blank stares) have forced me time and again to think more deeply about matters I thought I understood.

For this edition I want to particularly thank Eric Beane, a wonderful editor, and Nathan Gross, a gifted actor who offered many insights into his art. Anita Simons was very helpful in terms of research and Sandy Davis showed great patience in preparing the manuscript. Many of my current students provided valuable feedback: Kevin Bray, Kevin Chen, Janis Gallego, Sharolyne Griffiths, Cheri Hatanaka, Ana Himelic, Katie Hoole, Jessica Post, Kathleen Rapp, Sheila Schaeffer, Timea Shaeffer, Andy Stevenson, and Melissa Stuebner

Other folks helped on this or previous editions: Charles Ares, Stanley Feldman, Anna Medico-Stevens, Amy Wilkens, Laura McKinny, Mohyeddin Abdulaziz, Barbara Atwood, Bill Boyd, Dan Dobbs,

Carol Eliot, Jamie Ratner, Toni Massaro, Suzanne Rabe, Andy Silverman, Karen Waterman, David Wexler and Winton Woods. At one point, Kay Kavanagh read the entire manuscript, made great suggestions and was marvelously supportive.

My sister, Sherina Cadmun played the tough, constructive critic. My parents, Edwina Kenney and "Heg", taught me so much about writing. Thanks also to George Gross, who not only helped with this draft but taught me, long ago, the joys of writing (but not, alas, the difference between "that" and "which). My sons, Robert, Alex, Caleb, and Ben have all helped, as did, most of all, Barbara.

Excerpts from Scott Turow, *One L.*, reprinted with permission of G. G. Putman's Sons.

Finally, my two dear friends at U.C.L.A., Professors David Binder and Paul Bergman. In their wonderful books, they have always acknowledged the considerable intellectual debts they owe me. For example, in their recent *Lawyers as Counselors*, they admitted that my insightful suggestions were the core of the book's Chapter 23. The book runs twenty-two chapters. As Jack Benny once responded to such a humorless gag:

"You wouldn't dare talk to me like that if my writers were here."

OUTLINE

Law School: The best of schools,
the worst of schools.

Part One: Legal Analysis Made Simple

Chapter

Analyzing and distinguishing cases, dealing with cases of first impression and
an opportunity to practice lawyering.

Legal argument as ping pong; on overruling prior cases and the appearance of
permanence; and two more opportunities to practice.

Looking for underlying principles to
explain the bloomin' confusion of case
law; making law respectable by calling
it a "science." And yet another opportunity to practice.

Part Two: Study Skills

Part Three: Litigation

*

INTRODUCTION
TO THE
STUDY and PRACTICE OF LAW
IN A NUTSHELL
FOURTH EDITION

*

PROLOGUE
LAW SCHOOL

It is the best of schools; it is the worst of schools.

And it won't be the same old stuff.

As an undergraduate you sat and took notes while the professor lectured. You left, often inspired, occasionally depressed, but with the feeling that your life had advanced, that you had actually *learned* something, such as:

"Sartre believed that essence precedes existence" (or vice versa—I'll look it up for the final).

"The Second Law of Thermodynamics suggests that entropy (a measure of disorder) will continue to increase until the universe becomes a mush of completely undifferentiated chaos."

"Sartre, had he known of the Second Law of Thermodynamics, would have been even more depressed."

Naturally, when you get to law school, you expect to go to class, sit back and *learn* the law.

"Murder is the unlawful killing of a human being."

"Minors don't have contractual capacity."

"Torts are not English muffins."

1

It is not to be. Law professors seldom lecture, rehashing last night's Chapter 22 and offering additional insights to be noted and memorized. In fact, in law school you don't read chapters at all; you read "cases." What's a case?

When a court case is appealed to a higher court, such as a state supreme court or the United States Supreme Court, the appellate judges decide the matter and then write an *opinion* justifying their decision. Opinions generally begin by reciting the facts of the controversy then move on to discuss, and resolve, the legal issues raised by those facts. These opinions are the cases you will read in order to get ready for class.

When you get to class, professors will assume you have a fairly good grasp of the cases assigned for that day; their job is to put you to work, using the cases as starting points. You don't passively mull over interesting points; with your classmates, you actively analyze the cases you have read, testing their coherence, exposing their assumptions, and pondering their implications: "Let's change the facts of the case and see if it comes out the same way."

Classes are never boring, but they can be exhausting and confusing.

Often you leave class convinced that you lost ground: "Before class, I worked real hard on that first case and finally learned what 'murder' is. I felt good about myself. Then came class—people to the left of me, people to the right of me ... getting called on ... and questions, questions, questions.

Never any answers! Just confusion. When the person next to me answered, was she right or wrong? The professor only turned and called on someone else. What was the professor getting at? I no longer know what murder is.... Frankly, I don't think I even know what a human being is, much less an English muffin."

Preparing for class isn't a cakewalk either. You don't skim text looking for central ideas, nor do you sit long hours attempting to memorize key points. In law school you struggle with the ideas—expect, at first, to be whipped by a two-page case.

You think that's hype? Okay, try out this case; it's only a paragraph:

Nichols v. Raynbred

Nichols brought an assumpsit against Raynbred, declaring that in consideration, that Nichols promised to deliver the defendant to his own use a cow, the defendant promised to deliver him 50 shillings: adjudged for the plaintiff in both Counts, that the plaintiff need not to aver the delivery of the cow, because it is a promise for a promise. Note here the promises must be at one instant, for else they will be both nuda pactum.

That's the entire case.

Yes, it does has something to do with a cow. Good for you.

Stop trying to figure it out. It drives seasoned law students bonkers. But I have given it to you to illustrate an important point.

Much of your first year is not (optimistically) "learning how to think like a lawyer" nor (pessimistically) exposing yourself as the simpleton you know, deep down, you are. Much of the first year is simply vocabulary building, just like grade school:

"Marie, stand up and spell 'assumpsit.' "

"Good. Now Tommie, use 'assumpsit' in a sentence."

Don't beat yourself when you find yourself bewildered the first several weeks. You are not dumb; you just speak the wrong language. Picture yourself on a Greek island, in a crowded restaurant. People are talking, apparently about events of great moment, and you don't understand a word.

"Oh, no ... I'm an idiot. I should never have come. I'm going to flunk out of Greece."

Law exams are different, too. You won't be asked to recite what you have learned ("Define murder.") nor will you be given broad essay questions such as, "Is Law Just?" Law exams will require you to apply the law you have learned to new situations. You will be given little short stories filled with the stuff of human conflict: neighbors arguing over the location of a fence, business people arguing over the meaning a contract, and criminal defendants claiming "The Devil made me do it." It will be your job to "discuss" the case. What legal issues does it raise? What factors might a court use to resolve them? This is, by the way, exactly what lawyers do in real life.

Law exams are great fun to *take*, and you will be surprised at how much you have learned and how competent you are becoming. (Admittedly, law exams, particularly in the wee hours, are not great fun to *worry* about.)

The differences you are to encounter in law school are bewildering, threatening, challenging and exhilarating. It is the worst of schools; it is the best of schools.

You will read of real murders, of real scoundrels and of real heroes: of five-year-olds who pull chairs out from their aged aunts, of neighbors who fight over water wells, of New York executives who manipulate stock prices, of old fogies cutting off ungrateful kids (hopefully, the chair pranksters) and of lawyers standing tall in the fight against injustice. And you will share this dizzy ride through human experience with marvelous classmates and professors, folks with different lives and different outlooks. Like you, they are bright and challenging.

You will learn to read carefully—more carefully than ever before—and you will become sensitive to the ambiguities of language (almost to the point of losing old friends, friends who prefer the familiar sloth, their *"Can* you pass the salt?" to your *"Will* you pass the salt *to me?"*) You will come to suspect the rush to judgment (it seems there is nothing so sweet to humans as condemning others on the basis of third-hand gossip, overheard in crowded lunch rooms). You will come to appreciate that even the most despised among us have things that can be

said on their behalf. In fact, you will get so good at
seeing the other side that eventually you'll have a
hard time even getting mad at the plumber (all to
the chagrin of your friends and family).

You'll learn how to think "like a lawyer." A good
definition of this kind of reasoning came from the
late Paul Freund, the legendary Constitutional Law
scholar at Harvard. He said it was simply "*Yes,
but....*" reasoning. It contrasts sharply with our
traditional form of reasoning, honed on countless
playgrounds:

"Is so!"

"Is not!"

"Is so!"

"Is not, and I'm telling!"

Lawyers must make very difficult decisions.
These decisions have costs. All will involve some
negative consequences, and all will entail some compromise with principles. Rather than denying these
consequences and compromises (Not so! Not so!), a
lawyer acknowledges them: "*Yes,* all of that is true,
but there are other considerations." Throughout
this book I will stress "Yes, but" reasoning because
it forces you to consider both sides; ideally your
little voice will say it pretty all the time: "*Yes,* that
is a good point, *but* it does create problems down
the road."

Finally, and thrillingly, you will debate things
that *matter.* You will grapple with the problems of
free will and autonomy; with the quest to predict

and control the future (the stuff of Greek tragedy); with the nature of knowledge and the precision of language; with the deep human need to have rules and with the deep human need to be free of rules; with questions of justice and fairness and economic efficiency; and, at the end of the day, with the question that motivates all the others: what should we *do* in this particular case? Will *this* accident victim recover? Will *this* contract be enforced? Will *this* defendant walk free?

Law, and law students, muck around in the wonderful chaos of human existence.

Exciting stuff. It is the best of schools!

Welcome.

All good law schools are alike. Go to any law school in the country, and, once inside, you could be anywhere. Same cases, same books, same questions, and, thankfully, same Nutshells. This uniformity should comfort those who didn't get into their "first choice"; it should (but probably won't) humble those who did. But this is not a book of therapy.

Almost all law classes employ the "Socratic method," where students read cases before class and, under the questioning of the professor, extract from those cases the relevant rules of law. This is a very cumbersome way of getting at them. Wouldn't it be a whole lot easier to assign a text that simply comes out and tells you what you need to know, that, for example, torts are not English muffins? In short, what does the case method of legal education, the daily exhausting struggle, have to do with the practice of law?

Everything!

Day in, day out, trying murder cases, negotiating widget contracts, and counseling divorce clients, lawyers focus on the *interplay of law and fact*. Legal rules gain meaning only in relation to specific factual patterns. Conversely, the facts of a given dispute are only relevant to the degree that they trigger the application of specific legal rules. Staying up late struggling to understand the assigned cases, being battered around in the class with new fact patterns and competing legal rules, you are focusing on the interplay of law and fact, learning how to apply legal principles to the new situations and how to evaluate the legal significance of various real life events. In short, you are lawyering.

First year students get very uneasy about all of this. So, fine, but what is, when all is said and done, a tort? What is true about legal education is that, in twenty or thirty years, you will remember much of what you learned in your first year Property course, long after Sarte and the Second Law of Thermodynamics have become mere names. The reason this is so is that you will be asked to *apply* knowledge, not merely retain it. William James, a founder of modern psychology, taught that memory involves both retention and retrieval and that retrieval is improved as more paths leading to it are created. In his *Psychology: The Basic Course,* he warns of the shortcomings of cramming:

Speedy oblivion is the almost inevitable fate of all that is committed to memory in this simple way. Whereas, on the contrary, the same materials taken in gradually, day after day, recurring in different contexts, considered in various relations, associated with other external incidents, and repeatedly reflected on, grow into such a system, form such connections with the rest of the mind's fabric, lie open to so many paths of approach, that they remain permanent possessions. This is the intellectual reason why habits of continuous application should be enforced in educational establishments.

Here we are into continuous application. You will learn what a tort is at a level that will be with you when you need it, in perhaps twenty or thirty years.

The uniformity of American legal education means something else as well. All lawyers have gone through what you are about to. I don't care if your hero is Earl Warren, William Rehnquist, Thurgood Marshall, or Sandra Day O'Connor; I don't care if your hero prosecutes vicious criminals or defends the downtrodden; I don't care if your hero advises the President or advertises on the Late Show.

All of them once sat where you will sit; all of them read many of the cases you will read; all of them occasionally cursed the profs; all of them longed for clear rules; and, ultimately, all of them realized, "By Jove, I think I've got it ... really got it!"

You are now one of them; you are now part of a great tradition. And, despite all the jokes and calls for reform, it is a great tradition: that our country is as free and open as it is reflects in significant part the hard and often gutsy work of lawyers and judges. Don't you forget it! And don't forget to do it.

And don't forget one other thing. You have come to law school to become a lawyer. In the hurly-burly of law school, it is possible to get distracted and come to think that what matters most is being a successful law *student*. Some students, not getting the grades they wished for, grow despondent. Don't. You are here to be a lawyer. Even if you get straight C's, you can still become a great lawyer. The harder you work, the better you will be.

From now on it is no longer about you and how well you do; from now on it is about your clients and how well you will do for them.

Let's get to work.

PART ONE

LEGAL ANALYSIS MADE SIMPLE

Students complain that professors "hide the ball."

Here *is* the ball. Legal analysis.

Chapter 1 puts you in the position of a lawyer and gives you your first case. Working through it, you will consider the three questions that lie at the heart of our common law system: Should judges follow the rules announced in prior cases? Assuming they should, how does the system work? Finally, if there are no prior cases, how do judges decide?

Chapter 2 shows you how "cases" come to be and describes how judicial opinions are written. This will help you read cases for class. You will have the opportunity to practice an important lawyering skill: *arguing* and *distinguishing* cases. You will do a lot of this in your classes.

Chapter 3 describes the mechanics of *stare decisis* (the fancy name for following precedent). We will also look at *case synthesis*. While *case analysis* takes cases apart, *case synthesis* is the process of taking two or more cases and trying to find a rule that explains what at first may look like inconsistent

11

results. We'll see how this works and note that it responds to the deep human need to impose order on an unruly universe.

Chapter 4 looks at "cases of first impression" (those where there is no controlling prior authority). Chapter 5 discusses a key lawyering skill, interpreting language, here in the context of statutory construction. Does "No Vehicles in the Park" include Big Wheels?

Chapter 6 extends our discussion of precedent. I'll briefly introduce some competing schools of legal thought: legal formalism, legal realism, critical legal studies and the law and economics movement. These great debates inform how law is taught. I'll also discuss a central problem in law: the general and the specific.

Read this part now. It may not be as simple as advertised, law isn't, but it will be quite helpful in the storms that surely shall come.

CHAPTER 1

YOUR VERY FIRST CASE

There is only one game worth playing: the "Second–Case-in-the-World Game." It is the key to your legal education.

(There you have it, you have learned something profound in the very first paragraph! You're going to love this book.)

"Is it enough for us to know that the Second–Case-in-the-World *is* the only game worth playing or must we know *why* it is the only game worth playing?" Alas, a typical student question.

Alas, a typical professorial response:

"Knowing *why* is knowing *what.*"

("Wow, an incomprehensible, Zen-like sentence on the first page! This is gonna be great!")

The *what* of your legal education is the "law," such as the rule that minors don't have contractual capacity. Why is that? Grappling with why the law provides what it does teaches you what it is. Thus knowing why is knowing what.

But enough of riddles. Let's meet your first client.

Ms. K. sustained grave personal injuries when she tripped on a common stairway in her apart-

ment house. Inspection showed that the stairway was negligently maintained by her landlord: a step was defective.

This looks pretty good, exactly what you came to law school to do, help injured clients be compensated for injuries suffered at the hands of negligent landlords. But wait, there is an eegads! In the lease Ms. K signed, you find:

Tenant agrees and warrants that Tenant shall not bring any action against Landlord for negligently maintaining any common areas of the apartment house, including common stairs.

This is known as an "exculpatory clause" and, unless you can figure out how to get the judge to throw it out, it is bad news for Ms. K. The good news is that you remember from law school that judges can refuse to enforce contract terms if they are found to be against "public policy." The bad news is that you find a case that goes against your position.

Globe v. Credit Bureau

Scrooge, Chief Justice. Plaintiff Globe hired defendant Credit Bureau to run a credit check on a man named Jones who wished to borrow money from plaintiff. Due to defendant's neglect, it failed to find a mortgage that was on Jones' property; it reported that Jones had good credit. Had it found the outstanding mortgage, it would have labeled Jones a bad credit risk. Based on this favorable yet errone-

ous report, plaintiff lent Jones money that was not repaid.

Plaintiff sued defendant for negligence, arguing, "If it weren't for your negligence, I would not have lent the money, and thus, I would not have lost the money."

Defendant moved to dismiss plaintiff's case based on a clause in the contract between plaintiff and defendant wherein plaintiff agreed not to sue defendant for negligence. In response, plaintiff argued that the agreement not to sue should not be enforced by a court because it would violate public policy to do so.

We reject that argument. We do not believe that exculpatory clauses offend public policy and hence they will be enforced. We stress the importance of freedom of contract. If parties who make contracts cannot agree to limit the extent of liability, it is difficult to see where such a ruling would lead.

Judgment for the defendant.

Your life has become much more complicated. Not only must you figure out how to convince the judge who will hear your case that exculpatory clauses offend public policy and hence should not be enforced, but you must also convince that judge to ignore what Chief Justice Scrooge had to say in the Globe case.

If the case of Ms. K was truly the Second–Case-in-the-World, one argument you could make is that whatever Scrooge had to say has no bearing on the matter; what he had to say is no more important than what your neighbor had to say this morning over coffee. Why should current judges pay attention to what prior judges have ruled? Under our system, they are committed to do so.

Precedent

At the core of our jurisprudence is the concept of *precedent* or *stare decisis*. The root idea is that, in reaching decisions, courts should follow the rules laid down by judges in prior cases. If the first judge ruled, "Negligent drivers should pay, in addition to their victim's medical bills, compensation for their pain and suffering," then, the second judge, when faced with a case of a negligent driver, should apply the same rule and allow compensation for pain and suffering. It would be improper for the judge to say, "Well, I don't think victims should get compensated for pain and suffering, so I'm going to have my own rule and follow it."

Nonetheless, let's back up and consider the matter anew. I want you to argue that the doctrine of precedent should not be followed.

Won't that be a waste of time? The matter is already decided. *But never, not once, assume that the status quo makes sense*, that a group of wise folks sat down and planned things out and that they had "their reasons" and that we live in the best of all possible worlds. A lot of what we live is simply historical accident. Is law school three years because once a lot of professors and lawyers got together and after much study and debate decided three years was the time needed to educate a lawyer properly? No! Law schools are three years because the first law school was three years. That's the long and short of it.

It is only by questioning the "wise lessons of the past" that we can either embrace them or reject them. Learning today's Wisdom, don't just accept it, challenge it. Maybe there are better ways.

One way to challenge the status quo is to envision a different system and then compare it to what we have. To sharpen our inquiry as to whether judges should follow the rules laid down in prior cases, consider an alternative. We could have a system where, when folks got into a dispute, they'd go to the designated Wise One and tell their stories. Then the Wise One would decide, free from the obligation to decide as did other Wise Ones. What would the costs and benefits be of such a system? What are the costs and benefits of a system that requires the Wise One to decide the same way as previous Wise Ones?

Take a few minutes and write out your thoughts. Writing is simply a marvelous way of learning. I will repeat this again and again and again, and some of you might actually try it once, probably sometime in November. I am a man of few illusions. But I know this because I live this: *Writing out your thoughts slows the mind, highlights gaps and inconsistencies, and deepens analysis.*

Always consider counter-arguments. Remember *"Yes, but . . . ."* There are always good points on both sides, and we must test our arguments in the hot fire of competing positions. Finally, think concretely. Legal analysis falters when it gets too abstract. "Precedent: Yes or No?" Examples help. Following past cases is a familiar concept, no doubt employed by your parents ... sometimes ... and no doubt employed by yourself ... sometimes. Take an example from your past. "Last week, faced with the same situation, I did X. Should I do X now, merely because I did X last week?"

Now go ahead and write. Of course, you need not do this. You can keep on reading, confident in the knowledge that eventually I will discuss the issue. When I do, you will learn something ... but realize that the knowledge you get from others is a tad lifeless and dead, something to be memorized and forgotten. The knowledge you develop yourself, is, well, a triumph. Besides, it will be fun to compare answers.

Jotting in the margin is not only permitted but encouraged.

If you can convince your judge to ignore Scrooge on the basis that precedent should not be followed, then you can jump ahead and try to convince the judge that exculpatory clauses violate public policy. But what if you lose your first move? "Nope, I am committed to the doctrine of precedent and Justice Scrooge has said '*We do not believe that exculpatory clauses offend public policy and hence they will be enforced."'*

Is your goose cooked? Think. How might you respond?

Analyzing and Distinguishing Cases

Assume that we decide, as we have, that courts should follow prior cases. Assume now that we have two cases. In Case One, the judge announced Rule X. Under the doctrine of precedent, the judge in Case Two must apply Rule X but *only if* Case Two is sufficiently *like* Case One such that it would make sense to follow the rule of Case One.

As lawyers state the question, "Does Case One (and the rule of law it laid down) *control* Case Two?" This question introduces the art of legal analysis and legal argument. Its importance cannot be overstated; you will spend much of your first year perfecting this skill.

To say a case is *distinguishable* is like saying someone is quoting something out of context.

Take a close look at the facts of *Globe* and compare them with the facts of your case involving Ms. K. Based on these factual differences, you are to argue:

Your Honor, the rule laid down by Scrooge, that exculpatory clauses do not violate public policy, should not apply in this case because Globe is distinguishable in that . . . .

To flesh out your argument you must not only point to factual differences but also indicate why they would matter and why Scrooge, given the facts of Ms. K, would come to a different conclusion. For example, the fact that the plaintiff names are different in the two cases would not alone justify a different outcome.

Go ahead and jot.

Even if you convince your judge that *Globe* is distinguishable, all that means is that she need not follow the rule of that case. You still must convince her that the clause should not be enforced.

Cases of First Impression

Sometimes a judge is faced with a case where there is *no* controlling law and thus must decide it as a matter of *first impression*. This can happen if there have been *no* prior cases ruling on the issue or, if there have been, they are all *distinguishable* and thus do not *control*. (This also assumes that there are no controlling statutes on the subject, but we haven't gotten to statutes yet.)

What kinds of arguments should a judge consider in deciding a matter of first impression? Of course, a judge will want to do justice between the parties. While it is fairly easy to argue that justice is on the side of Ms. K, what would the landlord argue? Put yourself in his shoes. Most people think they are in the right. Why does he?

Another concern of the judge would be to create good law. That is because whatever she decides will become a precedent and must be followed by future judges. Why would it be a good rule to strike exculpatory clauses in apartment house leases? Yes, but what will the landlord say of such a rule? This raises a question that lurks in the shadows of every law school discussion: where should the line fall between *personal autonomy and freedom,* on the one hand, and *the well-being of others and community welfare* on the other?

Jot!

On the Need to See the Relationship Between Arguments

I have asked you to make three separate arguments on behalf of Ms. K.

1. That courts should *not* follow precedent; what Scrooge had to say is no more relevant than what Imus has to say.

2. That *Globe* is distinguishable.

3. That the exculpatory clause in Ms. K's lease violates public policy and should not be enforced.

You must understand not only the various points but also the relationship between them. Legal arguments get complicated. A lawyer (or judicial opinion) may make four basic points. Does the lawyer need to win all four points to win the case? Or will one victorious point carry the day?

To prey upon your math anxiety, let's say a lawyer makes four basic points as to why his client should win. There are several possibilities:

$1 + 2 + 3 + 4$ = VICTORY

> Here the lawyer must prevail on all four points in order to win; lose one and it's back to late-night advertising.

$(1 + 2)$ or $(3 + 4)$ = VICTORY

> Here the lawyer doesn't have to win all the points, only either (1 and 2) *or* (3 and 4).

1 or 2 or 3 or 4 = VICTORY

> Here, Hog Heaven. He wins if he prevails on only one point.

There are several other combinations, such as $(1 + 2 + 3)$ or 4 = VICTORY. In our case, Ms. K makes three points:

1. Precedent shouldn't matter.

2. *Globe* is distinguishable.

3. As a matter of public policy, agreements not to sue should be rejected.

For her to win, fill in the blanks:

1 __ 2 __ 3 = VICTORY

At this point, **STOP!!!** Fill in the blanks and take this last opportunity to write your thoughts on the three topics. In the next chapters, I give you mine.

CHAPTER 2

CASE ANALYSIS

Judicial argument is quite somber and grown-up: the judges fearsome in black, the audience nervous with anticipation, a lawyer opening with "May it please the Court" and, sitting in the corner, a little old bailiff, whispering "Hush."

I like to think of it as Ping–Pong.

One lawyer serves what he thinks will be a winner but his opponent fends it off, returning a crushing forehand which she believes will end the matter, but, with a quick turn of phrase, the first returns a deep one to her backhand, and on and on it goes until finally the judges yell, "Hold, enough!" and then scurry off to discuss and decide the case.

Let's do a play-by-play of the case we considered in the first chapter, *K v. Landlord*:

Landlord: You can't sue me because, in the lease you signed, you promised not to sue me.

Tenant: *Yes,* I made that promise, *but* it should not be enforced because it violates public policy.

Landlord: *Yes,* it might seem to, *but* the court rejected that argument in *Globe.*

Tenant: *Yes,* the court held that such clauses do not violate public policy, *but* the case is distin-

23

guishable because it involved a financial loss and not a personal injury. Second, *Globe* involved a contract signed by two business people, while our case involves a landlord and a tenant.

Landlord: *Granted,* there are factual differences between the two cases; *nonetheless,* the rule of *Globe* should apply, no matter the kind of injuries or the kind of contract, because the *rationale* of the case applies. It stands for the proposition that parties have freedom of contract and can make whatever agreements they please. The court in *Globe* stated, "The parties must be free to make their own contracts, and once the courts start rewriting them, there will be no end in sight."

Tenant: *Yes,* the Court said that, *but* those words were used in a particular factual context. The kinds of injuries do matter. It is one thing to agree not to sue for financial harm, but quite another to agree not to sue for doctors' bills and lost earnings. *True,* there is a great public interest in freedom of contract, *yet* there is also a great public interest in preventing physical injury. Allowing landlords to exempt themselves from liability will encourage them to be negligent, thus leading to more injuries. Further, as to the rationale of *Globe, we agree* that freedom of contract is important, *however* freedom of contract is premised on the notion of equal bargaining power, which assures both sides are making free choices. Who the parties are *does* matter. It is one thing to say that parties of equal bargaining power should be allowed to agree to what they will; it is quite another to allow a strong party to force a weak party into accepting his terms. And that's what we have in this case. Enforcing this term against Ms. K will violate her freedom of contract.

Judge Flintstone: (in desperation) *Hold, enough!*

Now, when lawyers actually argue a case, they don't go back and forth like this. One gets up and makes his argument, then the other gets up and makes hers, with the lawyer going first having a short time for rebuttal. Not to worry—there is a chapter on Legal Argument later. However, it is extremely helpful to think of legal argument as ping-pong because it helps you understand who is making what argument for what purpose.

So what happens after argument? The judges leave, discuss the case, and, probably several months later, a written opinion appears:

K v. Landlord

Flintstone, J. This case involves the validity of an exculpatory clause in an apartment lease where the tenant is suing for personal injuries caused by the alleged neglect of the landlord. **While it is true** *that this court, in* **Globe**, *upheld an exculpatory clause, we note that was in the context of a commercial contract and involved only financial loss.* **Even though** *we quite properly give contracting parties great freedom to fashion their own agreements, and* **despite the fact** *that we are fearful of where voiding such agreements will lead* *us, we feel we must invalidate this agreement. We note that there is inherent unequal bargaining strength between landlords and tenants and that, in this case, the tenant is seeking recovery for personal injuries. A landlord, under traditional doctrine, has a duty to take reasonable steps to keep common areas safe; if we allow landlords to escape this duty by the simple expedient of a standard lease term, physical injuries that could be avoided will not be.*

Note that legal writing is marked by *words of contrast* which you should begin using:

> *On the one hand . . . .*
>
> *Although this is so, that is so.*
>
> *Even though . . . .*
>
> *However . . . .*
>
> *While X is true, so is*

Judges *write down the middle* by collasping the competing arguments. They do not, for example, list all of Ms. K's points in one paragraph and then all of Landlord's in the next. That would be very awkward. It is much better to bring the competing contentions, point by point, together. This is very helpful and, as I will stress throughout this book, when contention meets counter-contention, one's analysis simply gets better: how can I resolve this conflict? Note that the court could have identified who was making which argument:

Landlord *argues that Globe upheld an exculpato-ry clause, and* **Ms. K** *responds that that was in the context of a commercial contract and involved only financial loss.*

This gets awkward itself. To avoid this, don't label:

While it is true *that this court, in* **Globe***, upheld an exculpatory clause, we note that was in the context of a commercial contract and involved only financial loss.*

Writing down the middle is the way to go: rub contention and counter-contention together and force your analysis deeper. In a sense you are res-taging the ping-pong game. Note, however, that you don't have to identify the players.

A funny thing happens when the judges don't identify the players. The case reads as if the judges made it all up themselves. They didn't. Judges are like Gilbert and Sullivan's Ruler of the Queen's Navy: *"And I never thought of thinking for myself at all."*

Every case judges cite, every point they make, they stole from one of the lawyers!

It is well that judges rest their decisions on points stolen from the lawyers. This is a manifestation of the adversary system and its commitment to have all positions considered in the heat of battle.

Say that Judge Flintstone decided *K* on the basis of a point not argued by counsel. Assume that K's lawyer argued only the personal injury aspect and did not bring up the matter of unequal bargaining. Now, if Flintstone, on her own, after the case was submitted, thought up that point and decided the case upon it, it would not be fair to the landlord. The landlord would not have had the opportunity to argue against it. And it might lead to a bad decision because, without a test in adversarial fires, we don't really know how good the point actually is.

Yes, but if judges rely *only* on the arguments developed by counsel, injustice can result. What if Ms. K hired a dullard as a lawyer who overlooks key arguments? Should she lose a substantial case simply because she hired an incompetent?

Tough call. Respected judges go both ways on it.

A great device to help you understand a court decision is to *restage the game*. Figure out which party raised which point and why. To get a feel for this, recall that Judge Flintstone mentioned three points in the opinion:

Globe

commercial loss

freedom of contract

Which side brought up *Globe* and why? Which side brought up "commercial loss" and why? Which side argued "freedom of contract" and why? Jot! You have room.

Some beginners answer only the "who brought it up?" question and not the "why?" question. Yes, Ms. K did bring up the matter of "commercial loss." But why?

Was she bringing it up as a knockout blow, one designed to convince the court to hold that the clause should not be enforced? Or did she bring it up only to counter the landlord's contention that the Court should follow the *Globe* case and enforce the provision?

Cases get complicated:

I. Plaintiff's main contention

    A. Defendant's response to defeat that contention

        1. Plaintiff's response to defendant's attack, arguing that defendant's attack in fact falls short.

            a. Defendant's answer to this response, which, if correct, would defeat the response.

Often the judges, in their opinion, will focus solely on the issue raised in (a) and go on at great lengths about it. You may well understand that the judges have decided that the defendant wins point (a) but, without Ping–Ponging, you may not understand how this impacts the ultimate outcome: "If the defendant wins (a), then plaintiff's argument in (1) fails, which means that defendant's argument in (A) is valid, and thus plaintiff's main contention fails."

Admittedly, a professor will seldom ask you, "Which side raised that point? Cited that case? And for what purpose?" So what's the value of replaying the game? Understanding.

Returning to the case of *K v. Landlord*, note that Judge Flintstone *distinguished* the case of *Globe*;

she did not *overrule* it. Judges can do this. Flintstone could have said:

> "The case of *Globe* is simply not well thought-out.
> It is overruled. All exculpatory clauses are invalid
> as being against public policy."

That Flintstone chose not to do this tells us a lot
about our case system.

On Overruling and the Appearance of Permanence

Sometimes courts *overrule* prior cases by admit-
ting that they (or, more likely, their predecessors)
got it wrong. The most famous overruling was in
Brown v. Board of Education, which overruled the
"separate but equal" doctrine of *Plessy v. Ferguson*
and held segregated schools to be unconstitutional.

Once a case is overruled, it can't even come to the
party. *Plessy v. Ferguson* is no longer good law: it
has been overruled. Lawyers cannot use that case in
their legal arguments. Had Flintstone overruled
Globe, the next case would be resolved by looking
only at *K v. Landlord,* with no reference to *Globe.*

Courts are very reluctant to overrule prior decisions. To do so presents a major theoretical problem. Judges, in reaching their decisions, are supposed to follow the law. If law comes from prior
cases, where do they get the law to overturn a case?
In addition, overruling tears at the notion of predictability. How can you ever rely on a case if a
later court can overrule it? Take *Globe.* Even if the

second case was on all fours, indeed involved the same parties and the same contract, a lawyer couldn't confidently advise, "The exculpatory clause will be enforced." The next judge might simply overrule *Globe*.

For these reasons, courts prefer to "distinguish" prior cases.

This preference has an interesting side effect. Law appears to be above history. Had Flintstone overruled *Globe*, we could see that things had changed. The world of *Globe* was likely a world where giants walked the earth and stern judges (Justice Scrooge, before the ghosts) let the chips fall where they might. The world of *K* and Flintstone is likely the world of judges committed less to freedom of contract and more to judicial intervention in the name of fairness. These are radically different worlds, but to read the opinion in *K*, which merely distinguished *Globe*, no one would know it. The seamless web of distinguished cases conceals great changes in society.

Change, of course, is inevitable, except from a vending machine.

Now, because Flintstone distinguished *Globe* rather than overruled it, both cases are still "good" law (when lawyers say something is "good" law they mean the case has not be reversed or, in the case of statutes, repealed; they do not mean they would necessarily take it home for dinner.) So let's take two cases and apply *Globe* and *K*.

An Opportunity to Practice:
Cases Three and Four

Case Three

Assume a statute provides that tenants must be given a 30–day notice before they can be evicted. Joe, a single father earning a low wage, moved into an apartment house with his two children. He signed a lease waiving his right to a 30–day notice. The landlord has brought an eviction action which could not be brought under the statute. The landlord asserts that the protection was waived.

Under *K* and *Globe*, who wins?

Case Four

At a tyrannosaurus riding stable (this gets boring for me too), a rider (a lawyer) is eaten (alas, bringing great joy to the audience). Nonetheless, the lawyer's heirs bring suit based on the owners' negligence (they forgot to feed it). Needless to say, as part of the riding agreement the lawyer signed on that fateful day, there was a clause providing, "Riders cannot sue for negligence."

Under *K* and *Globe*, who wins?

Discussion of Cases

Hopefully, with pencil in hand or with computer running, you took advantage of the two problems to begin to develop your skills in case analysis. If not, it's still not too late.

Both cases raise basically the same issue: will the court enforce the exculpatory clause? Both also raise the issue of whether, to avoid the clause, you need *both* unequal bargaining power and personal injury (as you had in *K v. Landlord*) *or* whether it is enough if you have only one of the two?

Hopefully, when you read the problems and began to think about them, these issues more or less jumped out at you. This illustrates the first of several points I want to make about the exercise.

You learn the law by struggling with it, not by closing your eyes and memorizing it. As you worked your way through *Globe* and *K v. Landlord* you were not trying to learn contract law; you were struggling to understand the cases and why they were decided the way they were. Your knowledge of contract law and your ability to spot contract issues came as *a by-product of that struggle.*

On the other hand, you can leave the driving to someone else. You can buy study aids that tell you such things as:

Exculpatory clauses are enforced in commercial contexts but have been held unenforceable in apartment house leases.

I don't care how many times you underlined that, copied it on flash cards, or put it to music, it would not have helped you when it mattered, when you had to answer the questions.

The second point I want to make about this exercise is the need to focus on the relationship between elements. Is the relationship between unequal bargaining and personal injury an *"and"* relationship or is it an *"or"* relationship? In other words, must there be both unequal bargaining strength *and* personal injury before the court will throw out the exculpatory clause, or is one enough? If it is an *"and"* relationship, then both Joe and the lawyer's heirs would be out of luck. While Joe did not have equal bargaining power, there was no personal injury; while the lawyer suffered personal injury, she had oodles of bargaining power (not only was she a lawyer, but, unlike a tenant who needs a place to live, she did not need to go riding and could therefore easily walk away if she didn't like the contract).

To figure out the relationship between the elements, let's review what Judge Flintstone said in *K v. Landlord*:

> *We note that there is inherent unequal bargaining strength between landlords and tenants and that, in this case, the tenant is seeking recovery for personal injuries. A landlord, under traditional doctrine, has a duty to take reasonable steps to keep common areas safe; if we allow landlords to escape this duty by the simple expedient of a standard lease term, physical injuries that could be avoided will not be.*

This raises my third point. Judges often take the easy way out. In *K v. Landlord*, we had both elements and Judge Flintstone did not have to decide between them. Note that she does not tell us the relationship between the two; she just mentions them and then decides. It will be up to the judges deciding the next cases, like those of Joe and the lawyer's heirs, to decide the issue.

Rather than being faulted for "taking the easy way out," Judge Flintstone could be praised for following the judicial tradition of deciding *only* the case before the court. Because the case had both elements, Judge Flintstone did not have to decide whether one would be enough. We follow prior decisions because we believe that the prior judges thought deeply about them before coming to their decision—because Judge Flintstone did not *have to* decide the issue in *K v. Landlord*, she would not have thought deeply about the issue. Therefore, it was better for her to just keep quiet.

My final point is that legal analysis is more than simply spotting the issues. Issues give you a framework for analysis. To illustrate this, in the case of Joe the tenant, one might write:

> While Joe lacked equal bargaining power, there was no personal injury. *While it is true* that courts have refused to enforce exculpatory clauses if they deny recovery for personal injury, and this is not the case here, *a case might be made* that the requirement to give a 30–day notice before eviction *also* protects public safety in that it allows individuals like Joe to find a

new place to move his family before he is thrown out in the street.

Always remember *"yes, but."* *Yes,* there are no personal injuries here, *but* maybe I can equate the possible harm to Joe with personal injury.

Don't be upset if you didn't "get" this point in your answer. You probably got some that I didn't. In any event, I will have more to say on this subject in later chapters. You will be given another opportunity to practice, and then I will give you model answers to work with.

This has been a long chapter. Goodnight.

CHAPTER 3

CASE SYNTHESIS

In our prior chapter, we tore apart *Globe* and *K v. Landlord*. This is known as *case analysis*. The process of putting two or more cases together is known as *case synthesis*. Expect to do a lot of it during your first year. A casebook will have a couple of cases, usually from different jurisdictions, which face the same general issue but which come to apparently different results.

"Consistent or inconsistent?" the prof will puff.

You will long to make them consistent. There is a deep human need to reduce the "bloomin' confusion" of our world to patterns that we can understand and, eventually, control. We need to understand the apparent randomness of things. If every event in our lives were a specific instance reflecting no underlying cause or theme, we could never learn from our experiences, for there would be nothing to learn. If sickness, floods, and famines had no causes we could understand, we would huddle in our caves fearing vicious and irrational gods (which are an explanation in their own right but not much of one).

William James wrote of "our pleasure at finding that a chaos of facts is the expression of a single underlying fact" and that, in our chaotic world, "each item is the same old friend with a slightly altered dress." He continued:

Who does not feel the charm of thinking that the moon and the apple are, as far as their relation to the earth goes, identical; of knowing respiration and combustion to be one; of understanding that the balloon rises by the same law whereby the stone sinks?

How does a scientist reduce the world's complexity? By finding a "law" that explains apparently different phenomena. An apple falls and the moon circles the earth: at first blush, these seem to be very different kinds of phenomena, but, wait, both are but different manifestations of the law of gravity. How do lawyers reduce complexity? By stating a rule of law that explains what appear to be inconsistent cases.

That science and law are similar is not a fanciful suggestion. In fact, the father of modern American legal education and, in 1870, the first dean of the Harvard Law School, Christopher Columbus Langdell, claimed that law *is* a science. Just as botanists go to botanical gardens to study plants in order to discover the laws of nature, lawyers and law students go to the law library to study judicial opinions to discover the basic principles underlying law. According to the law-as-science thesis, while there may be a great number of cases, careful analysis of them will lead to the realization that they are really specific manifestations of a relatively small number of basic legal principles, with each case then becoming the same old friend, in a slightly altered dress. Once we understand these principles we can predict with great confidence the outcome of cases yet to be conceived.

Let me show you how this works. You will learn in your first-year Contracts class that gift promises are unenforceable. Say I promise to give you $50 tomorrow. If I do, fine, but if I don't, the courts will not enforce my promise. To explain this result, the courts came up with the doctrine of consideration: to be enforceable the person making the promise must "get something" for the promise. For example, if a father asks a stranger to care for his sick adult son and promises to compensate the stranger for his expenses, then the father's promise would be enforceable: he "got something" for it, the care of his son.

But what happens if the father's promise comes *after* the stranger cared for his son? Then the father *"got nothing"* for his promise (the care had already been given) and hence his promise would be unenforceable. This is the case *Mills v. Wyman*, a case you're likely to read in your Contracts class. Wyman, the father, heard that Mills had played the part of a Good Samaritan in caring for his son during his last illness. He wrote Mills promising to pay his expenses but thereafter refused to do so. Mills filed suit.

"My promise," argued the father, "is not enforceable because I got nothing for it. When I made it, Mills had already cared for my son."

At this point, Mills, the Good Samaritan, brought to the court's attention a series of cases where the courts enforced promises even though, like the father, those making the promises had "gotten nothing" for them. The cases were of two types:

Bankruptcy Cases.

1. A owes B $1000 pursuant to a previous transaction.

2. A goes to bankruptcy court and has his debt to B discharged; he is now under no *legal* obligation to pay B.

3. Thereafter, A promises to pay B $1000.

In this kind of case, the courts had enforced A's promise even though he didn't seem to get anything for it (anything that he didn't already have).

Statute of Limitations Cases.

1. A owes B $1000 pursuant to a previous transaction.

2. Under the *Statute of Limitations*, B has only four years in which to file suit on the debt. Thereafter it is barred.

3. B allows the four years to pass without filing suit; A is now under no *legal* obligation to pay B.

4. Thereafter, A promises to pay B $1000.

In this kind of case, the courts had enforced A's promise even though he didn't get anything for it (anything he didn't already have).

Of course, neither of these kinds of cases involved fathers promising to pay for past care of their children. But the theory is that these specific instances (bankruptcy and statute of limitation cases) are simply manifestations of an underlying legal principle, much like the specific instances of orbit of the moon and the fall of an apple are manifestations of the underlying law of gravity. To decide whether to enforce the father's promise, the judge simply finds the underlying legal principle and applies it.

The judge puts on a white coat, assumes a somewhat crazed look, and weird background music comes up: what is the underlying legal principle that explains the Bankruptcy and Statute of Limitations cases? The judge studies the cases and notes that, in both kinds of cases, the person making the promise to pay the debt *once* had a legal obligation to pay it. *Eureka*! The underlying legal principle:

> *Even if the promisor did not get something for the promise, the promise is enforceable if the promisor had a prior legal obligation to pay.*

This principle neatly explains the prior cases: in each the promisor had the required prior legal obligation. Now, if we were to apply this newly discovered legal principle to the case at hand, the father's promise would not be enforced because he did not have a prior legal obligation to pay the Good Samaritan.

But not so fast there! Are we sure we got the right legal principle? The ancient Greeks explained the movement of moons and apples with the notion of indwelling spirits; maybe there is a different principle to explain the Bankruptcy and Statute of Limitations cases. Studying those cases, we could conclude that in all of them the promisor had a *moral* obligation to pay the debt. We could come up with an alternative explanatory legal principle:

Even if the promisor did not get something for the promise, the promise is enforceable if the promisor has a moral obligation to keep it.

If this is the correct explanation of the prior cases, then the father's promise would be enforced because he has a moral obligation to pay the expenses. Obviously, a great deal is at stake in deciding what theory to adopt.

How is the judge to choose ? Sometimes there will be language in the prior cases that points in a certain direction. Judges often include such language to help future judges who will be applying their decision as precedent. For example, in the bankruptcy cases, the judges could have written:

We note that the person who made the promise to pay had a prior legal obligation to do so, and this is critical.

Or they might have written:

We note that the person who made the promise to pay had a prior legal obligation to do so, but we do not think this is critical; it is more important that he had a moral obligation to pay.

Such language points the way. What if there is none? How is the judge to choose? In the next chapter I will review some *good* arguments that can be used, but here, however, is the essential point: the result is not dictated by the "science of law" because the science of law has produced two equally logical explanations of the prior cases. As Oliver Wendell Holmes once wrote:

> *The life of the law has not been logic: it has been experience. The felt necessities of the time, the prevalent moral and political theories, intuitions of public policy, avowed or unconscious, even the prejudices which judges share with their fellow men, have had a good deal more to do than the syllogism in determining the rules by which men should be governed.*

For a fascinating look at how scientists decide between competing scientific theories, see Kuhn's *The Structure of Scientific Revolutions*. His basic argument is that the choice is *not* a scientific one, in that the competing theories usually come out pretty much the same in terms of explaining (and in failing to explain) the observed data. He argues that the choice is often based on aesthetics: on which theory is more elegant and which presents more exciting research possibilities.

Today no one believes law is a science in the sense that all of the cases can be explained by a series of underlying basic principles. Langdell himself might have had his doubts: when he came across a case that he couldn't fit into his scheme, one he couldn't make consistent with other cases, he would simply label that case as "wrong" and move on. No scientist could make this move: "This tree doesn't seem to be growing the way my theory says it should. This tree is wrong."

There are inconsistent cases out there. They raise a host of theoretical problems: just what *is* the law if it can be "X" in California but "Not X" in Arizona? Lawyers, bless them, have a short fuse for theoretical problems; when they come across inconsistent cases, they label "X" the *majority rule* and "Not X" the *minority rule* and then go out for coffee.

In any event, a lot of good lawyering goes into trying to make cases consistent by discovering underlying legal principles, and a lot of good lawyering goes into arguing why one explanatory principle is better than another. It is great intellectual training to try to make cases consistent; work hard at it in your studies. But don't get comatose if you can't. Here is an opportunity to practice.

Let's return to a problem considered in the last chapter. You must decide whether to enforce a term in a residential lease that waives the statutory requirement of 30–day notice before eviction. There are two prior cases:

Globe: enforcing a contract term that prevented a party from being sued for negligence resulting in financial loss.

K v. Landlord: refusing to enforce a contract term that prevented a party from being sued for negligence resulting in personal injury.

On its face *Globe* (exculpatory clauses are *valid*) is inconsistent with *K* (exculpatory clauses are *invalid*). One's an apple falling to earth, the other's the moon orbiting the earth. Take a few moments to try to articulate a legal doctrine that makes them consistent. "*Globe* and *K* seem to be inconsistent with one another, but really they are just different manifestations of one underlying rule, which is...."

I'll give you my answer in a minute. This will be more helpful to you if you stop reading now and try to come up with your own. Jot!

Two alternative theories come to mind that make *Globe* and *K* consistent:

> *Exculpatory clauses are* **valid** *unless they relieve liability for physical injury.*

> or

> *Exculpatory clauses are* **invalid** *unless they relieve liability for financial loss.*

Neat. *Globe* and *K* are no longer specific instances; just as the falling apple and the circling moon are different manifestations of the same underlying physical law, these two cases are different manifestations of the same underlying rule of law. We have explained both cases in that we were able to fashion rules that explain both. Good for us.

Note that, although both rules explain both decisions, they point to radically different outcomes downstream. Under the first rule, most waivers of exculpatory clauses would be valid, and, by analogy, so too would a term waiving statutory notice requirements because they do not trigger physical injury. Under the second, most exculpatory clauses would be invalid, and, by analogy, so would the waiver of the right to receive adequate notice before eviction because it does not involve financial loss. Which is the correct reading of the cases? Again we leave logic and turn to "felt necessities."

Controlling Authorities

Let's clear up some technical matters concerning what we mean by such terms as "controlling authority" and "primary authority."

Several years ago, a juvenile court judge in Florida was asked to decide the right of a surrogate mother to retain custody of her child. Paid to carry the father's baby to term, the surrogate mother changed her mind and wished to keep the child. The father filed an action to gain custody based on her promise to give the child to him and on the fact that he was the biological father. It was the first such case ever, the ultimate case of first impression.

The press wrote as if the trial judge's decision would conclusively establish the respective rights of surrogate mothers nationally and for all time.

Not so.

Under the doctrine of *stare decisis*, courts are *obligated* to follow *only* the law set down by higher courts in their *own* state and those of the United States Supreme Court. These cases are known as *"controlling authority."* Trial courts in, say, Iowa *must* follow the law laid down by the Iowa Supreme Court; they are not obligated to follow the law as laid down by the California Supreme Court or any other state courts. Note that, even in Florida, the judge in the next courtroom could ignore his neighbor's surrogate decision. He would be bound only by the decision of a higher court, a Florida appellate court.

This does not mean the Florida decision would have no impact elsewhere. If a judge were faced with a similar case in Montana, the Florida decision could be cited as *"persuasive"* (as opposed to *"controlling"*) authority. It is significant, but not conclusive, that a judge in Florida came to a particular decision: he spent a lot of time thinking about the issue and what he decided is probably right. There are several sources of "persuasive authority" (things that lawyers can cite to judges in support of their positions). They include decisions from other states, statutes from other states, Restatements, law review articles, and state bar journal articles.

There are two other terms you will come across that may cause confusion: *primary authority* and *secondary authority*. Primary authorities are the cases and statutes themselves; secondary authority is what commentators say about them, perhaps in law reviews or legal reference books.

Finally, in terms of definitions, be aware that lawyers use the word "control" in two different senses, a status sense and an application sense. If we are in a Missouri trial courtroom, all Missouri State Supreme Court decisions "control" legal controversies in that courtroom in the status sense of that word: the trial court judge must follow them if they apply to the case before him. Cases from the Supreme Court of, say, Maine, do not "control" in this status sense; the Missouri trial court judge can ignore them even though they address the exact same issue that he must decide.

All of this is straightforward enough, but lawyers muddy the waters by arguing that a case that clearly controls in the status sense, say a case from the Missouri Supreme Court, does not "control" the particular decision the trial judge must make if that case is "distinguishable." So in our little corner of the world, you can have a "controlling" case which doesn't "control."

But what if there is no controlling authority, no persuasive authority, no secondary authority? In the case of first impression, the judge stands alone on the desolate shore. Is "freedom" just another word for no where else to look?

CHAPTER 4

CASES OF FIRST IMPRESSION

Thus far we have looked at how judges analyze and synthesize prior appellate cases in order to guide their decisions. But what if there are no prior decisions? Indeed, how was the *first* case decided? This presents something of a chicken and egg problem.

In practice, most cases that are appealed are of "first impression" in the sense that there is no prior controlling case (or statute) that is directly on point. If a case or statute clearly stated what rule of law should be applied, then the only argument the losing party would have is that the case should be overruled or, in the case of a statute, that it should be found unconstitutional. Most of the cases you will read are something of a mixed bag, with lawyers arguing and distinguishing "cases" and, in addition, making the kinds of arguments we will review in this chapter:

Arguments based on hypotheticals and analogies

Policy arguments

Slippery slope arguments

We'll see how these work and look at typical responses.

Hypotheticals and Analogies

Hypotheticals are quite popular in legal discourse. Take the case of Ms. K, where the issue is whether the court should refuse to enforce a clause in her lease releasing her landlord from negligence liability. Assume that no court has ever refused to enforce a contract term. The lawyer asking the court to throw out the provision would think of a hypothetical case where a court would do just that. The argument becomes:

> *Your Honor, in the situation I am about to describe, I am sure you will agree that no court would enforce the contract. Well, enforcing the exculpatory clause in this case would be basically the same thing.*

Can you think of a contract, or a provision in one, that a court would *obviously* not enforce? Take your time. I am in no hurry. Jot.

My case of non-enforcement: A six year-old promises to give his allowance, every week, to his big brother. No court is going to enforce that deal.

. Of course, the attorney arguing for enforcement of the term will make up her own hypothetical case, one in which a court would surely enforce the contract, perhaps one signed by two major corporations after months of negotiation by competent lawyers.

Now we have two cases, neither of which happened, but so what? The next step is to decide whether our case, the one involving the exculpatory clause, looks more like the kid's contract or more like that of the corporations.

"Your Honor, this is basically like a case where a six year-old agrees to give up his allowance; that agreement would not be enforced and neither should this one."

"No, Your Honor," replies the other side. "It's more like an agreement between two corporations, one we would surely enforce. You should enforce this one as well."

How do we decide which it is more like? By articulating why the hypothetical cases are easy ones. Why, exactly, is the six year-old case an easy case? Once we understand that, then we can look and see if those reasons (policies) apply to the case at issue.

"We don't enforce kids' contracts because we don't think they know what they are agreeing to. Ms. K didn't know what she was agreeing to because the clause was buried in the lease."

"No," replies the other side. "We don't enforce kids' contracts because we feel that they are not capable of understanding what they are agreeing to. Ms. K, as an adult, surely is capable of knowing what she agreed to; if she didn't take the trouble, that's not our concern."

What we have done is made up easy cases and, by asking ourselves why they are easy, we have, in effect, written the supporting opinion. We have created two new first cases, along with their supporting rationale. Presto! What was the first case now becomes the third, and we land safely on familiar ground.

Neat trick!

As to the chicken/egg quandary, easy. The egg came first and, to explain its existence, created a hypothetical parent, the chicken, and the rest is history. Okay, sure, it might have been the other way around, with the chicken coming first and then creating a hypothetical egg to explain itself. Maybe we still don't know which came first, but at least now we know how they pulled it off.

An Aside On Intuition and Free Radicals

It is often thought that legal analysis and argument are matters of logic but intuition plays a huge role. It is the engine that starts the whole process.

Split-brain research suggests that the two sides of the human brain have different roles. The right side is the intuitive side: it sees relationships, draws pictures, and sings. Unfortunately, it has grunts for words. The left side is organized, logical, and has a brilliant vocabulary: alas, it has nothing much to say, pretty much limited to such things as "Pass the salt."

Split-brain research helps us understand how we think. Prize both your logic and your intuitions.

Facing a new problem, your mind might throw out, "Gee, Ms. K's problem strikes me as the same as that of a six year-old giving away his allowance." This is the brain's right side, grunting. Standing alone, it is a *free radical*. While we may have only the vaguest idea what "free radicals" are, we do know they are bad. In law, free radicals are free-standing "good points" tied to no proposition of law. I knew a very talented lawyer who did prison-reform work. After several years, she quit: "I am sick of trying to make filthy and dangerous jail conditions into 'cruel and unusual punishments.'" But courts have no power to do anything about filthy and dangerous conditions; they can only act to prevent "cruel and unusual punishments." Filthy and dangerous conditions are free radicals; they must be tied to legal requirements.

Free radicals are the product of the right side of our brain. They are often brilliant. In briefs and memos, beginning students just write them down. However, standing alone, they don't make any sense. Other students, realizing that they don't make sense, run away from their free radicals and never mention them. Both approaches are wrong. Your right brain is generally pretty insightful. Neither simply record the grunts nor run away from them: use the left side of your brain to tie your intuitions to legal principles. One device is to ask of them: "So what?"

Intuition is not the solution: it is an invitation to do the hard analysis needed to get to a solution.

Policy Arguments

As a first year law student, one of my biggest shocks came when I was talking with a second year student about his Moot Court and he mentioned he was going to make some policy arguments.

"Policy arguments? You can *do* that?" In my first several months of law school I had somehow picked up the notion that law was pretty mechanical: find the law and apply it. (Alas, this was an era pretty much without Nutshells.) But policy considerations obviously are of critical importance in judicial decisions: those decisions create law and in turn become precedent. Looking ahead, will the decision be good law?

In the chapters on legal argument, I will go into policy arguments in greater detail: where do you find policies and how do you support them? Here I just want to give you a sense of the arguments and of one kind in particular, the Slippery Slope argument.

In the case of Ms. K, the landlord's attorney would no doubt argue for a rule that promises should be enforced because that furthers the policy of freedom of contract. "Ms. K agreed to the term; if you allow her to get out of her agreement, you have reduced her to a child, someone whose decisions we ignore."

There are two ways to meet policy arguments; the first is to come up with your own.

Yes, there is a great public interest in freedom of contract, but there is also a great public interest in preventing physical injury. Allowing landlords to exempt themselves from liability will encourage them to be negligent, thus leading to more injuries.

There is no established pecking order that ranks policies, such as:

Freedom of contract trumps public safety, or

Public safety trumps freedom of contract.

When conflict emerges, the judge will simply have to choose. This is very much like the judicial choice between two competing explanations of a series of prior cases and, indeed, very much like the judicial choice involved in determining whether a prior case controls or is distinguishable.

The second response to a policy argument, and one that is great fun if you can pull it off, is to steal your opponent's argument and turn it around:

Yes, freedom of contract is important, but freedom of contract is premised on the notion of equal bargaining power, which assures both sides are making free choices. To allow a strong party to force a weak party into accepting his terms denies the weaker party freedom of contract.

Note that these arguments have focused on the policy implications of the decision at issue. Another kind of policy argument focuses not so much on the decision itself but on where it might lead. These arguments go by "Slippery Slope," "Opening Floodgates," or, for some reason, "Allowing the Camel's Nose in the Tent." They are so common that they deserve special treatment.

Slippery Slopes

"Your Honor, if you do what my opponent wants you to do, X, which may be a very sensible thing to do, then in the next case the judge will have to do Y, which we all agree would be a bad thing to do, so don't do X."

We saw a slippery slope argument in *Globe*: "If we void this term, then we don't know where we would stop rewriting contracts"). There are *three* responses to slippery slope arguments.

1. Pre-distinguish.

Once you step onto the slope, you need not tumble to the bottom because there are things to grab on your way down. "Your Honor, if you void the exculpatory clause, this will not mean that in the next case you will have to rewrite a *rent term*, as there are obvious distinctions between the two. Exculpatory clauses affect public safety; rent terms do not." What you are doing is inviting the judge to "pre-distinguish" the opinion, thus effectively slamming the door on those poor fools who are paying too much rent.

"We note that our decision merely goes to the narrow issue involving physical injury and would not apply to lease terms not involving such injury."

2. So what?

Another response to the slippery slope argument is that falling all the way down might not be such a bad idea. "Hey, that's not a bad idea. Given that many landlords take advantage of their tenants, courts should rewrite unfair leases."

3. Reverse the slope.

The final possible response to a slippery slope argument is to counter with your own. Whenever a judge is asked to make a decision, he stands on a sharp pinnacle with slippery slopes falling sharply on all sides. *All slippery slope arguments are reversible.*

> *Your Honor, if you enforce this clause because you don't want to get involved in rewriting contracts, then in the next case you will have to enforce a clause which requires the tenant, if one day late, to forfeit her first born.*

Meet slippery slopes with slippery slopes.

The *floodgate* argument is essentially a slippery slope argument.

> *"Your Honor, if you do justice in this case, all manner of ragamuffins will be pounding down your door asking for justice. You might as well kiss your golf game goodbye."*

This argument, although quite popular, has always struck me as curious. One response is that justice isn't such a bad idea. The other, more solicitous to the golf industry, is to suggest to the court that the rule could be drawn quite narrowly so that ragamuffins stay where they belong.

CHAPTER 5

STATUTORY INTERPRETATION

A city ordinance makes it a misdemeanor to "operate a vehicle in a public park." Ben, driving his Big Wheel, which is a fancy tricycle, is busted in the park. Is he guilty?

If you said no, YOU ARE WRONG.

Perhaps you assumed that Ben is probably a toddler and, as such, can't be guilty of a crime. But you must read more closely: Ben's age is not mentioned. More significantly, you probably just assumed a definition of "vehicle," one which included large oil tankers but excluded children's toys. Never assume definitions!

If there is one quote I want you to remember, indeed, if there is one thing I want you to remember, it comes from Robert Bolt's wonderful play, *A Man for All Seasons*. It deals with personal integrity and the importance of law. Why not cut down the laws to get at the Devil?

"And when the last law was down, and the Devil turned round on you—where would you hide, the laws all being flat? ... d'you think you could stand upright in the winds that would blow then?"

Keep this in mind when friends start attacking your career choice and the "technicalities" of the law. As good as that quote is, however, it is not the one I want to stress.

To set the scene, King Henry VIII has broken with the Pope in order to marry Anne Boleyn. He demands, upon the penalty of treason, that all of his subjects take an oath approving of the marriage. Sir Thomas More, a Catholic, disapproves of the marriage. When he first hears of the oath, as a careful lawyer, he entertains the possibility that he can sign it and remain faithful to his beliefs.

More: What is the oath?

Roper: It's about the marriage, sir.

More: But what is the wording?

Roper: We don't need to know the wording—we know what it will mean.

More: It will mean what the words say.

Train yourself to read closely. No more picking up the gist and speeding ahead. "Wait a minute, 'Vehicle.' Can that include Big Wheels?"

Thus far we have been dealing with judicial opinions as sources of law. Statutes are another source of law, and we have two questions:

1. If an irresistible statute meets an immovable judicial opinion, which wins?

2. If a statute is ambiguous, how do we figure out what it means?

Finally, we will discuss the question that may have led you to buy this book in the first place: just what is "an argument that eats Pittsburgh?"

On Statutes and Cases

Both statutes and case law are sources of law—judges must follow controlling statutes and controlling cases. As a general matter, statutes trump: legislatures can overrule the rules laid down in judicial opinions by simply passing a statute, unless the judicial rule rested on the United States Constitution, which trumps everything, or on the state constitution, which trumps state statutes. Judges can throw out statutes *only* if they contravene the Constitution.

To illustrate, if a court said, "Exculpatory clauses in leases are valid," the legislature could change that result by simply passing a statute saying they were void. On the other hand, if the legislature passed a statute saying, "Exculpatory clauses in leases are valid," a court *could not* change that rule unless it found it to be unconstitutional.

Bottom line, in terms of what you want to be when you grow up, if you want to change the world, become a legislator, not a judge. (This sentence entirely ignores the Civil Rights Movement and other great moments in our legal history, but Nutshell Writers have to make tough choices.)

On Statutory Construction

Statutory interpretation is a variation of the Second-Case-in-the-World (*everything* is).

Assume a statute in the following form: "No vehicles in the Park." Ben, age 4, drives his Big Wheel in the Park. Has he violated the statute?

Obviously the question turns on the meaning we attribute to "vehicle." Much of your legal education (and much of your legal practice) will deal with the interpretation of language. You will face the issue in interpreting contracts, statutes, cases and even criminals' confessions. The question is always one of *intent*: when the person or parties used the word in question, what was their intent?

Often you don't have to go any further than the word itself. For example, if Ben's big brother, Caleb, was driving a large gasoline transport truck in the park, there is little doubt that he was running afoul of our rule about "vehicles" in the park. Unfortunately, few of your cases will be that easy. Those cases are never litigated. However every day you will meet situations like the one raised by Ben's Big Wheel, where it is unclear whether the chosen word was intended to cover such a case.

Unless the language has a plain meaning that applies to the case at hand (Caleb's gasoline truck), the first move in interpreting language is to put it in *context*. If "No vehicles in the Park" had been announced in a judicial opinion, we would have the *facts* of the case to help guide us. Did the judges, in using the word "vehicle," intend to cover such things as Big Wheels? If the rule had been announced in the context of a dispute over heavy trucks in the park, then we might conclude that the court, in using the word "vehicle," meant things of that ilk—things that could run people over and things that pollute the air and things that make loud noises. Ben's Big Wheel does none of these things, and hence, the word "vehicle" should not be interpreted to include it.

Note that distinguishing cases required the same process: "Yes, the Court said 'No vehicles in the park,' but that was in the context of discussing heavy trucks. Surely that rule should not be applied to a case involving a Big Wheel; the case is distinguishable."

Further, if the rule "No vehicles in the Park," had been announced in a judicial opinion, we would have the court's *rationale or justification* to help guide us as to meaning. Assume the judges said:

> *"Public safety, noise abatement, and pollution control all require us to prohibit vehicles in the Park."*

We would then have some sense of how the judge was using the word "vehicle" and whether it would include Big Wheels.

Again, the first move in interpreting ambiguous language is to look to the *context* in which the language was used. In the case of judicial opinions, rules are announced in the context of specific facts and asserted rationales. What about statutes? Occasionally it is possible to put a statute into context as an aid to interpretation. For example:

1. Sometimes there will be *legislative history* in which the legislature writes out what it has in mind.

2. Sometimes what appears to be an isolated statute was in fact a part of a larger legislative package. Perhaps "No vehicles in the Park" was part of a "Clean Air Act." If it was, one could argue that, in using "vehicles," the legislature intended only those vehicles that pollute the air.

3. Sometimes statutes amend prior statutes. If the old statute read "No cars or trucks in the park," one could argue that, in substituting the word "vehicle," the legislature intended an inclusive definition.

In your Legal Research class, you will learn how to check out all of these possibilities.

Unfortunately, most statutes come to us as simple declaratory sentences, with no description of the kinds of situations the legislators had in mind in passing the statute (the "facts" in a case) and with no statement of why they adopted the statute. Statutes simply appear, like the ghost of Hamlet's father.

Let's assume all you have is a statute that reads, "No vehicles in the Park." Does it include Ben's Big Wheel? How would we go about analyzing this problem?

We assume that the legislature must have had its reasons in passing such a law, and then we ask ourselves what that reason might have been. Once we have decided upon that reason, we have a context in which to interpret the language.

> *"Your Honor, the legislature must have intended not only to abate noise and pollution in the park, but also to prevent clutter and to protect public safety. A park filled with Big Wheels is not a pleasant place for adults to be, and Big Wheels do in fact present a risk of injury."*

Of course, the opposing lawyer would posit different legislative purposes.

Here too, lawyers put forth *hypotheticals* and *draw analogies*. Let's see how this works. The lawyer would first make up two easy cases: a gasoline transport truck would surely be a "vehicle" within the meaning of the statute, while a child's toy model truck would surely not be. Then the argument would be by analogy:

> *"Your Honor, a Big Wheel is more like a gasoline transport truck than a toy model car for the following reasons...."*

To make these arguments by analogy, we are forced to tease out why our easy cases are in fact easy cases. Why is the gasoline transport case an easy one? Does that reason apply to Big Wheels?

Don't put this entire discussion down as an instance of bad legislative drafting. Let's say the legislature envisioned the problem and passed a statute reading:

No vehicles in the Park, and this includes Big Wheels!

Ben drives his Big Wheel in the Park and gets busted. Easy case? You don't know Ben.

He will argue: "My Big Wheel was *on the road*, not *in the Park* and the purpose of the rule is to prevent damage to grass and flowers. The rule reads '*in* the Park' and not '*on* the road.' The very precision of the rule shows that the legislature was drafting very carefully. Besides, I had only *one* Big Wheel. The rule specifically says 'Big Wheels.' Probably the rule was aimed against vendors or people putting on races. So there!"

Let the legislature throw some more words at the problem; soon we will have an Internal Revenue Code—much too big to fit on a Yellow Sign. Park signs will read:

Warning: Certain rules may or may not apply. Read them!

No matter how carefully language is drafted, a situation will arise that renders the language ambiguous. That is the stuff of life; that is the stuff of law practice.

Turning briefly to a question of political science, it tells us a lot about courts and legislatures that courts must publicly justify their decisions while legislatures just vote. Judges have to write opinions, justifying the rules of law they lay down. This is because judges have limited power. Very few are elected. Their decisions should rest on reason, and that reasoning should be made public in order to prevent possible abuses. Legislators are elected, and if they misuse their power, they can be thrown out of office. Further, political decisions can be irrational as long as they are those of the majority.

Arguments That Eat Pittsburgh

Sometimes a word in a statute will be interpreted in such a fashion that it turns and devours the statute itself. Let's assume a burglary statute that requires, among others things, a "forced entry." Let's further assume a fact pattern where the culprit walked into the house though an open door.

If we were to interpret "forced entry" to include walking into a house, because walking requires "force," we have effectively defined that provision of the statute out of the statute. All entries are now "forced entries," and the requirement vanishes. The response is, "That cannot be a proper interpretation because the legislature, in requiring a *forced entry,* must have wanted to distinguish some kinds of entries from others."

Be sensitive to these kinds of arguments. Would the proposed definition turn upon and consume the rule?

I call these arguments "arguments that eat Pittsburgh." I do not have any good reason to call them that. In fact, I have never been to Pittsburgh. But that kind of argument deserves a name and until you come up with a better one, I'll let mine stand.

CHAPTER 6

THE DOCTRINE OF PRECEDENCE, RULES, STANDARDS, AND JURISPRUDENCE

My first job was with California Rural Legal Assistance, and one of my first clients was a farm worker whose family was cut off welfare because he refused to work raking leaves in a local park. The welfare law provided that recipients could be terminated if they refused to engage in "work-training programs." My theory was that raking leaves was not such a training program: my client knew how to work and worked long and hard when he did; however the season was over, and there was simply no work for him. His family needed food. I appealed his termination and discovered, talking with another lawyer in another poverty law office, that the very same hearing officer who was slated to hear my case had heard an identical case of hers and had written an opinion upholding my contention.

Hog Heaven! "Send me a copy of her opinion."

Several weeks later, near the end of our hearing, I opened my closing argument by reading from her opinion. It was quite elegant. I sensed, however, that she was getting restless: "Where did you get that? What I wrote in *that* case was for the parties to understand my reasoning. It has nothing to do with *this* case!''

Apparently the written decision of welfare hearing officers had no precedential value. Oh well, you can't learn *everything* in law school.

Fast forward to the International Court of Justice, where the governing statute seems to reject the notion of precedent: "the decision of the Court has no binding force except between the parties and in respect to that particular case."

Precedent is not inevitable, but we have it. Why devote a chapter to it?

This chapter will help you as a first-year student because it raises some background jurisprudential concerns. We look at the law's central dilemma (the general versus the specific), introduce some important concepts, such as the differences between rules and standards, and take a quick look at a significant debate: the degree to which law actually controls judges. We'll end with some questions of ethics.

Television to the contrary, most lawyers spend a great deal of time drafting documents, such as employment contracts, franchise agreements, and buy/sell deals. To what degree is it possible to foresee future difficulties? Should you draft with precision, spelling out how possible conflicts should be handled, or should you draft more loosely, counting on the parties to cross that bridge successfully if they have to? This chapter will get you thinking about the choices you and your clients will face.

Following precedent has its costs. First, it makes dispute resolution more expensive. Without a doctrine of precedent, folks would simply go to a judge, cite the controlling law ("Work Training Programs can be required") and make their arguments ("This one isn't one"). There would be little need for lawyers, and there would be no need for the specialized knowledge on how to find and analyze the "prior cases." (There goes Westlaw!)

Second, cases can be wrong; early Supreme Court decisions upheld segregation. If judges were not obligated to follow prior decisions, errors could be *ignored*; under a doctrine of precedent, they must be *corrected*. The common law corrects errors by creating new duties or defenses, by distinguishing bad cases into oblivion, or by overruling them, as in the case of *Brown v. Board of Education*. However, before these bright shining moments, the errors were still good law and, in our celebration of the common law's "working itself pure," we should pause to consider all of the people who suffered due to previous errors, faithfully followed.

Third, to work at all, precedent must work at a general level even though justice may reside in the details. We'll come back to this point, but let's now turn to the justifications *for* the doctrine of precedent.

1. *Predictability*. For people to plan their lives and for lawyers to advise their clients, it is important to know, once and for all, whether

Park Cleaning Projects are proper "Work–Training Programs."

2. *Universalization.* In order to filter out personal biases, the philosopher Immanuel Kant advised us to universalize our decisions: we should do only that which we would have everyone in a similar situation do. The doctrine of precedent works this way and hence helps check judicial abuse.

3. *Correctness.* The strongest case for following prior cases is that they are *right.* Cases could be right in one of two senses: that law in some sense exists "out there" and can be "discovered," or, even if law doesn't exist out there, human reasoning is such that it would lead, after much hard work, to the same conclusion. If either of these possibilities is correct, then it would be a waste of time to litigate issues, because the discovery or conclusion would be the same. If neither of these possibilities is correct, then the case for precedent is weakened, for, as we shall see, the first two justifications are problematic.

Predictability

Precedent promises both predictability and control of judicial whim. Once the first judge rules "Park Cleaning Projects are not legitimate," people can plan their lives without worry that a future judge, perhaps out of racial animus, would rule that they are. Two questions come to mind:

1. If there was not a doctrine of precedent, would judges be all over the lot?

2. Assuming they would be, does precedent deliver on its promise of predictability and control?

"If there were no laws, what would happen?" Young children, asked that question, predict doom: "There would be all kinds of murders and stuff." It has always struck me that this does not reflect early Hobbesianism. I think it reflects something of a self-fulfilling prophecy. Children believe in grown-ups: why would they have laws unless, without them, there would be all kinds of murders? Why would we have a doctrine of precedent unless, without it, judges would be all over the lot?

Say we have ten welfare hearing officers and no doctrine of precedent. If five were to rule that Park Cleaning Projects weren't valid training programs, while five would rule that they were, life becomes something of a crap-shoot. However, if the tally was nine to one, then we would have a fairly predictable system and people could plan their lives around it. Note, as we shall shortly see, the doctrine of precedent does not deliver 100% predictability because controlling cases can be distinguished or overruled. The question is whether precedent delivers more predictability than would a system where judges decided on their own. Again, merely because we have a system of precedent, don't just assume that it does. Think of situations in your own life where you have made, or others have made, decisions without reference to prior decisions. Were they all over the lot?

One's take on this may be more philosophical than empirical. If judges shared basic values or if human reason could lead us to similar conclusions, then we could more confidently leave the judges to their own devices. They would generally come out agreeing, perhaps even 9 to 1. However, if values and rationality are subjective, arbitrary, and individualistic, then allowing judges to make decisions in a vacuum would create chaos: 5 to 5. We'll return to this issue in a moment.

The more common critique of precedent is not that it is not needed, but that it doesn't deliver. Cases can be distinguished and statutes interpreted. Is there so much play that the system really doesn't control judges at all, that they can always make it come out the way they want to? If so, then the whole house of cards comes crashing down: *stare decisis* cannot deliver on its promise of predictability (or on its promise to control arbitrary decision-making by judges).

Law professors in the "Critical Studies Legal Movement," known more affectionately as *Crits* (not to be confused with the street gang), write law review articles asserting that judicial rules are a sham. Take the Constitutional requirement that the President must be at least 35 years old, a clear rule if there ever was one. Not so, claim the Crits.

If a judge wanted to validate the election of a teenager, he could rely on the well-known theory of statutory interpretation: statutes should be interpreted in light of their purpose. The purpose of the age requirement, he would opine, was to ensure the President was well-educated and mature, and this teen candidate is both. As to plain language in the Constitution, the judge could turn to the theory of literary interpretation known as *deconstructionism,* which suggests that the meaning of a text resides in the reader and that all readings are equally valid. The good news of this theory is that you need to buy only one book, sometimes reading it as *Huck Finn*, and other times reading it as *Cases and Materials on Civil Procedure.*

As a quick aside, the substantive argument of the Crits is that law oppresses minorities and women and that it justifies illegitimate hierarchies. While Crits long for the 1960s, the other major intellectual movement pines for the 1870s. The "Law and Economics Movement" looks at the effect of legal rules on the market and tries to figure out what rules are most efficient. At some point, you will get caught up in these debates whether you know it or not: your professors are involved and that will affect their takes on law.

Many students, sometime in the first semester, become closet Crits: "Now that I understand it, it's a sham; judges do what they want." Four things to consider: First, casebooks have only close, difficult cases, those which are bound to be the most uncertain. A word to the wise: if a teenager asks you whether he or she can run for President, say "no."

Second, the judges I have talked with feel bound to decide matters in ways they don't necessarily want to. Third, the debate assumes that judges have overriding political or moral values that they are just itching to impose on us. More likely, they just want to go home to dinner. Few legal contests are about whether one should stay home to care for one's aging mother or leave her alone to go off and join the underground to fight the Nazis. Most legal contests are about rather mundane disputes, such as which side of the road to drive on. Judges will turn to prior cases to decide them and then go home. They will not stay up all night figuring out how to attack those cases, writing tenure pieces on how recent advances in relativity theory have rendered the notion of "the right side of the road" meaningless.

But let's assume that there is a lot of play in the system and that prior cases seldom dictate specific outcomes. Does this make it a sham? *Legal Realism*, a movement started in the 1920s, argued that there was vastly more to judicial decisions than simply logic. It was a reaction to the conservative bent of the then-prevailing view of law, *Legal Formalism*. Formalists contended that prior cases logically compelled certain outcomes (usually conservative ones). A typical legal realist law review article would line up cases pointing in different directions and thus conclude that there was more to judging than logically applying prior cases. Professor Llewellyn, whom you will probably meet in your first-year readings, was a leading realist. His take on precedent is worth noting. Even though a prior case was not determinative, it can contain "good and shrewd judicial discussion of useful criteria to use—persuasive, too, I suggest, to any court to which it might be quoted—*because it helps*."

If I were a judge faced with a difficult issue, it would help me to read what other judges have said.

Legal uncertainty, however, remains a problem. When the common law system was young, there weren't that many cases, and the system worked. When you have hundreds, it starts to break down. A diligent researcher could find, somewhere, a case standing for about any possible proposition. To help solve that problem the *Restatement Movement* was started. Groups of law professors and leading practitioners would sit down to distill the common law rules, add their own thinking, and, when common law rules clashed, pick the one that made the most sense. Alas, old habits die hard. Now, like barnacles, scores and scores of judicial opinions hang on the Restatements "interpreting" them. Now, with computer-retrieval systems, research becomes cheap and easy. Lawyers used to look for cases in their own state; it was just too hard to search nationally. Now, however, lawyers in San Diego can quickly access cases from Boston; the flood of relevant authority has expanded vastly. Who knows what eventual effect this will have on our system?

The *bright line rule* is another device to reduce legal uncertainty. Assume our welfare-hearing officer writes "Programs offering little in the way of teaching new work skills are not legitimate 'Work Training Programs' for individuals who have a proven work record." This rules makes it somewhat difficult to plan your life or advise your client: does a specific program offer "new work skills," and does a given individual have a "proven work record?" A bright line rule would be "A program offering only manual labor is not a legitimate Work Training Program."

Let's stop to introduce some very important concepts and vocabulary: "rules v. standards" and "over- and under-inclusiveness." Wanting to improve highway safety, you could have a rule ("Don't go over 65") or a standard ("Drive at a safe speed"). Rules are *easy to administer* (Did they or didn't they?), but are often both *under-inclusive* (not including cases they should: unsafe slow driving) and *over-inclusive* (including cases they should not: safe fast driving). To solve these problems, you could have a *standard*: "Drive at a safe speed." Standards, at least in theory, avoid both the over- and under-inclusive problems: you can target unsafe drivers every time, whether they are going too fast or too slow. However, standards are very hard to administer because they require individual assessment.

The more bright-line the rule, the more it will act as a rule; the more fuzzy it is, the more it will act as a standard. This is a fundamental legal quandary, one which will haunt you, or entertain you, from here on out. Justice Cardozo, writing in *Jacob &*

Young v. Kent, stated the issue in his wonderful prose:

> *Those who think more of symmetry and logic in the development of legal rules than of practical adaption to the attainment of a just result will be troubled by a classification where the lines of division are so wavering and blurred. Something, doubtless, may be said on the score of consistency and certainty in favor of a stricter standard. The courts have balanced such consideration against those of equity and fairness, and found the latter to be weightier.*

Others have taken a different view. For example, years later another Justice on the New York Court of Appeals, Justice Jasen, wrote:

> *As in every situation where the law must draw a line between liability and nonliability, between responsibility and nonresponsibility, there will be borderline cases, and injustices may occur by deciding erroneously that an individual belongs on one side of the line or the other. To minimize the chances of such injustice occurring, the line should be drawn as clearly as possible.*

There is a lot to consider. Let me add to the mix two things that might not jump quickly to mind:

First, it is all well and good to decide matters on the basis of "equity and fairness" as long as you are the one making the decision. However, what if you are asserting unpopular positions or are simply unpopular? It can be argued that your only chance would be in a very formalistic system, one with very clear rules, one where the judge could not take away your rights to achieve equity and fairness.

Second, and on the other hand, something can be said for "wavering and blurred" lines, even without the claim that they can produce more justice. "Negotiating in the shadow of the law" suggests that one look at not only how law plays in the courtroom but also how it plays in the street. When the law is uncertain, there is an incentive for the parties to compromise their dispute. If both the plaintiff's lawyer and the defendant's lawyer are telling their clients the same thing, "Gee, I don't really know if we will win or lose if we go to court," cooler heads are more likely to prevail, triggering serious negotiations. It can be argued that the more certain the law is, the more pig-headed people can become: "I want it all! I don't have to compromise. I gotcha!"

How we come out on the issue may be less a product of intellectual assessment and more a product of our psychological bents. Cardozo seems to suggest this: some people seem instinctively to lean towards "symmetry and logic" and seek "consistency and certainty," while others lean towards "equity and fairness" and embrace "wavering and blurred" lines.

Universalization

The doctrine of precedent has the good effect of forcing judges to universalize their decisions. This raises their gaze from the specifics of the case toward long-term goals and also reduces the opportunity that judges have to decide on improper, case-specific grounds. (Other checks on judicial abuse include the requirements that judges follow prior decisions and justify and publish their decisions; as we will see elsewhere in this book, another check on judicial abuse can be law students analyzing judicial opinions in law reviews.)

The problem with universalization is that it may blur significant details. Take another problem researchers give children:

Carl's wife is dying. The druggist has a drug that will save her life but costs $1000. Carl doesn't have the money. One night he breaks into the drugstore and steals the medicine. He gives it to his wife, and she gets well. Did Carl do the right thing?

Graduate students will answer at the level of "property rights" versus "human rights." But maybe this is wrong-headed. Young kids want more details:

Does Carl love his wife? Did he try real hard to get the money? What's the druggist like? Does he kick puppies who accidentally wander into his store?

Laugh as you will, but when you actually make decisions (as opposed to discussing them in class), you probably consider any manner of specific details. Maybe there are no two cases that are really "alike" and it is simply a mistake to believe that they are.

The conflict between the general and specific is endemic to law. You cannot have a rule of law that reads:

*It is okay to steal medicine, at least up to $1000
worth, if it is needed to save the life of your wife,
as long as you love her and as long as you tried
really hard to get the money and provided further
that the druggist is a bad guy who kicks puppies
for no good reason.*

Such a law does not work; it is too specific. Lawyers
could not rely upon it to make predictions; judges
could not rely on it to make decisions. Our dilemma
is this. Legal rules must be somewhat general, or
they won't work at all; if they are somewhat general, they may be suppressing specific facts that
should matter.

The last justification for our doctrine of precedent
is one you seldom hear of: the first judge got it
right. The problem with this justification is that it
suggests natural law, partisan religion, and weird
stuff.

Natural Law, Right Answers

*Stories are found things, like fossils in the
ground.... Stories are relics, part of an undiscov-
ered pre-existing world. The writer's job is to use
the tools to get as much of each one out of the
ground intact as possible.*

So says Stephen King in his book, *On Writing*. To
suggest, however, that judges find the law would be
laughable in today's law school; so too the suggestion that human reason will lead us to correct
solutions. We all know that judges create law, not

find it, and that human reason is but the facile servant of political or psychological dictates.

Ours is a world of relative value and power politics. We rejoice in debunking ideas and authorities and love to point to political or psychological factors as the "real" reasons behind decisions. As undergraduates, we analyzed Marx in terms of Freud and Freud in terms of Marx. It is difficult for us to believe that judicial decisions are "right" in any strong sense of the word. But others have so believed.

Once, people believed in "natural law," that law somehow exists "out there," independent of us. Under this view, judges don't make law, they discover it. Scientists, after all, did not *invent* gravity. We don't buy natural law anymore. We believe that judges are not *discovering* the law; they are *creating* it. But if that is so, how can we say any law or practice is unjust? Slavery? Dictatorship? Cruel and unusual punishment? Are these just matters of convention, or individual opinion, or whim?

I can understand why those who thought they were discovering the law believed that they were; thinking hard on a subject and writing on a subject feels a lot more like discovery than invention. Sitting here, watching the cursor blink, I get stuck; I begin to rethink my life, and then, suddenly, something will pop into my mind. That seems like discovery. Of course, it is easy to discount how things seem. Richard Pryor, caught in the act with another woman, yells at his wife: "Things are not as they seem. I am not having an affair; do you believe me or do you believe your lyin' eyes?" Nonetheless, during your studies, consider this: if Stephen King can discover *Cujo*, why can't we discover law?

Some Concluding Thoughts on Ethics

A cartoon shows a middle-aged couple in shock and surprise: "Oh, no! We forgot to have children!"

To conclude this section of the book, the section on legal analysis, with some thoughts on legal ethics smacks of "Oh, no! I forgot ethics!" It isn't. Once you get the mechanics of legal analysis down, and you will, it becomes a lot easier. In practice, you will probably tend to specialize in a few areas of the law, such as criminal law, security law, elder law, or entertainment law. You will quickly learn the substantive doctrines in those areas.

The hard parts of legal practice are dealing with people (and I can't help you there; novels might) and resolving the tough ethical issues that seem to arise almost every day. To get you thinking about such issues, consider the following problems that could arise in your first case, that of Ms. K and her landlord.

1. If a landlord comes and asks you to draft a form lease, do you automatically include an exculpatory clause (assuming they are legal in your jurisdiction)? Should you discuss the issue with the landlord, expressing your feelings about the propriety of the clauses?

2. Assuming exculpatory clauses have been held unenforceable in your state, what if the landlord says, "Draft one anyway. Maybe the courts will change their minds; in any event, most of my tenants don't know the law and won't sue."

3. Assume that exculpatory clauses are valid in your state. A landlord who has been quite negligent and whose negligence has seriously injured a tenant seeks your representation. Reviewing the store-bought lease, you find an exculpatory clause buried on the second page. Would it be proper for you not to raise the defense? If you do raise it, should you tell your not-too-bright opponent that similar clauses have been found invalid in other states?

4. Should you decide these issues yourself or should you do whatever the official ethics code dictates?

Most law schools have courses in legal ethics, a legacy of Watergate, where it was discovered that a great many of the bad apples were lawyers. All states have adopted ethical codes for lawyers to follow. However often they lack suggestions about how one can go about making difficult ethical decisions. Surely you start with the controlling rules, and surely you will want to talk to others, both lawyers and non-lawyers. Here are some other ideas.

"Act only on that maxim by which you can at the same time will that it should become a universal law." So advised Kant. Say I am tempted to cheat on my taxes. But must the maxim be very abstract ("Everyone can cheat") or can we put in some needed qualifications ("Minor cheating is OK as long as you are a nice person who has earned a piddling amount from Nutshell royalties")?

Along these lines it might be well to write a rule that would either allow you to do what you are considering or prohibit you from doing what you do not wish to do. In discussions of ethical matters, law students are often rather quick with the approval or condemnation of certain activities lawyers engage in. Pressed to write a rule governing such conduct often helps them think thorough their positions.

Another method is so simple it sounds ridiculous: think of a person you respect and ask yourself what he or she would do.

One final matter concerns the debate you will no doubt engage in time and again. As a lawyer, should you be a "hired gun" do whatever your client wants, as long as it is legal?

Professor Thomas Shaffer has a brilliant analogy. You are a druggist and someone comes in to buy a hypodermic needle. You believe he is a heroin addict. One choice is to sell him the needle; what he does with it is his business. This is the "hired gun" response. Another choice would be to refuse to sell it to him because you don't want to facilitate such behavior. The problem with both approaches is that they are settled by power: in the first, the buyer has it; in the second, the druggist does. Shaffer gives us a way out. The druggist should begin a conversation: "I think you are going to use this to shoot heroin, and I believe it is wrong to be an addict." The important aspect of this solution is that the druggist must be open to being convinced by the buyer, must be open to the possibility of agreeing that it is fine for this person to be an addict. Otherwise, it will be a feigned discussion, one we are likely to engage in with our young children: "You think it is fine to stay up all night watching *South Park*. O.K. Let's talk about it."

This doesn't mean that you check your common sense and your ethical sense at the door. As Elihu Root once said, "about half the practice of a decent lawyer consists in telling would-be clients that they are damned fools and should stop."

*

PART TWO

STUDY SKILLS

"What is it, exactly, that I'm supposed to be learning?"

You will be exposed to a bewildering set of materials: "cases" from different states and from different times, Restatements, law reviews, Uniform Codes, state and federal statutes and maybe even snippets of the United Nations Charter. What's going on? What are you to make of this mess? Should you memorize case names? Dates? The language of the Restatements? How a state statute differs from a Uniform Code provision?

What do lawyers do? Clients come, seeking help. When they explain their situation, their lawyers will spot the legal problems that must be resolved. Based on their training, these lawyers will know the law's general solutions to these problems and, based on that knowledge, will ask their clients to amplify certain portions of their stories in order to determine how the law's general solutions would play out in the clients' situations.

In law school, you are learning how to be a lawyer. You are learning:

1. To spot legal issues (problems) lurking in any fact pattern;

2. To know the general solutions the law has adopted to solve these problems; and

3. To apply these solutions to the case at hand.

This, and nothing more fancy, is what it is "to think like a lawyer." This is the essential format you will follow in your various tasks, from writing memos to taking exams. Law students, when I tell them that, have a hard time believing it. "Yeah, well, that's cool, but do I have to memorize dates?" Hopefully, as you work your way through this Part, you will get a hands-on sense of what I mean. Knowing what you are trying to learn will inform your understanding of how to learn it.

In Chapter 7, I expand on your educational goals and relate them to educational methods.

Most of your time will be spent reading and briefing cases. Chapter 8 gives you some tips on how to read cases and gives you one to work on. Chapter 9 goes into the matter of case-briefing, and it too gives you a case to work on. Do the work. Not only will you understand the general advice better, but you will also be getting a head start on your Contracts class; the two cases I use are classic first semester fare.

Chapter 10 offers general study tips on such topics as how to get the most out of your classes, the use and abuse of study aids, and "outlining" your courses (a grand law school tradition).

Read all of these chapters early because you will be reading and briefing cases from the get go.

Chapters 11 and 12 can wait until mid-semester. They focus on law school exams and will make better sense once you have some law behind you. You will be given a test to take and two model answers to analyze.

The last chapter in this Part, "Fear and Loathing in the First Year," is basically therapy. Read it when you suddenly realize that you are the dumbest person in law school. Because this insight strikes different students at different times, there is no set time for that chapter.

CHAPTER 7

STUDYING LAW: APPLICATION, NOT MEMORIZATION

Once upon a midnight dreary,
while you ponder, weak and weary,

Over many quaint and forgotten cases,

While you're nodding, nearly napping,
suddenly will come a tapping,

As if someone gently rapping,
rapping at your chamber door.

" 'Tis some professor," you will mutter,
"tapping at my chamber door—"

Quote the professor, "Application! Application!
That's the core! "

Law is not something we *know*; it is something we *do*. The late Grant Gilmore, from the lofty halls of Yale, said it reminded him of baseball.

Baseball? A professor? From Yale?

Baseball. Something we do. Knowing all the rules won't get you to first base. You have to hit, throw, run. How do you get better? How do you get better playing the piano, dancing ballet, acting Shakespeare or painting pictures?

Practice!

Learn law by *practicing* law. View your assignments, not as tasks to learn specific legal doctrines, but as opportunities to practice lawyering skills. Don't be a passive observer ("Hey, how about them apples?"); be an active participant ("How can I apply that?"). Struggling to understand a case, struggling to see if two cases are consistent, struggling to make sense out of a statute, you are doing what you will be doing when you are a lawyer, practicing law.

Let me illustrate what I mean by practice. In your Contracts class you will learn about modification of contract. Often parties to a contract will, during the life of the contract, change its terms and the question is whether the modification is enforceable. You will probably read some cases on the issue and then be presented with a Restatement Section, which I have slightly rewritten, that covers the situation:

Section 89: Modification of Contract

A promise modifying a duty under a contract not fully performed on either side is binding if the modification is fair and equitable in view of circumstances not anticipated by the parties when the contract was made.

You can't read this quickly and move on. Restatements and statutes are drafted with great care, and every word matters. Carefully reading the section, you note that three factors or elements are set out. It would help to set them out separately, either on a separate piece of paper or as notes in the book's margin.

1. The contract must have "not been fully performed";

2. The modification must be "fair and equitable"; and

3. The circumstances must not have been "anticipated."

So far, so good. Now, if you were to approach this as an undergraduate, you would sit down and memorize these three elements. You would *know* the law and this would work fine if law school exams (or clients) asked:

Name the three elements a court would consider to find a modification binding.

But law school exams don't ask questions like that. Rather they give you little problems to solve, problems similar to those you might meet in practice.

Homeowner and Pool Person sign a contract for the construction of a pool for $20,000. After the Pool Person is half done, he comes to homeowner and says "I have run into difficulties. I have hit solid rock only three feet down. I will need another $5000 to complete the pool." Reluctantly, Homeowner agrees to pay the extra $5000 and the pool is finished. Thereafter, Homeowner refuses to pay the extra $5000. Is the modification enforceable?

Knowing the three elements of the law would help you answer this question, but more is required: you must be able to do law by applying the elements. How do you learn how to do that? Practice before the game. Once you have parsed a Restatement or statute for its elements, as to each, (1) *ask why the drafters included the element, and (2) make up easy cases to which it would apply.*

The drafters required that the contract must not be fully performed. Why would that be? If the Pool Person came *after* he had completed the pool and asked for more money, Homeowner's agreement to pay it would not be enforceable. Why would the drafters make such a distinction? What problem were they addressing?

The drafters required that the circumstances were unanticipated at the time the contract was made. Why would they do so? What problem were they addressing? In the pool case, what would be an easy case of *anticipated* circumstances? What would be an easy case of *unanticipated* circumstances? Once you have the easy cases before you, tease out why they are easy.

These are tough questions, but I'm not going to answer them for you. If I did, it would be like me taking batting practice for you, rehearsing your lines, or practicing your scales. The key point is not that you get the right answers; neither Babe Ruth nor Barry Bonds woke up hitting home runs. The key is that you keep forcing yourself to practice.

Still the fear: "I'm just getting more and more confused in asking all of these questions and who knows if my answers are right? What I have to do is memorize the three elements or were there four?

I've had it!" The surprising thing is that by asking yourself hard questions you are learning the elements at such a level that they will "jump" out at you during an exam.

In the pool example, you wouldn't waste time discussing the first element, that the contract hadn't been completed. You might do so if you were working from a memorized checklist. On the other hand, the fact that the Homeowner agreed to pay the entire cost of the additional work will likely trigger, "Wait a minute, that seems suspicious. Oh yes, the modification must be fair and equitable. Is one side paying for the whole thing fair?"

That Pool Person hit solid rock at three feet will trigger: "Was that anticipated?" That is a tough question. What did the drafters intend by that term? Because you have already thought about that question, by considering easy cases and teasing them out, you are ready to rumble!

Recall the problem I gave you in the second chapter.

Assume a state statute provides that tenants must be given a 30–day notice before they could be evicted. Joe, a single father earning a low wage, moved into an apartment house with his two children. He signed a lease waiving his right to a 30–day notice. The landlord has brought an eviction action that could not be brought under the statute. The landlord asserts that the protection was waived. Discuss.

If you read that chapter, you could take a good stab at answering the question even though you never sat down to try to memorize the law. Your knowledge came from making sense out of the two cases we were discussing, *Globe* and *K v. Landlord.*

In the Prologue, I quoted William James. Memory involves both retention and retrieval. Closing your eyes to memorize, using flash cards and cramming are efforts to improve *retention*. However the hard part is *retrieval* and that is improved as more paths leading to it are created.

Speedy oblivion is the almost inevitable fate of all that is committed to memory in this simple way. Whereas, on the contrary, the same materials taken in gradually, day after day, recurring in different contexts, considered in various relations, associated with other external incidents, and repeatedly reflected on, grow into such a system, form such connections with the rest of the mind's fabric, lie open to so many paths of approach, that they remain permanent possessions. This is the intellectual reason why habits of continuous application should be enforced in educational establishments.

All of this is not to suggest that memorization has no role in legal study. But make it your last move, not your first. Once you have spent time practicing, it would be very helpful to write out, for later review, the key points you have discovered. But remember the tapping at your chamber door, *"Application! Application! That's the core!"*

CHAPTER 8

DISSECTING CASES

"Who's on first?"

"No. Respondent's on first."

"Who's he?"

"The appellee."

The staple of the first year diet is the appellate case. Something happens, and a lawsuit is filed; at the trial court, someone loses, perhaps the plaintiff, perhaps the defendant. The loser, filing an appeal, now becomes the "appellant" while the other side is called the "respondent," or, sometimes, the "appellee." To make matters worse, occasionally the appellant will win at the first appellate court and his adversary appeals and now the appellant becomes the respondent. Whatever.

You read appellate cases to extract rules of law, what lawyers call "holdings." Why don't we just tell you what the law is? Partly to give you practice, not only in the lawyer's task of analyzing cases, but also in struggling with tough material. Additionally, learning legal rules this way gives you a much better understanding of their operational worth: when they have been applied (the facts of the case) and why they were applied (the court's rationale).

There is another reason to read cases: to get an intuitive sense of good practice. Thomas Kuhn, in *The Structure of Scientific Revolutions,* discusses the training of scientists. They are asked to repeat the grand experiments of the past, not to learn the laws those experiments disclosed (they're in the textbook), but to get a feel for how science is done. Later asked to define good science, they can't; but they can recognize it and, more importantly, they can do it. Working cases you are gaining an intuitive sense of good lawyering.

One more matter before we begin. You are not only a student of law; you are a student of legal writing. Every now and then, step back from the opinion and consider matters of style. If it reads well, how so? If you find it confusing, how come?

Reading cases is hard. As a first cut, consider three simple questions:

1. Who are the parties?

2. What is the argument (in legal jargon, the "issue" the court must decide)?

3. What should I get from this case?

Given these three questions, read my slightly altered version of a famous case, that of *Walker–Thomas.* Underline parts you feel are important. Write notes in the margins. Don't just read the case; go after it.

WILLIAMS v. WALKER–THOMAS FURNITURE CO.

U.S. Court of Appeals, District of Columbia Cir., 1965.

J. SKELLY WRIGHT, CIRCUIT JUDGE. *Walker–Thomas Furniture Company operates a retail furniture store in the District of Columbia. During the period of 1957 to 1962, Ms. Williams purchased a number of household items from Walker–Thomas, for which payment was to be made in installments. The terms of each purchase were contained in a printed form contract which provided that, in the event of a default in the payment of any monthly installment, Walker–Thomas could repossess the item.*

The contract further provided that "the amount of each periodical installment payment ... shall be credited pro rata on all outstanding bills...." The effect of this rather obscure provision, known as a cross-collateral clause, was to keep a balance due on every item purchased until the balance due on all items, whenever purchased, was paid. As a result, the debt incurred at the time of purchase of each item was secured by the right to repossess all the items previously purchased by the same purchaser.

On April 17, 1962, Ms. Williams bought a stereo set of stated value of $514.95. At that time, she had an outstanding balance of previous purchases of $164. The total of all of the purchases she had made at the store over the years came to $1,800. Over the years she had paid $1,400. At the time of this purchase, Walker–Thomas was aware of Ms. William's financial position. The reverse side of the

*stereo contract listed the name of her social worker
and her $218 monthly stipend from the government.
Nevertheless, with full knowledge that Ms. Williams
had to feed, clothe, and support both herself and
seven children on this amount, Walker–Thomas sold
her a $514 stereo set.*

*Shortly after purchasing the stereo, Ms. Williams
failed to make her payments, and Walker–Thomas
brought this action to repossess every item she had
purchased at its store over the years. The court below
found that, under the contract, Walker–Thomas had
the right to do so and granted judgment for it. Ms.
Williams appeals that decision to this court.*

*Ms. Williams' principal contention, rejected by the
trial court, is that cross-collateral clauses are unconscionable and, hence, not enforceable. The trial court
explained its rejection of this contention as follows:*

*"I cannot condemn too strongly appellee's con-
duct. It raises serious questions of sharp practice
and irresponsible business dealings. A review of
the legislation in the District of Columbia affecting retail sales and the pertinent decisions of the
highest court in this jurisdiction disclose, however, no ground upon which this court can declare
the contracts in question contrary to public policy.
I think Congress should consider corrective legislation to protect the public from such exploitative
contracts as were utilized in the case at bar."*

*We do not agree that the court lacked the power to
refuse enforcement to contracts found to be unconscionable. In other jurisdictions, it has been held as*

a matter of common law that unconscionable contracts are not enforceable. While no decision of this court so holding has been found, the notion that an unconscionable bargain should not be given full enforcement is by no means novel. In Scott v. United States (1870), the Supreme Court stated:

"If a contract be unreasonable and unconscionable, but not void for fraud, a court of law will give to the party who sues for its breach damages, not according to its letter, but only such as he is equitably entitled to."

Since we have never adopted or rejected such a rule, the question here presented is actually one of first impression.

Congress has recently enacted the Uniform Commercial Code, which specifically provides that the court may refuse to enforce a contract which it finds to be unconscionable at the time it was made. The enactment of this section, which occurred subsequent to the contracts here in suit, does not mean that the common law of the District of Columbia was otherwise at the time of enactment nor does it preclude the court from adopting a similar rule in the exercise of its powers to develop the common law for the District of Columbia. In fact, in view of the absence of prior authority on the point, we consider the Congressional adoption of that section persuasive authority for following the rationale of the cases from which the section is explicitly derived. Accordingly, we hold that where the element of unconscion-

ability is present at the time a contract is made, the contract should not be enforced.

Unconscionability has generally been recognized to include an absence of meaningful choice on the part of one of the parties together with contract terms which are unreasonably favorable to the other party. Whether a meaningful choice is present in a particular case can only be determined by consideration of all the circumstances surrounding the transaction. In many cases, the meaningfulness of the choice is negated by a gross inequality of bargaining power. The manner in which the contract was entered is also relevant to this consideration. Did each party to the contract, considering his obvious education or lack of it, have a reasonable opportunity to understand the terms of the contract, or were the important terms hidden in a maze of fine print and minimized by deceptive sales practices? Ordinarily, one who signs an agreement without full knowledge of its terms might be held to assume the risk that he has entered a one-sided bargain. But when a party of little bargaining power, and hence little real choice, signs a commercially unreasonable contract with little or no knowledge of its terms, it is hardly likely that his consent, or even an objective manifestation of his consent, was ever given to all the terms. In such a case the usual rule that the terms of the agreement are not to be questioned should be abandoned, and the court should consider whether the terms of the contract are so unfair that enforcement should be withheld.

In determining reasonableness or fairness, the primary concern must be with the terms of the contract considered in light of the circumstances existing when the contract was made. The test is not simple, nor can it be mechanically applied. The terms are to be considered "in the light of the general commercial background and the commercial needs of the particular trade or case." Professor Corbin, a leading expert in the field, suggests the test as being whether the terms are "so extreme as to appear unconscionable according to the mores and business practices of the time and place." We think this formulation correctly states the test to be applied in those cases where no meaningful choice was exercised upon entering the contract.

Because the trial court did not feel that enforcement could be refused, no findings were made on the possible unconscionability of the contracts in these cases. Since the record is not sufficient for our deciding the issue as a matter of law, the cases must be remanded to the trial court for further proceedings.

So ordered.

———————

Take a few minutes to jot down what you learned from this case.

Discussion

No doubt you read carefully but not as carefully as you will. Can you answer these questions?

1. What was the precise issue before this court? How was it resolved?

2. Remembering that judges are like the Ruler of the Queen's Navy, and never think of thinking for themselves, which side called the judge's attention to *Scott v. United States*? What argument was made based upon that case?

3. Why didn't the court simply apply the UCC to this case? Congress had passed it and made it the law.

4. What argument did the store make based upon the fact that Congress passed the UCC?

5. Two elements of unconscionability are discussed. What are they? And what is the relationship between them? For a term to be found unconscionable must both elements be found or only one?

If you can't answer these questions, reread the opinion. Get used to rereading opinions. It's not like I'm asking your to reread *War and Peace*. Once you have, take a stab at the questions. Write your answers. Then we can compare notes.

Don't panic: you are not expected to *know* which party cited what authority or which party made what argument. I am not talking about what you want to take away from a case; that is the subject of the next chapter on case briefing. What I am talking about is the intensity with which you read cases; better yet, *dissect* cases.

Recall my comparison of legal argument and ping-pong. It is extremely useful to restage the game: as to each argument and as to each case, which side was relying on it and for what purpose. A careful reader would know, as she read along or with a moment's reflection, which side cited *Scott* and for what purpose; a careful reader would not, however, try to "learn it." Who cited *Scott* in terms of legal doctrine doesn't matter.

My answers:

1. The precise issue was whether the courts of D.C. have the *power* to refuse to enforce parts of contracts if they are *unconscionable*. The court below didn't think it had the power. This case does not decide whether the particular clause was unconscionable; the case is sent back to the lower court to make that determination.

   This raises an interesting point. The case appears in Contract books, not to teach you anything about the power of the D.C. courts, but rather to teach you something about unconscionability. Hence what you are supposed to get from a case may not be what the case was technically about.

2. The customers brought up *Scott* in support of their argument that the courts have an inherent power to refuse to enforce contracts, at

least not to their "letter," if they are "unconscionable."

A somewhat plausible "wrong answer" would be that the store cited *Scott* for the proposition that the courts enforce, even if not to their "letter," unconscionable contracts. The problem with this answer is that the store, given the tenor of trial court opinion, knows that the "letter" the court would refuse to enforce would be the cross-collateral clause.

3. The court couldn't just apply the UCC to the case because the contracts in question were signed *before* the UCC was passed. Statutes, generally, cannot have *retroactive* effect.

This raises a fascinating jurisprudential issue: *Congress* can't retroactively change the rules on Walker–Thomas ("unconscionable contracts will not be enforced") because that would be unfair to Walker–Thomas. But apparently there is nothing wrong with the *courts* changing the rules ("unconscionable contracts will not be enforced"). Of course it can be argued that the court really wasn't changing the rules at all; that in some sense the common law in D.C. always had a doctrine of unconscionability; it's just that no one realized it before Judge Wright came along and told us.

But what happens when a court overrules prior decisions? Aren't they changing the rules, upsetting apple carts, retroactively? Ask your profs.

4. What argument the store made based on Congress's passage of the UCC is a difficult question, as you must *infer* what the argument was. The argument is that, prior to the passage of the UCC, the courts of D.C. could not refuse to enforce contracts on the basis of unconscionability: if they already had that power, why would Congress have to pass the UCC?

Note here the reversibility of many legal arguments. The court, adopting something of an "in your face" style, writes:

> *The enactment of the UCC does not mean that the common law of the District of Columbia was otherwise at the time of enactment. In fact ... we consider the congressional adoption persuasive authority for following the rationale of the cases from which the section is explicitly derived.*

5. To show a contract provision unconscionable, the customer must show *both* lack of meaningful choice *and* terms unreasonably favorable to the other party.

> *Unconscionability has generally been recognized to include an absence of meaningful choice on the part of one of the parties **together with** contract terms which are unreasonably favorable to the other party.*

It is critical that you focus on the *relationship* between elements. In our prior math notation, here we find a $1 + 2 = $ VICTORY equation, not a 1 **or** 2 $=$ VICTORY one.

A Few Tricks to Reading Closely

1. First, figure out what the *issue* is: what legal point must the court decide in order to resolve the case?

2. Be clear on the basics:

   What happened in the court below?

   Who is appealing?

   On what theory?

   Who wins and why?

   What happens next? Is the case over or is it sent back for a new trial?

3. As to each case cited, and as to each argument the judges make, ask, "Who did they steal that one from?"

4. Be clear about the *relationship* between arguments and between elements. If the court is making two points, the relationship can be:

   $1 + 2 = $ VICTORY

   or

   1 or 2 $=$ VICTORY

   Again, to prevail on unconscionability, the customer must show "lack of meaningful choice" **and** "unreasonable terms"; one is not enough.

5. Play loser. Pretend you are the lawyer representing the losing side in the case and that the court's opinion is simply your opponent's argument. How will you respond to it? Often, opinions seem so clearly right that we ask ourselves, "Why did the losing side even bother?" Always remember that the losing side thought that it would win! Judicial opinions are "winners' history."

Now that you have some idea of the intensity with which you should read cases, we turn to what you are supposed to learn from them.

CHAPTER 9

BRIEFING CASES

Briefing is a brilliant educational device. I will begin by asking you to brief a case.

"You can't do that. You haven't told us *how* to brief a case!" A better point: I haven't told you *why*.

One reason is for review; you don't want to have to reread all those cases reviewing for finals. The real worth of briefing, and why you must do your own, is that it forces you to grapple with the cases and to reduce them to their core. Brevity is a virtue in both regards.

An appellate opinion is a *rule of law* announced in a specific *factual context* and justified by a particular *rationale*. The *traditional briefing format* uses these categories of analysis:

1. Facts

2. Issue/Holding ("Rule of Law")

3. Rationale

If you are called on in class to recite a case, you will say something like, "The facts of the case are ... and the issue before the court was ... and the court held that ... for the following reasons...." (assuming that you don't just freeze up and die).

The "issue" is the legal question the court must decide. Recall that in *Walker–Thomas*, the case you read in the last chapter, the issue was whether the court has the power under common law to void unconscionable contracts. Recall, in *Globe*, our old favorite, the issue was whether exculpatory clauses violated public policy.

The "holding" of the case is how the court resolved the "issue." It becomes the "rule of law" for which the case stands. So many terms, so little difference.

Issue: Does the court have the power to void unconscionable contracts?

Holding: The court has the power to void unconscionable contracts.

Rule of Law: The court has the power to void unconscionable contracts.

Issue: How to define unconscionability?

Holding: Unconscionability involves two elements . . . . .

Rule of Law: Unconscionability involves two elements . . . . .

The essential thing is not the label but the learning; you must be able to state the legal question the court had to decide and how it decided it.

You are about to meet two extraordinary people, Justice Cardozo (a true common law giant) and Lucy, Lady Duff–Gordon (who is seen, alas, not at her finest—in law, people are seldom seen at their finest). Lucy was a well known designer of women's clothes and, leading the way for today's superstars, was one of the first celebrities to endorse products. Whether she was a role model is lost in the historical record. She did, however, survive the *Titanic*.

But we are not here to gossip.

To help you brief the case, there is a contract doctrine called "mutuality of obligation." Unless both sides are bound to do something under the contract, neither is. In this case Lucy, the defendant, promised Wood, a marketing agent, the exclusive right to market her endorsement. Lucy cheated by making some deals on the side! When Wood sued, she defended on the basis of "mutuality of obligation."

"Sure, I made a promise to Wood, but Wood never actually promised to do anything for me. He could walk away from the contract any time he wanted to. Because he didn't have any promises to live up to, under the doctrine of mutuality, I don't have to live up to mine."

Your brief shouldn't be more than a page and should follow the traditional format: facts, issue, and rationale. Before you can begin a brief, you must read the entire case, maybe more than once. However, as you read it, underline what you think is important and, yes, jot ideas in the margins. The basic questions you will have to answer are: What was the question the court had to decide? What were the important facts in the case? Why did the court decide as it did?

WOOD v. LUCY, LADY DUFF-GORDON

New York Court of Appeals, 1917.

CARDOZO J. *The defendant styles herself "a creator of fashions." Her favor helps a sale. Manufacturers of dresses, millinery, and like articles are glad to pay for a certificate of her approval. The things which she designs, fabrics, parasols, and what not, have a new value in the public mind when issued in her name. She employed the plaintiff to help her to turn this vogue into money. He was to have the exclusive rights, subject always to her approval, to place her indorsement on the designs of others. He was also to have the exclusive right to place her own designs on sale, or to license others to market them. In return she was to have one-half of "all profits and revenues" derived from any contracts he might make. The exclusive right was to last at least one year from April 1, 1915, and thereafter from year to year unless terminated by notice of 90 days. The plaintiff says that he kept the contract on his part, and that the defendant broke it. She placed her indorsement on fabrics, dresses, and millinery without his knowledge, and withheld the profits. He sues her for the damages, and the case comes here on demurrer.*

The agreement of employment is signed by both parties. It has a wealth of recitals. The defendant insists, however, that it lacks the elements of a contract. She says that the plaintiff does not bind himself to anything. It is true that he does not promise in so many words that he will use reason-

able efforts to place the defendant's indorsement and market her designs. We think, however, that such a promise is fairly to be implied. The law has out-grown its primitive stage of formalism when the precise word was the sovereign talisman, and every slip was fatal. It takes a broader view today. A promise may be lacking, and yet the whole writing may be "instinct with an obligation," imperfectly expressed (Scott, J., in McCall Co. v. Wright, 133 App. Div. 62, 117 N.Y.S. 775). If that is so, there is a contract.

The implication of a promise here finds support in many circumstances. The defendant gave an exclu-sive privilege. She was to have no right for at least a year to place her own indorsement or market her own designs except through the agency of the plain-tiff. The acceptance of the exclusive agency was an assumption of its duties. Many other terms of the agreement point the same way. We are told at the outset by way of recital that:

"The said Otis F. Wood possesses a business orga-nization adapted to the placing of such indorsement as the said Lucy, Lady Duff–Gordon, has approved."

The implication is that the plaintiff's business organization will be used for the purpose for which it is adapted. But the terms of the defendant's com-pensation are even more significant. Her sole com-pensation for the grant of an exclusive agency is to be one-half of all the profits resulting from the plaintiff's efforts. Unless he gave his efforts, she could never get anything. Without an implied prom-

ise, the transaction cannot have such business "efficacy, as both parties must have intended that at all events it should have." Bowen, L.J., in the Moorcock, 14 P.D. 64, 68. But the contract does not stop there. The plaintiff goes on to promise that he will account monthly for all moneys received by him, and that he will take out all such patents and copyrights and trademarks as may in his judgment be necessary to protect the rights and articles affected by the agreement. It is true, of course, as the Appellate Division has said, that if he was under no duty to try to market designs or to place certificates of indorsement, his promise to account for profits or take out copyrights would be valueless. But in determining the intention of the parties the promise has a value. It helps to enforce the conclusion that the plaintiff had some duties. His promise to pay the defendant one-half of the profits and revenues resulting from the exclusive agency and to render accounts monthly was a promise to use reasonable efforts to bring profits and revenues into existence. For this conclusion the authorities are ample.

The judgment of the Appellate Division should be reversed . . . .

Try your hand at briefing the case; then we'll discuss it.

Issue/Holding/Rule

Stating the issue is a matter of art and, occasionally, contention. Sometimes courts come right out and tell you "The issue we have to resolve is . . . ." or "We therefore hold that . . . ." When they do, hog heaven. But generally they don't; you have to root around some. (Sorry for the imagery.)

In *Lucy,* you had to root around. How did you state your issue? Consider two possibilities:

Issue: Will the contract be enforced?

Issue: Will the court imply a promise on the part of an agent to use reasonable efforts to market endorsements of a famous woman where both sides signed the contract and where they agreed to split the profits and he agreed to account for them.

What do you make of these statements of the issue? Jot!

The first is wildly too broad: it's always the issue (except in Torts, where it's "Was it a tort?"). State the issue so that it can be turned into a useful rule of law: "Contracts can be enforced" isn't one.

The second rendition illustrates the frying pan: being too specific. It can become a rule of law, but not much of one.

Rule of law: The court will imply a promise on the part of an agent to use reasonable efforts to market endorsements of a famous woman where both sides signed the contract and where they agreed to split the profits and he agreed to account for them.

As a rule of law, this wouldn't do much work in future cases because it seems to encompass very specific facts. You must strive for a statement of the issue that, when answered, can become a useful rule of law, neither too broad nor too specific.

Issue: Will the court imply a promise to use reasonable efforts on the part of an agent who has been given an exclusive contract?

Lawyers can argue as to the precise issue. Some might include, for example, additional matters:

Issue: Will the court imply a promise to use reasonable efforts on the part of an agent who has been given an exclusive contract *and who has made some promises in the contract*?

The question is whether the case stands for a broad or narrow proposition of law. Will it apply only in cases where the agent has made "some promises" or in all cases where he has an "exclusive"? There are no right answers, only good arguments.

Facts

Include only *operative facts,* those that make a difference in the court's decision. The others, let's call *tidbits*. Tidbits are easy to recognize. In *Lucy,* some of the tidbits were that Lucy designed parasols, that the contract was dated a certain date, and, alas, that her favor helps a sale.

Reread your statement of facts: have you included tidbits, facts that played no part in the court's decision? Including tidbits is a "no-no." They make your brief longer, and hence less helpful when it comes time to review. More importantly, including tidbits may indicate that you are "looking busy" and sticking things in without forcing yourself to consider their relevance.

What were the *operative facts*? Some are clear, such as the fact that Wood did not, in so many words, promise to undertake any work for Lucy. Your brief should have included that. Reasonable minds can differ on some of the facts at the margin. Is Wood's promise to "account monthly" an operative fact, or is it a tidbit? Another way of asking that question is, "If he hadn't made that promise, would the court refuse to imply the promise of *reasonable efforts*?" I don't think so. As I don't think the court's decision would have been different, I don't think "monthly accounting" was an operative fact. But who am I to say? Perhaps, down the road, a court might distinguish *Lucy* on that very basis:

"In the case before us, we are asked to imply a promise as was done in Wood v. Lucy. *However, in that case the agent had made some express promises, including to account monthly to his principal. Given the fact the agent made some express promises, it is easy to imply others. In the case before us, the agent made no express promises at all, and hence we refuse to follow* Wood v. Lucy *and will not imply a promise to use reasonable efforts."*

This illustrates a central point: what is, and what isn't, an operative fact is very much at issue in applying and distinguishing cases. Recall our discussion in Chapter 2 of whether *Globe* controlled *K v.*

Landlord or whether the cases were distinguishable based on the factual differences.

Given uncertainty as to centrality, there may be a tendency to err on the side of inclusion. "Well I'm not sure if that fact matters, so I'll put it in." Bad idea. Best to do your work *now*, before you think of another excuse later: "Is this fact important or isn't it?'

Warning. You will work hard on a brief and, at class, discover that others (alas, perhaps including the Prof) saw things differently, saw your tidbits as pivotal, and your operative facts as beneath mention. Don't get depressed. You brief cases, *not* to get them right, but to get into the thick of things. It's OK to be wrong as long as you're muddy.

Rationale

Restate the court's reasoning in your own words. Copying is tedious and mindless.

The law has outgrown its primitive stage of formalism when the precise word was the sovereign talisman, and every slip was fatal. It takes a broader view today. A promise may be lacking, and yet the whole writing may be "instinct with an obligation," imperfectly expressed.

I don't care how many times you copy that over. To understand it, you simply must try to express it in your own words. What does it mean? Talk about "imperfectly expressed"!

What did you have for the rationale in *Lucy*? I would have put something to the effect that the court seems to justify its decision on the common-sense notion that, "Come on, the parties obviously intended that Wood would sing for his supper. If he didn't Lucy would be too vulnerable because she had given him an exclusive. Even though he didn't come out and say so, we will imply a promise to use reasonable efforts."

Viewing cases as opportunities to practice doing law, don't overlook the intellectual dividends that can flow if you *challenge* the court's reasoning. Can you think of any reasons why Wood would *not* want to promise Lucy that he would use "reasonable efforts?" Can you think of any reasons Lucy might have agreed to give him an exclusive contract even though he didn't promise "reasonable efforts"?

A Way to Check Your Brief

A good way to check your brief is to put it in the following form:

We decided X (holding) because

    1. Of these operative facts and

    2. For these good reasons (rationale).

If you do put your briefs in this format, you may find some strange constructions:

*We decided to imply a promise of "reasonable efforts" on Wood's part **because** Lucy designed parasols.*

This raises the issue of whether you should always follow the traditional format: facts, issue and holding, rationale.

Alternative Format

How do we know what facts are operative unless we know the issue? What had been just an interesting tidbit becomes the smoking gun if the issue is "Is Lucy a woman of many talents?"

*We decide that Lucy is a woman of many talents **because** she designs parasols.*

Consider putting the issue first, and then the facts. It then becomes much easier to tell which facts are operative and which are tidbits.

Another problem with the traditional format is that it suggests that facts, issue, and rationale are all quite distinct. They aren't. They often meld together. For example, a statement of the issue must include at least some operative facts or it will soar off into "Will this contract be enforced?" That said, however, the categories can be helpful.

The last problem with the traditional format is that it doesn't handle the *holding/dicta* problem very well.

Holding/Dicta

Holdings are statements of law necessary for the decision in the case; *dicta* are statements of law which aren't necessary for that decision. Recall Walker–Thomas. The court discussed two matters: first whether the courts had the power to void unconscionable contracts and, second, the elements of unconscionability (lack of meaningful choice coupled with unreasonably favorable terms). Which the holding and which the dicta?

The holding was that the courts have the power; it was needed to decide the case. The dicta was the discussion of what constitutes unconscionability; it was not necessary to decide the case because the court did not decide whether the contract was unconscionable. Why do we split these hairs?

It goes to the heart of *stare decisis*. When something is really at issue, when the case turns on it, the court will think long and hard about it before reaching a decision. The reason we follow prior decisions is that we respect that effort. Compare that to a statement of law that has the quality of, "Oh, by the way, did you know that . . . ."

Dictum is not ("are" not, for you real hair splitters) worthy of the same respect because it is not the product of long, serious thought; this is because nothing in the case turned on it.

To see how this works out, assume a case following *Walker–Thomas* where the issue is how to define unconscionability.

Lawyer One: Your Honor, in *Walker–Thomas* the court defined unconscionability, and you should follow that definition.

Lawyer Two: No, Your Honor, that discussion of unconscionability was dicta.

Judge: That's right. The court didn't have to define unconscionability to decide the issue before it. Therefore that definition doesn't bind me.

The distinction between holding and dicta is a useful analytical ploy. It forces you to think deeply about the precise issue. But don't ignore dicta. Much of the law you will learn will come from judicial asides. That is why the traditional briefing format doesn't always work; had your brief of *Walker–Thomas* not covered the elements of unconscionability, you would have missed the main point.

Clutter

Should you include citations, dates, names of judges, and procedural history? Or are they just clutter?

> Wood v. Lucy, Lady Duff–Gordon
> New York Court of Appeals, 1917
> 222 N.Y. 88, 118 N.E. 214
> Opinion by Justice Cardozo

Is this information necessary?

No, hardly ever. It won't help you review, nor does it further your understanding of the case. In Constitutional Law courses, it's interesting to see how a particular Justice's philosophy plays out in several areas. However, in most courses, who wrote the opinion is of little interest. That said, in the development of common law principles, some courts are more equal than others. The opinions of the New York Court of Appeals (the highest state court in New York) with Justice Cardozo and the California Supreme Court under Justice Traynor carry particular weight.

Dates are important *if* you are studying the historical development of a particular legal doctrine.

Sometimes you are. *Usually* you aren't. Most cases are included in casebooks not to show you what the law *was* but to show you what the law *is*.

Legal education generally ignores history. Reading old cases as current law may give you the sense that the problems facing the law have always been the same, that the law itself is above history, that it is the product of neutral rational principles rather than the clash of competing philosophical, economic, and political positions. It isn't.

Oliver Wendell Holmes, in his great essay, "The Path of the Law," said it best:

> *I cannot but believe that if the training of lawyers led them habitually to consider more definitely and explicitly the social advantage on which the rule they lay down must be justified, they sometimes would hesitate where now they are confident, and see that really they were taking sides upon debatable and often burning questions.*

Law cannot and should not escape its historical context. Yet we tend to teach law as a set of timeless principles. I lament this with great fanfare. But, bottom line, I am part of the problem. Don't include dates. Include them only if you think them important. And be explicit as to why the date is important. Do you feel the case would not be followed today because it reflects different times?

Procedural History of the Case

Some profs *insist* on it and, well, it's their nickel. For my money, don't *routinely* include the procedural history of the case.

Jury found for plaintiff. Defendant appeals on basis of improper jury instruction.

Appellate court reversed and plaintiff appeals. Affirmed.

This tells you nothing about the law and simply takes up space. Your interest is in what the error was in the jury instruction.

This is not to say, however, that procedural history is irrelevant. I return to the notion that I developed in the last chapter. There are things that you should understand about a case (such as which party cited which case) that you need not "take away" from the opinion. The procedural history of a case is one such thing. Forcing yourself to sort it out will help you to understand how courts operate and will help you understand which party is arguing what.

The procedural history of a case can also tell you some very interesting things. *Lucy won at the lower court.* Reading the flowing prose of Justice Cardozo, we are swept along, "But of course a promise should be implied." Before Cardozo, the courts were reluctant, in the name of party autonomy, to "imply terms" to contracts. Cardozo was working a major shift in the law, but he doesn't seem to be making a ripple. Recall our earlier discussion about the reluctance of courts to overrule prior decisions. Instead they distinguish them or, as here, add certain refinements which in fact change the basic rule. In the common tradition, our revolutions are pretty much invisible.

In addition to the procedural history of a case, be sure you are clear about *what happens next*. Often the decision will put an end to the matter, once and for all. But what about the case of *Wood v. Lucy*? Has Wood won his case? Think.

Final Pointers

1. Leave wide margins so that you can add points from class discussion and make further notes when you review.

2. Don't expect to write your brief the first time you read the case.

3. Some advise *not* to brief a case until you have read all of the cases in the same assignment. This helps you see how the particular tree fits in the forest.

4. Include a "puzzling points" section at the end. What don't you understand about the case? Do you agree with it?

Here is a format you might try out. If you find that it doesn't always work (and it won't), this discovery doesn't make me an idiot; it makes you a genius. It shows that you are not mechanically filling in the blanks; it shows you are struggling with the material.

1. Issue/holding (What legal issue did the court have to resolve and how did it resolve it? Note: in some cases you will find more than one issue.)

2. Operative facts (don't include the kitchen sink ... unless the case is about a plumber).

3. Rationale (in your own words).

4. Procedural history and what happens next (when of interest).

5. Puzzling points.

"That's it? That's the end of the chapter? I'm puzzled."

CHAPTER 10

STUDY TIPS

"Tell them to take one day and go work in a soup kitchen. That's what I would tell them."

Second semester, first-year student

This is a chapter of odds and ends: how to get the most out of your classes, the traditions of outlining and study groups, how much time most students put in, and the critical importance of getting involved with the material by writing. Before we begin, a cautionary tale. After finals, some students come to discuss their grades.

"I thought I would do better. I really *know* Contracts."

That might be the problem. If your goal is to know the subject, two bad things happen. First you will memorize rather than apply the law. Tap, tap. Second, you will protect what you know by ignoring the ambiguities and the nagging questions that threaten your understanding. Rather than knowing your subject, your goal should be to deepen your understanding of it. Then you will play with the material and relish the ambiguities and the difficult questions. If you push yourself, if you refuse to be satisfied with easy understandings, you never walk away smug. You simply run out of time.

Writing

Writing, like the prospect of being hanged, concentrates one's mind wonderfully. Write in the margins; when you run out of room, draw arrows to the top and write upside down. A well-used casebook is a mess.

Reading, you skim along and all is right with the world. When you put pen to paper or fingers to keyboard, your mind slows. "Wait, that point really doesn't make sense. And how did the court get from point A to point C? I thought I understood that."

Underlining and decorating your book with various color markers gives you a sense of accomplishment but leaves the real work of understanding to a later day. Do it now.

In order to *write,* you need room. Leave *sufficient margins* on your briefs, class notes and outlines.

Classes

There's not as much to learn as you think. Get used to it.

Using the "Socratic method," a professor calls on students to recite the assigned cases. Once the basic facts and law are given, the professor asks the student a series of questions attempting to test and then apply the law.

"If the facts showed X instead of Y, would the court have come out the same way? Why?"

"Is that case consistent with the one we studied yesterday?"

"Which makes the better argument, the majority or the dissent?"

"Do you think this rule makes good sense? What policies does it further? Hinder?"

The goal is not so much to teach you the law as it is to help you understand how judges and lawyers apply the law. A class may struggle with a single word for an entire hour without there being *any* significance to the result of that struggle. The goal was *not* to define the word; it *was* to show you how lawyers and judges go about defining words.

True, some law professors lecture. But they probably have few major points, perhaps three or four, five on a busy day. The rest, surely not fluff or chaff (these folks are friends!), is supporting detail, examples, and, of course, the ever present academic throat-clearings and neat qualifications.

That there is very little to learn takes some of the pressure off. You aren't missing anything. Let the wild rumpus begin!

Warming up

Take five minutes *before* class to review your briefs of the cases you will discuss. You won't waste valuable time trying to remember who the plaintiff was or what the dispute was about.

Volunteering

Jump in to test your ideas and your ability to think on your feet. You owe it to yourself and your classmates. I can never understand students who sit on their hands, complaining that so-and-so talks all the time. On the other hand, don't volunteer too much because there is a cost. While your arm waves, in order to hold on to your comment, you will of necessity be blocking out what is happening in class.

Volunteer early in the semester just to get it out of the way. You don't want to sit there all semester thinking, "Well, will today be the day?" Psychologically the longer you wait, the harder it gets, "Hey, you never raise you hand. This better be good."

Don't wait until you have a profound question or "something really good to say." That idea can freeze you for semesters, for years. You won't know if what you have to say is really good until you say it. Jump in with some obvious point; it may be quite profound.

Studies show that minorities, women, and even certain parts of the classroom tend to volunteer less. But once one does, others follow. Consider yourself a trailblazer.

Taking notes

The ability to take good notes is an important skill. It does not involve writing fast and getting most everything down. It involves close listening and making judgments about what to include, what to skip. Making judgments, as opposed to merely transcribing what you hear, keeps you engaged and will trigger a more meaningful memory when you review.

As a lawyer, you will take notes in the heat of battle as bullets whiz. For example, when an opposing witness is testifying at trial, you need to listen for improper questions while also listening carefully to the answers, deciding whether they are consistent with the witness' prior statements and whether they help or hurt your case (and, if they hurt, whether there is anything you can do about them on cross). Clearly you can't transcribe the testimony; at best you can "jot down" key points, perhaps a word or two, simply enough to remind you of where you want to go on cross-examination. The same kind of note taking under pressure occurs during depositions, negotiations, and the scads and scads of meetings lawyers attend.

Recording everything offers a sense of safety. It's scary going only for the key points. "What if I'm missing something important?" But it's scary in trials, negotiations, and board meetings too. Practice now, when there is so little at stake.

Cooling off

Leaving class with few notes is fine, unless, of course, your short-term memory is worse than mine, unless, of course, your short-term memory is worse than mine. You will not miss anything important *if* you conduct a *mini-review* after each class. Right after class, or surely some time the same day, take ten minutes to read over your class notes, filling in the points you missed and qualifying those you couldn't understand. You may find that there was method after all.

Laptops

If you are going to use a laptop in the classroom, be aware of some of the dangers. There will be temptations (the Internet, Instant Messenger, Breaking News, and, of course, Solitaire), and you will kid yourself: "A quick look, nothing more; it is, after all, a News Flash." "I can do two things at once, in fact it *helps* me to do two things at once. I did it as an undergraduate and I was gang-busters!"

You can't do two things at once (at least not very well), and the harder you work in law school the better lawyer you will be. Would you want take a cruise on a ship designed by an engineer who had played Solitaire during Basic Buoyancy? Three years from now, clients will rely on you.

Once you turn off the Internet and the games, there are still dangers. Some sit staring at their screens like grim court reporters, fingers poised, committed to transcribing *every* word. You'll miss subtleties. Anna Quindlen, in *Blessings*, writes of an elderly woman:

"After so many years of living alone, she had to remind herself that part of saying the right thing was reading the face of the person to whom you were speaking. It was no wonder that her own mother, who had tended to look down at her own rings whenever she talked, had so often gotten things wrong."

Without the gestures, the grimaces and the grins, you may capture the words but get things wrong.

Then there's the matter of class participation. It is important for you, for your classmates and, indeed, for your professor, for you to offer an insight, answer a question or two. If your focus is on the screen, you will be something of an outsider, missing the movement and excitement of the class; volunteering becomes more of a knock on the door than an excited utterance. Further, and perhaps surprisingly, you participate by "being there." You have no idea how much you contribute to the class *merely* by looking at the professor. Professors, like Quindlen's character, need to read the audience, its gestures, grimaces, and grins. "Am I making things clear?" "Is it time to move on?" "Is my favorite footnote really that boring?"

Visualize making a speech when everyone is facing the other way.

The final potential problem with computers is that they may prevent active review. Handwritten notes cry out for margin notes, arrows, and additions. The need is always to be *involved* with the material, not just *rereading* your notes but *reworking* your notes, restating the rules, considering new hypos, asking if what you learned yesterday is consistent with what you learned today. This requires *writing*, not just cutting and pasting.

Bottom line, if you are using a laptop, fine, but consider some pledges:

> *I will <u>not</u> keep my hands on the keys at all times.*

When a question is asked, I will think, not scroll.

I will look up and participate.

I will only write down key points, and never, not once, complete sentences.

Don't get the notes but miss the class.

Outlines and Old Exams

"Outlining" is a grand law school tradition and, like briefing, a brilliant educational device. Outlines combine case briefs, class notes, and any outside reading you have done. There is nothing magical about outlining except doing it. Its value is not the product but the production. It is yet another way to be actively involved with the material. ("Where does this interesting tidbit fit? Should it go under Topic A or Topic B and, come to think of it, what's the difference between A and B?") As for the major categories, the pompous Roman Numerals, the Table of Contents of your casebook can be helpful.

"Have you started your Property outline yet?" Dreaded words. I am reminded of the nightmare we all have had, something along the lines of walking to take a final and suddenly realizing you forgot to take the class.

"Property?"

Most students begin outlining about halfway through the semester.

Some find it helpful, toward the end of the semester, to review old finals, either by themselves or in a study group. Many schools maintain files of them, and there are books giving typical exam questions. Writing the answers will help, although, as a student, I would look at an old exam and simply freeze—there was simply no way I could answer it. On the real test I thanked my Little Voice shouting "You're doomed!" and moved on.

If you are going to take a multiple choice, as opposed to essay, test, old tests and books showing models might be very helpful. They will give you a good sense of the format and how you should approach it.

Study Aids, Canned Briefs, and Commercial Outlines

Most professors advise not to rely on canned briefs or commercial outlines knowing, full well, that you will believe the second-year student who assures you that someone in his class used nothing but canned briefs ("Didn't even buy the book!") and did great. Probably the most important advice in this entire book: *Never believe second-year students*.

One problem with study aids is that they cover more than you need to know. I recall a short story:

A man commits murder in the victim's living room. "I must wipe my fingerprints off the glass I was drinking from!" Fair enough, he does. "What about the table? Did I touch it? Why take a chance?" He wipes the table. "Maybe I went into the kitchen! I don't think I did, but I can't

> *be too sure, it will take just a few minutes!" The*
> *next morning, the murderer is found in the attic*
> *... slavishly wiping off old trunks.*

There are scores and scores of legal doctrines that you just don't cover in your classes. Treatises cover them all. The risk is getting further and further from the topics you did cover and eventually finding yourself in the attic.

Outside materials can be valuable if you make them your last, not your first, choice. If you are having a particularly difficult time with an area, a treatise might help. Once you have finished a topic, it is helpful to read a Nutshell or commercial treatise as a method of coming at the material from a different perspective. It is helpful to see how others have organized the material, to read how others have described the rules, and to think about examples others have used to illustrate the doctrines. Treatises can also help overcome the discreteness of the case method by showing where a particular topic is in the forest.

Study Groups

One of the best things about practicing law is talking cases with colleagues. After law school I practiced with a Legal Services Program. Every Friday afternoon, we sat around the table in our small law library and talked cases. I was representing a group of low income families, mostly farm workers, and their complaint was that a large cattle feedlot had moved next to their small community along with flies, smells, and general health hazards. The Friday meeting went something like this:

"How is your feed-lot case going?"

"Great! I found a wonderful case, right on point. It holds a feedlot's a public nuisance. I'm moving for an injunction next week."

"But won't you have a problem with the Knowles case?"

"No, I can get around Knowles by arguing X."

"Yeah, but if you argue X, won't they come back with Y?"

"I thought of that. If they do, I'll argue Z."

"I dunno. Do that and they'll come back with W."

Exciting, hard-headed legal analysis. A reporter, who sat in, had a slightly different take:

"Oh, no! They've overrun the Nitpicks! Retreat to the Quibbles!"

So be it; some people don't appreciate Mozart. Once you get into your studies, law will be about the only thing you want to talk about, to the great consternation of friends and significant others.

Many students find formal study groups productive. Working with others is a tricky business. Some may dominate; others seek free rides. Study groups will require you to negotiate, often implicitly, the critical dynamics of working with others, including, perhaps, some explicit breaks:

"Let's stop for a few moments. This group doesn't seem to be working out. We never get as far as we

plan. There are too many distractions. What can we do to improve this?"

Or, more to the point:

"Lee, shut up!"

A few tips:

1. Everyone should feel comfortable enough to ask "dumb questions" and to admit confusion. Learn. Don't maintain image.

2. Structure the sessions. Will you go over more than one subject? Will you review by discussing the cases or by working on problems, possibly old exam questions? How much time will be spent?

3. Consider having discussion leaders. Rotate them. "Next week, you do Property, I'll do Contracts." One effective way to learn is to teach: planning and conducting a review session can be quite educational.

4. It is *not* a good idea to divide the first-year curriculum among the group to prepare outlines. "Kingsfield, you take Contracts." The true value of outlines comes in putting them together. Each person should outline each course.

5. One really fun thing to do, near the end of the semester, is to come up with a list of categories, such as "Worst Case," "Funniest Case," "Most Pathetic Plaintiff," "Most Dastardly Defendant," and then, at the next session, report back. It is a

marvelous way to review cases and to see how much you have learned.

Don't feel bad if you're not in a study group. You can do brilliantly without one, and they are not for everyone. Some people work better alone. So be it! But, outside the formal structure of study groups, be sure to "talk law" with other students every chance you get.

How Much Time?

About half way through the first semester one of my students came to me.

> *"I'm doing all the reading and briefing and have even started on my outlines. But I still have time for my family and going to an occasional movie. What am I doing wrong?"*

Don't get all caught up in the law school hype. Sure, it is demanding, and, sure, it will probably take more time and intense preparation than you are used to. But you don't have to become a mole. Several years ago there was a national study that indicated that law students average about two and a half hours of study for each hour in class. Assuming you are carrying 15 units, this works out to about 53 hours per week. This is surely a full-time load, but don't think that all your classmates are studying all the time and that you must do so to keep up. Realize that we all like to play games with each other. Some will claim that they hardly study at all, others will claim that they study all the time, have already finished their outlines (although they haven't taken the course), and have found secret study aids that, in addition, help you lose weight.

You may be setting a pattern that you will follow your entire career. If you are doing just enough to get by, I surely don't want you for my lawyer. On the other hand, if you put your studies before your family or health, it is likely your job will come first when you graduate. Actually, this might not be such a bad thing: some of the happiest people I know are "workaholics." It is, however, lousy for your family. No one ever dies thinking, "I should have spent more time at the office."

If you, like me, planned your entire undergraduate life around a single guiding principle, "No classes before 11," you will be shocked to learn that studying in the early morning hours is the most productive. After you wake up, you are as alert as you will be; thereafter, it is all downhill. I find that if I start working around 6 a.m., I can get as much done in one hour as I can in two or three in the late afternoon or evening.

Trees and Forests

Usually your focus will be quite narrow, on a particular case or, indeed, a particular paragraph. Every now and then, step back and try to get an orientation as to where you are and how a particular case fits with the others you have read.

A good table of contents helps. Assume that you're using Dobbs, *Torts and Compensation*, and have just read a case by the name of *Cullison v.*

Medley. Where it fits in the big picture? Turn to the table of contents and see where the case is.

To put a case in context, begin with it and expand outward along the book's outline.

a. What does *Cullison v. Medley* add to your understanding of "Assault" that the other cases did not? Was it added to the casebook to show the same rule of law in a different factual context? To show a variation on the rule of law?

b. How does the subsection "Assault" relate to the one of equal rank: "Battery"? How are the cases in those two sections the same? How are they different?

You can use this technique to go where no one has gone before: the future.

"Wow, look here. Next we'll read about 'False Imprisonment.' I wonder what that is. How

might it be different from the assault cases?
How might it be the same? How will it fit into
the general topic of Chapter 2?"

The periodic journeys into the vast unknown
shouldn't take very long, only a few minutes. I
don't even suggest you write anything: just sit, look
at the table of contents, and ask yourself questions.

At first it will be difficult even to begin to answer
the questions I have suggested, and indeed, some
may be without rational answer. (Some cases seem
to be in casebooks simply "Because they're there.")
Still, the questions take you beyond the narrow
focus of the particular case and, ever so slowly, the
overall picture clears. The trick is knowing both the
particular and the general, in seeing both the tree
and the forest.

Treatises, hornbooks, nutshells and law review
articles can also help put the tree into the forest.

As you wander the halls of your first year, you
are something of a tree yourself. How can you keep
your orientation?

Journals

Law study is turbulent and overwhelming. Expect
moments of exhilaration and expect moments of
deep self-doubt. Every now and then, quit the hurly-burly and step back to reflect on what is happening to you. Consider keeping a journal. Take 20 to
30 minutes a few times a week to be with yourself
and your thoughts.

My students, after initial grumbles, tell me they got a great deal out of it. Graduates tell me that they reread with great interest.

Write your thoughts, because, until you write them, you really don't know what they are. In your head they are just vague impressions and fragments of ideas; on paper they take shape and content. Write *now* while you are experiencing what will be an intense and highly significant period in your life. Next year it will be too late:

"First year? I liked it, at least some of it, I think."

Many journal entries will be first-year gossip. But occasionally force yourself to attempt something in the nature of an essay.

- *Reflections on a particular case or legal doctrine.* Did you find it just? Were there certain aspects of the case that you found of special interest that your classmates and professor did not?

   Once an anthropology graduate student was sitting in a Torts class. The plaintiff went to the circus in Ames, Iowa, and, as fate would have it, an elephant backed up and defecated on him.

   "I wasn't interested in assumption of risk," the student told me. "But why would someone in a rural state be so upset to sue?"

- *Reflections on law school.* How is it affecting you? Is it what you thought it would be? How does law school compare with undergraduate education? What about competition? What of male/female reactions in the classroom? Do you participate in class? Why or why not?

- *Reflections on lawyering.* Based on what you see, do you think you will like being a lawyer? What do you think the lawyers who handled a particular case were feeling? Were thinking? Could they have done something to avoid litigation?

Consider writing yourself a letter. Address it to yourself as a third-year student. What will you want to tell that person about you? "Why I came to law school" might be a good topic. In the years to come, maybe even next year, when you are considering what kind of job to take, it will be good to recall why you came to law school.

Finally, what if you think keeping a journal is a waste of time? Write an essay: "Why keeping a journal is a waste of time."

You can't win. It's my book.

CHAPTER 11

WRITING LAW SCHOOL EXAMS: THE ONLY SKILL WORTH HAVING!

The first thing you'll notice is that law school exams are written in Greek. You will confront an indistinguishable mass of words, all blurred, all running together. Let me give you an example from an exam I gave last year.

Question 1

Acme Construction Inc. *allkdfj pqwiur nbvmznx kdk ieur pire jdjo ghjhgfiyr oiyu re otjhg lkpqyr pqlxh plvhgfd qwert yuiop asdf fgh zxcvb mjuik opk kiuy juyhgr dqwsxcgy plmbht fdghj qmpzwno hyde nhyu cdew mkoiy asdfqwer.* Discuss. Be concise but don't overlook anything. Pay particular attention to *kuzt op mdzopor yuiopt.*

You look around the room. Everyone else has already started writing. Sweat runs into your eyes and drops onto the page, smudging the only words you understood.

Take a deep breath. Remember this: All law school exam questions relate to the material you covered in the course. Eventually you will be able to understand the question, and you will be able to answer it. The folks who have started writing are writing home.

Don't worry that you didn't get "enough" sleep the night before. While advisable, sometimes sleep just doesn't come. No one has ever, not ever, gone to sleep during a law school exam.

What should be your *goal*? It is not to fill up a lot of space, nor is it to use a lot of legal terms. More surprisingly, it is *not* to show how much law you learned during the semester, nor is it even to appear brilliant.

All good legal writing is alike. Your goal is always to *help* the reader (here, the professor) understand how the law would impact a specific factual situation. Law school exams generally give you a fact pattern which ends with folks being disappointed, mad or injured. (There are no happy endings.) How can you help the reader understand how the law would resolve the conflict? You must tell the reader the legal issues that would be involved in the dispute, the law governing such issues, and then give your best thinking on how a court would come out in resolving the matter.

Issue

First, you must identify the *legal issues* buried in the problem. Most law exams have several issues and each must be discussed separately in its own paragraph or so. One error I want to flag. Assume a problem raises three issues. It is a mistake to discuss the plaintiff's arguments as to all three and then turn to defendants argument as to all three. Discuss both positions on each issue. When you bring contention and counter contention together, your analysis goes deeper.

Rule

Second, you have to tell what *legal rule* or *legal doctrine* a court would look to in order to resolve the issue presented. There is no need to have memorized the exact wording of the legal rule you are to apply; it is enough to give the reader a fairly accurate statement of it. As to form, again there are no magic words:

> *"The law is that . . . ."* or
>
> *"The courts have held that . . . ."* or
>
> *"The U.C.C. requires that . . . ."*

Lawyers encounter two kinds of problems: first trying to figure out what the controlling legal rule is or should be, and, second, applying a given legal rule to a fact pattern. You will encounter both on exams.

Recall *Walker–Thomas*. The buyer was resisting enforcement of a particularly onerous contract term on the basis that it was unconscionable. The first issue the court had to decide was whether the law allowed it to refuse to enforce unconscionable terms. This is a legal issue, a fight over the law. I call these Type 1 problems. These problems are frequent: Is a prior case distinguishable? What is the proper interpretation of a statute? In the context of *Walker–Thomas*, which was a case in Washington D.C., if a similar case arose in Nebraska, the first question would be whether to follow that case in the sense of finding that the Nebraska courts also have the power to declare contracts unconscionable.

Assuming the court has that power, the next question is whether the particular term is unconscionable. Here the court would apply the law (the tests of unconscionability) to the facts, the contract term at issue. I call this Type 2 problem: the fight is over how the controlling law applies in a given factual situation. In practice these problems are frequent as well: the definition of murder is fairly clear and the question is whether the defendant did it.

To resolve Type 1 problems (legal questions), you consider questions of policy, draw analogies, and put hypotheticals. To resolve Type 2 problems, you focus on the facts.

Analysis

Third, you must give the reader your best thinking as to the factors the court would consider in either deciding what rule to apply or in applying the legal rule to the facts of the case. Consider *both sides*. An big error is *taking sides*. Once you conclude one side should win you become a partisan and will tend to overlook the good arguments the other side might have. To help the reader understand how the law might resolve the issue, both sides must be presented with equal vigor. You must adopt *"yes ... but"* reasoning: *"Yes,* the plaintiff has this good point, *but* the defendant can answer it with...."

Another typical error is the failure to be *explicit*. It may be clear to you why you are discussing certain facts or legal principles but you must tell that to the reader. Discussing a fact or legal principle, ask, *"So what?"* and then the rest of us.

Thus far I have given you the famous *IRAC* approach to exam-taking, without the *C*.

*I*ssue

*R*ule

*A*nalysis

*C*onclusion

The reason I leave off the "C" is that it tends to suggest that you must resolve the case—*"Plaintiff will win."* Such conclusions generally don't help the reader understand how a court might resolve the conflict. Write as if the reader is the decision-maker. That reader wants your best thinking on the issues presented and is not particularly interested in your conclusions unless they further your analysis: "Having looked at the plaintiff's and defendant's arguments as to this point, it strikes me that the plaintiff has the better arguments in that...."

That said, *IRAC* works well for individual issues. However, it fails to draw your attention to the need to account for the relationship *between* the issues. Let's say there are three issues, A, B, and C. To prevail, must the plaintiff win on all three issues (A *and* B *and* C) or is it enough if the plaintiff prevails on only one (A *or* B *or* C)? Or are we dealing with some form of new math: ([A *or* B] *and* C)?

After you have identified the issues a problem presents, be clear on the relationship between them before you start to write. Then, when you move from one issue to the next, tell the reader the relationship between the issue you just discussed and the one you are about to discuss. I'll show you a neat way of doing this later in the chapter.

Practice Test

What follows is a typical (at least for me) law school exam question. I follow it with two possible answers which I then analyze. If you wish, you can try your hand at writing an answer before you see my answers, or you might wish to wait until after you read them.

Isn't the latter cheating? No. It is one thing to read something and say, "That's good." It is something more to articulate why it is good. However, you must learn not only to recognize good writing and how to describe what constitutes it. You must *write* it.

In art museums, you will see aspiring artists copying the pictures of the masters; aspiring poets copy the work of masters as well, calling this "playing the sedulous ape." Play the ape: find a good piece of legal prose and *copy it* just to get a hands-on sense of how it is put together.

Rules of Law to Apply

These legal rules will come into play in answering the practice test. Reread them a couple of times before you begin writing your answer, and it is OK to refer back to them while you are writing.

1. If one is sued for breach of contract, it is a good defense to say, "I wasn't making a serious offer, and the person who is now suing me should have known it!" The law is that, after looking at the surrounding circumstances, if a reasonable third party would conclude that the person making the promise was not serious, then that promise is not enforceable.

2. The Statute of Frauds requires that some, not all, agreements be in writing. It generally goes something like this:

    The following contracts are invalid, unless the same, or note or memorandum thereof, is in writing and signed by the party to be charged:

    1. An agreement for the sale of real property.

    2.   * * *

    Cases interpreting the Statute of Frauds have indicated that it fulfills two purposes. The first purpose is to protect against false claims. A writing is good evidence that the parties actually agreed and that no one is making things up. The second purpose of the Statute is cautionary. People shouldn't enter into important legal transactions, such as the sale of realty, orally.

Written contracts ensure greater reflection on the part of the contracting parties.

3. Contracts for an illegal purpose are void and unenforceable. For example, a "contract," as in "there is a contract out on the Godfather," is unenforceable. Even if the assassin does his part, he can't sue to recover his promised fee. Such contracts are illegal on their "face" in that the illegality appears in the agreement itself: "I'll shoot Jones for $5,000." Some courts have extended the rule to prevent someone who has performed a contract in an illegal manner from suing on it.

The Question

Sleazy Sam and Billy Bigmouth ran into each other at the Lazy J Bar. After several drinks, Billy said, "You know, I think I'll blow this town and get into pictures."

"Oh yeah? How are you going to support yourself in Hollywood until they discover your major talent?" asked Sam.

"Why, I'll sell my house. You can have it for $60,000. Last week it was appraised at $120,000."

"You must be joking; that deal is too good to be true," replied Sam, having another drink.

"Man, it's just that you don't have the money."

"Look, I can have $60,000 cash at the end of the week."

"Bring it by."

"Are you serious?"

"Sure," laughed Bigmouth.

"Well, I need a new place for my bookmaking activities."

"That's illegal, but what you do with the place is your business," said Bigmouth. "Let's shake." The men shook and left the bar.

Three days later Sam received the following letter from Bigmouth:

Dear Sam,

Of course I was joking when I promised to sell you my house for $60,000 cash at the end of the week. In any event I don't want to do it. So there.

Yours truly,
(Signed) Billy
Bigmouth

Discuss.

Taking an exam, before you start writing, it is well to jot down some ideas on a separate piece of paper which will then serve as a rough outline. Do some jotting now.It's okay to go back and read the law and the problem.

Issue One:

Issue

Rule

Analysis (What P will argue; what D will argue as to that issue)

Issue Two

Issue

Rule

Analysis (What P will argue; what D will argue)

Issue

Issue

Rule

Analysis

If you wish, you can write an answer now or wait until after my discussion of the model answers.

Model Answers

As you work your way through these two examples, jot down what you like and don't like about them.

Answer Number One

This case is about Sam and Bill, who met in a bar and began to talk about the selling of Bill's house to Sam for $60,000. The issue is whether the alleged contract is enforceable or not.

First, Bill was clearly drunk.

Second, Bill was joking. He said as much in his letter to Sam. Who on earth would sell a $120,000 house for $60,000 in order to get into pictures? Sam was going to use the house for bookmaking activities, and that's illegal. And remember that Sam didn't think Bill was serious because he asked him "Are you serious?" Sam knew Bill was joking.

Because this deals with the sale of real property, the Statute of Frauds applies. The first English Statute of Frauds was enacted nearly 300 years ago to prevent fraud. In California the Statute is Civil Code § 1624. Many commentators in law reviews have argued that the statute, which has been adopted with modifications in many states, causes more fraud than it prevents. That is, it allows people who have made promises to get out of them simply because they are not in writing. Courts often try to get around the Statute of Frauds.

Bill will clearly win.

Answer Number Two

[Ed. Note: I put words of contrast in bold to illustrate their importance.]

There are several issues to be considered in this question:

1. *Did Bill make a serious offer to sell his house to Sam?*

2. *the Statute of Frauds applies, does the letter from Bill to Sam satisfy it?*

3. *Is the contract void because Sam intended to use the house for an illegal activity?*

The first issue is whether Bill was making a serious offer to sell his house. If he wasn't, then he has a good defense to any suit Sam files. The test will be, considering all of the circumstances, would a reasonable person conclude Bill was making a serious offer? Bill will claim he was joking and that Sam should have known it. He will point out that both men accidentally met in a bar. There is no indication that they met to discuss the sale of the house. He will also point out that both men were drinking. (If Bill had been drunk, that would be another defense.) He will argue that no reasonable person would believe he wanted to sell a $120,000 house for $60,000 in order to go into pictures. Note that there was nothing put in writing—it is reason-

able to assume that if Bill were seriously thinking about selling a house, it would be in writing.

On the other hand, Sam will argue that Bill appeared seriously to want to sell his home. First, Bill initiated the discussion. Second, he mentioned that the house had been recently appraised—one does that when one is planning to sell. Third, Bill told Sam he was serious, and both men shook hands, a traditional way to conclude a deal. If Bill had been joking, he would have told Sam just that rather than shake hands. Finally, Bill himself thought the deal serious because he wrote the letter to Sam—had the joke been clear, he wouldn't have thought to write claiming it was a joke.

Even if it is found that Bill was making a serious offer, the agreement might still be unenforceable under the Statute of Frauds. The Statute applies because the deal concerns the sale of real property. It requires that some writing be signed by the party to be charged (here Bill). The original agreement was oral. However, Bill wrote Sam saying he wanted out of the deal. He signed that letter. **The question becomes**, then, can a letter denying the seriousness of a prior oral promise be used to satisfy the Statute of Frauds? **On the one hand**, it appears as though it might. One of the purposes of the Statute is to prevent fraud—by signing the letter, Bill admits he made the promise to sell the house. Sam didn't make up the agreement. **On the other hand**, another purpose of the Statute is cautionary—to ensure that people reflect before committing themselves to important deals. Obviously a letter trying to get out *of a deal cannot be said to fulfill any cautionary function: it comes too late.*

Assuming *Bill was serious in making the offer and* **even if** *his letter satisfies the Statute of Frauds, there* **is another** *possible defense, that of illegality. The law states that contracts illegal on their face are unenforceable.* **However,** *this contract isn't illegal on its face—it is not for bookmaking, it is for the sale of a house. Assuming a seller knows that the buyer is to use what is purchased for an illegal activity, can he, must he, refuse to go ahead with the deal? I assume that contracts for illegal acts are not enforced in order to deter illegal activity. That policy would apply here and make the contract unenforceable.*

Before continuing, I would advise you to go back and reread both answers, noting in the margins what you liked and disliked about each. The more you put into this exercise, the more you will get out of it. Again I hope you will take the opportunity to write an answer yourself.

Given the length of this chapter, and your growing weariness, I'm going to stop right here and pick up my analysis of the two answers in the next chapter. Get some rest.

CHAPTER 12

A TALE OF TWO ANSWERS

Dickens is in the office of his agent and the agent is clearly irritated, "Come on Charles, which was it? The best of times or the worst of times?"

We'll look at the two answers given to the practice exam in the last chapter. Most would agree that Answer Two is better. I wrote both and the first illustrates common first-year errors:

1. Taking sides.

2. Failing to state the controlling law and making implicit statements.

3. Failing to note the relationship between issues.

4. Mixing legal categories.

5. Discussing law "because it's there."

The second answer I wrote to give you a feel for a really good answer. Don't be depressed by it; it took me a long time to write it, and I *wrote* the question. Reading and analyzing it will, however, give you a feel for good legal writing.

Before you look at my analysis, reread Answer One, looking for the errors I just mentioned. Then reread Answer Two to see how it avoided them.

Answer One

Answer One begins:

This case is about Sam and Bill, who met in a bar and began to talk about the selling of Bill's house to Sam for $60,000. The issue is whether the alleged contract is enforceable or not.

This is a rather weak opening. How so? Jot!

It tells the reader nothing that is not already known and does not focus the issues at all. The issue "is the contract enforceable" is so broad as to be meaningless.

The major fault, however, is that one senses that the student just started writing without first *analyzing* the problem. You must spend some of your allotted time, but not too much, thinking about and organizing your answer.

Look at the opening paragraph in the second answer:

There are several issues to be considered in this question:

1. *Did Bill make a serious offer to sell his house to Sam?*

2. *Assuming that the Statute of Frauds applies, does the letter from Bill to Sam satisfy it?*

3. *Is the contract void because Sam intended to use the house for an illegal activity?*

Why is this such an improvement?

Here the student *planned* before writing. The student has a good sense of the issues to be discussed and probably a sense of how they all fit together. It is *not* necessary to list all of the issues up front. You can start:

The first issue is whether Bill made a serious offer.

Still, before you being writing, have a fairly good idea of all of the issues. Don't suddenly take off on the first issue you see.

Stating the issues up front does have some advantages. It forces you to organize your thoughts and gives you instant credibility (as long as you have listed most of the issues the prof is looking for).

Answer One continues:

First, Bill was clearly drunk.

I see two problems with this. Jot!

First the student has *manufactured* facts—the question did not say Bill was drunk, simply that he was drinking. Be careful to get the facts straight and be aware of the critical distinction between *observed data* and *inference*. Don't jump to conclusions. Why do you think the student jumped here? (It is never enough to identify bad practice; one must also get at its root cause.) Here the student had taken Bill's side and figured his being drunk would help him get out of the contract. Always maintain your neutrality: you don't care who wins.

The second problem is that the statement is implicit: *So what* if Bill was drunk? Is this a legal point or just an interesting comment? We don't know. Observe how the second answer avoids both of these problems:

"If Bill had been drunk, that would be another defense."

This doesn't assume Bill was drunk and tells us the legal significance of being drunk.

The first answer continues:

Second, Bill was joking. He said as much in his letter to Sam. Who would sell a $120,000 house for $60,000 in order to get into pictures? Sam was going to use the house for bookmaking activities, and that's illegal. And remember that Sam didn't think Bill was serious because he asked him "Are you serious?" Sam knew Bill was joking.

There are multiple problems here: no law, taking sides, and mixing categories. See how? Jot!

Law. There is no attempt to state the controlling law. Without some knowledge of the legal principles to be applied, the reader will not be able to understand how they would apply in the specific case. Merely calling the reader's attention to the fact that Bill was joking forces the reader to tie that fact to a controlling legal principle. Here is how Answer Two handles this problem:

The first issue is whether Bill was making a serious offer to sell his house. If he wasn't, then he has a good defense to any suit Sam files. The test will be, considering all of the circumstances, would a reasonable person conclude Bill was making a serious offer?

Unless your prof says otherwise, in stating the controlling law, you *don't* have to cite case names, Restatements, or statutes. All you have to do is alert the reader to the governing law. You can use your own words in describing it.

Taking sides. The student is simply making arguments for Bill. The right question to ask is "What would the other side say when Bill's lawyer argued Bill was joking?" All the counter facts will jump out. The problem with "taking sides" is that you fail to see the other side's point of view: without rubbing contention against counter-contention, your analysis is doomed to remain superficial.

Always ask, "How will the other side respond?" Or, more simply, keep in mind, *"Yes,* that's true, *but . . . ."*

Mixing categories. The business of illegality is thrown into a discussion of seriousness. Not good. Legal analysis is *analysis by category*. "Illegality" and "seriousness" are *separate* legal categories; each, on their own, could make the contract unenforceable. Always keep categories separate. (We will see, however, that the same fact can be used in more than one category, *viz,* the lack of writing going to the seriousness issue and triggering the Statute of Frauds issue.)

Because this deals with the sale of real property, the Statute of Frauds applies. The first English Statute of Frauds was enacted nearly 300 years ago to prevent fraud. In California the Statute is Civil Code § 1624. Many commentators in law reviews have argued that the statute, which has been adopted with modifications in many states, causes more fraud than it prevents. That is, it allows people who have made promises to get out of them simply because they are not in writing. Courts often try to get around the Statute of Frauds.

This paragraph reads like a good undergraduate essay. Why is that a fatal flaw?

Writing law always *involves the interplay of law and fact*. Recounting the history of the Statute of Frauds does not help the reader understand how the law would impact the controversy between Bill and Sam. Note that *"So what?"* applies to long discussions of law as well as long discussions of fact. You must explicitly tie the law you are discussing to the facts of the case, and you must explicitly tie the facts you are discussing to the law.

Fortunately, there is usually little need, in law exams, to cite specific code sections ("Civil Code § 1624") or, for that matter, specific case names. Case names may be important in some courses, such as Constitutional Law. In most first year courses, however, case names are not significant. Ask your professor.

Finally:

Bill will clearly win.

If it were that clear, the question would not have been asked.

IRS Transitions

A final criticism of Answer One is that it fails to show the relationship between the issues and, when it introduces a new issue, fails to indicate its legal significance. Consider the first sentences of the first two paragraphs.

First, Bill was clearly drunk.

Second, Bill was joking.

What is the legal significance of Bill being drunk? He would have a defense to the contract action, and it would be helpful to the reader to know this. Let's rewrite:

First, Bill was clearly drunk, and this would constitute a defense to any suit filed by Sam.

We should rewrite the second topic sentence as well:

Second, Bill was joking, and the law says that individuals are not to be held to their jokes.

But what is the relationship *between* the *intoxication* issue and the *prankster* issue? It could be either an *and* relation or an *or* relation. To successfully defend the action, must Bill show both that he was drunk *and* that he was joking, or is it enough if he shows one or the other?

To show an *or* relationship:

Second, assuming Bill could not show he was drunk, if he could show he was joking this would constitute a defense.

To show an *and* relationship:

Not only must Bill show he was drunk, in addition he must show he was joking.

Compare the two major transitions in Answer Two:

1. *Even if* it is found that Bill was making a serious offer, the agreement might still be unenforceable under the Statute of Frauds.

2. *Assuming* Bill was serious in making the offer and *even if* his letter satisfies the Statute of Frauds, *there is another* possible defense, that of illegality.

I call these *IRS* transitions. Not only do they introduce the next topic, but also relate it to the last topic or topics discussed *and* tell the reader the legal significance of the topic.

*I*ntroduce

*R*elate

*S*ignificance

Forcing yourself to think and write in terms of IRS transitions not only will help the reader understand your writing, but also will help you to think through the relationships. I return to this topic in my chapter on legal writing.

Before turning to the good cop, Answer Two, note that the seriousness issue is a Type 2 legal issue. You must test the facts against a relatively clear legal standard. The issue concerning whether the letter of revocation satisfies the Statute of Frauds, as well as the impact of the planned illegal use, are Type 1 issues. Here you must decide what would be the appropriate legal rule in a given factual context. In Type 2 cases, the facts are at issue; in Type 1, the law is.

Answer Two

There are several issues to be considered in this question:

1. *Did Bill make a serious offer to sell his house to Sam?*

2. *Assuming that the Statute of Frauds applies, does the letter from Bill to Sam satisfy it?*

3. *Is the contract void because Sam intended to use the house for an illegal activity?*

The first issue is whether Bill was making a serious offer to sell his house. If he wasn't, then he has a good defense to any suit Sam files. The test will be, considering all of the circumstances, would a reasonable person conclude Bill was making a serious offer? Bill will claim he was joking and that Sam should have known it. He will point out that both men accidentally met in a bar. There is no indication that they met to discuss the sale of the house. He will also point out that both men were drinking. (If Bill had been drunk, that would be another defense.) He will argue that no reasonable person would believe he wanted to sell a $120,000 house for $60,000 in order to go into pictures. Note that there was nothing put in writing—it is reasonable to assume that if Bill were seriously thinking about selling a house, it would be in writing.

This is really good. How come? Jot!

It starts off discussing the law. Again *precise statements of law* are not required, nor need you memorize the language of statutes or Restatements or the key language from opinions.

The seriousness issue requires the student to apply a relatively clear legal standard to an ambiguous fact pattern. The paragraph shows good factual analysis. For example, note the use of the fact that the deal was not in writing. There is a *separate* issue concerning the Statute of Frauds, but here the fact of no writing is skillfully used as evidence of lack of serious intent. Well done!

On the other hand, Sam will argue that Bill appeared seriously to want to sell his home. First, Bill initiated the discussion. Second, he mentioned that the house had been recently appraised—one does that when one is planning to sell. Third, Bill told Sam he was serious and both men shook hands, a traditional way to conclude a deal. If Bill had been joking, he would have told Sam just that, rather than shake hands. Finally, Bill himself thought the deal serious because he wrote the letter to Sam—had the joke been clear, he wouldn't have thought to write claiming it was a joke.

This paragraph answers the essential question, "What will the other side say?" (or, to state the matter differently, employs *"Yes, but"* analysis). Is it necessary to reach a conclusion as to which side has the better arguments? Not necessarily.

This is a tricky point. Physicians often don't make good law students as they have been trained in a system where coming to the right answer is crucial: "Does the patient have TB?" In law, it is our analyses, not our conclusions, that matter. Take the issue of whether Bill's letter satisfies the Statute of Frauds. The competing contentions would be:

> *Bill: My letter could not satisfy the Statute of Frauds because the goal of the Statute is to force people to reflect before they enter into important deals. My letter was written after I made my hasty promise. To allow it to satisfy the Statute would defeat its purpose.*

> *Sam: Not so. The main purpose of the Statute of Frauds is to prevent false claims from being made. It requires that before one person can sue another for the breach of certain kinds of promises, that person must produce written evidence that the promise was made. And there is that evidence, Bill's letter.*

Developing the competing contentions is your main work. It helps the reader see how a court would approach the issue, and it shows that you know how to analyze problems as a lawyer would. To further that analysis, it may be proper to reach a conclusion—not because it is necessary to reach the "right" conclusion, but rather to round off the analysis, to show the reader that you have a legal sense that some arguments are better than others. Two important lessons come from this discussion:

> *1. Don't freeze up in fear that you won't reach the proper conclusion.*

2. *Don't simply assert your conclusion; always justify it.*

Take the following conclusion:

I think that Sam will win the Statute of Frauds issue.

Well and good. Perhaps, in a real court, he would. Yet, as written, the conclusion tells us nothing about the only thing we are really interested in: the student's ability to analyze problems. Perhaps the student simply made a lucky guess—after all, the odds aren't all that bad. Compare:

I think Sam will win the Statute of Frauds issue. Although Bill's letter was written after the promise, and hence could not fulfill any cautionary function, it seems that the main thrust of the Statute is to prevent false claims. Here we know Bill made the promise because we have his signed letter to prove it.

In sum, while analysis may stand without conclusion, conclusion can seldom stand without analysis.

Continuing with Answer Two:

Even if *it is found that Bill was making a serious offer, the agreement might still be unenforceable under the Statute of Frauds. The Statute applies because the deal concerns the sale of real property. It requires that some writing be signed by the party to be charged (here Bill). The original agreement was oral.* **However**, *Bill wrote Sam saying he wanted out of the deal. He signed that letter.* **The question becomes**, *then, can a letter denying the seriousness* *of a prior oral promise be used to satisfy the Statute of Frauds?* **On the one hand**, *it appears as though it might. One of the purposes of the Statute is to prevent fraud—by signing the letter, Bill admits he made the promise to sell the house. Sam didn't make up the agreement.* **On the other hand**, *another purpose of the Statute is cautionary—to ensure that people reflect before committing themselves to important deals. Obviously a letter trying to get out of a deal cannot be said to fulfill any cautionary function: it comes too late.*

Another job well done. Nice transition. It shows we are dealing with an **"or"** relationship between seriousness and the Statute. Good statement of the law and of the issue.

Note that this analysis is essentially different from the "seriousness" analysis. There we had a clear legal standard and had to apply it to an ambiguous fact pattern. Here the facts are clear and the law is ambiguous: Should the letter satisfy the Statute? The model answer uses the proper mode of analysis. Because the Statute does not tell us what it means by "note" or "memorandum," we must define those terms in light of the **purposes and goals** of the Statute. Would they be furthered or defeated by allowing the letter to count? This is something a court would have to decide.

Continuing with Answer Two

Even if *Bill were serious in making the offer and* **even if** *his letter satisfies the Statute of Frauds,* **there is another** *possible defense, that of illegali-*

*ty. The law is that contracts illegal on their face are unenforceable. **However**, this contract isn't illegal on its face—it is not for bookmaking, it is for the sale of a house. Assuming a seller knows that the buyer is to use what is purchased for an illegal activity, can he, must he, refuse to go ahead with the deal? I assume that contracts for illegal acts are not enforced in order to deter illegal activity. That policy would apply here and make the contract unenforceable.*

This starts well. There is a good transition. We know that even if Sam wins on the serious issue and on the Statute of Frauds point, he still may be a loser if he blows the illegality point. The discussion of illegality would be much improved had the student asked, "What will the other side argue?" There are powerful arguments against Bill's position here, so powerful, in fact, that courts will likely reject the defense—although that is an issue I will leave to your Contracts course.

Finally, one last point. You are to discuss *all* issues that are *fairly raised* in the problem *even though* you may think one would be determinative. For example, even if you were convinced Bill would win his case on the Statute of Frauds point, you must still discuss seriousness and illegality because they are fairly raised in the problem.

CHAPTER 13

EXAM TIPS

The last chapter focused on how to write law exams. Here I will discuss spotting issues, organizing answers, and deepening analysis. There may be some repetition. While repetition on an *exam* is a vice, generally, repetition is a virtue. This stuff is difficult; hearing it more than once should help.

At the end of this chapter I will address Multiple Choice exams. A lot of what I have to say first, about the need to focus and to spot issues, applies both to essay and multiple choice exams.

The basic points I'll cover are:

-Your goal.

-Staying focused.

-Spotting issues (the law exam as art).

-Outlining your answers (briefly).

-Asking "So what?" and "Yes ... but ..."

-Writing down the middle.

Your Goal

Your goal in writing an exam is *not* to discuss as much law as you can, it is *not* to use as much legal jargon as you can, and it is *not* to resolve the question in this sense: "The plaintiff will win this one." The goal of all legal writing is the same. It is to *help* the reader understand how the law will apply to a specific factual situation. This is true whether your reader is a law professor, a senior partner, a judge, or, indeed, a client.

Write as if the reader *is* the decision-maker; he or she wants your best thinking on the factors that should be considered in making the decision. Faced with a tough decision, the reader is not helped by long discussions of the law, nor by being bamboozled with a lot of legal jargon, or even by being told what to decide. What this person *needs* is your help in sorting out the problem.

What do you know about your reader? If the reader is a lawyer, he or she has a background knowledge of the law *but* is *not* 100% on top of the specific law that applies to the case at hand. I stress this because often students fail to mention the controlling legal rule or standard on their exams.

"I didn't bother telling the law, I mean, like, you know, you're the professor."

This is error; you must always state the controlling law. First, you must show you know it. Second, once you have stated it, it will structure your analysis.

What does this reader need to know?

1. What legal issues the problem presents;

2. What legal rules will apply;

3. Your analysis of how these rules will apply to the given facts; and

4. The relationship between the issues you discuss.

This is basically the traditional exam writing format, IRAC (Issue, Rule, Analysis, Conclusion), without the C, but with an added emphasis on the relationship between issues.

The reason I drop the C from IRAC is not that conclusions are inappropriate, especially if they further analysis. However free-standing global conclusions ("The plaintiff will win") are not needed and do nothing to help the reader figure out why the plaintiff should win. Further, most issues on exams will be close ones; as long as you analysis them, don't worry if you cannot conclude them. Rather than conclusions, I stress the need to tell the reader the relationship between issues because it helps both the reader and *you* sort out the problem.

So, forget IRAC and embrace IRARI (Issue, Rule, Analysis, and Relationship between Issues).

Staying Focused

After all that study, after all that struggle, one morning you will enter the room, and it's just you and the exam, now the size of a telephone book. You sit, waiting further instructions. Sweat pours into your eyes. Your little voice will go bonkers. Thank it:

"Thank you, Little Voice of Doom. I know you think this was all a terrible mistake. But I have a

pretty good handle on this stuff and I will be able to understand and answer the questions. Now hush!"

After the panic, you will *enjoy* the exam. It will be a fascinating intellectual puzzle. It will push you, confound you, and ultimately delight you. *Exams are not awful.* The prospect of exams is awful. Grades may be awful. Exams themselves are adrenaline, discovery, and adventure. The hard part about exams is generally not having too little to say, but having too much to say.

Be with the exam. Ooommm. Thinking of things outside the exam, such as "Do's and Don't of Taking Exams," will shift your focus. Some use "checklists," ones which reduce all the learning of a course into one mnemonic device, perhaps "Tippecanoe and Tyler too." Checklist are thought to be a good ways of picking up the issues. There are dangers. While there may be a "Tippecanoe," there might not be a "Tyler too," but, because you are looking for it, you might think you see it. And there will be issues on the exam that you didn't put in your mnemonic, perhaps an "I like Ike." Focusing on the checklist you may overlook them.

Advice of second year students diverts your focus. "Professor Rehnquist is a liberal, so always take the bleeding-heart position," or "Professor Cro–Magnon isn't that sophisticated; you really have to draw pictures for him." Second year students don't know what worked for them. Perhaps Rehnquist, deep down, loves hard-headed, heartless analysis, and the very thing that prevented the student from doing much better on the exam was his wishy-washy, bleeding-heart position. And, as for Professor Cro–Magnon, how many stick drawings of bison can one person take?

No one is smart enough to psych out the professor. Don't try a special writing or analytical style based on what you think the professor wants. You're going to be busy enough just sorting out the problem.

Of course, there are no controlled studies as to what is effective exam writing. However, some hunches are better than others. To reassure yourself as to this matter of "no controlled studies," look at the lower-right hand corner of the title page of this book: make sure it doesn't say, in teeny-tiny print,

Placebo Edition.

Spotting Issues

After your Torts exam, the person you had thought was your best friend will ask, "Did you see the assumption of risk issue?"

Don't discuss exams with others. Nothing will make you more miserable. But take heart. Few students, no students, get all of the issues. Usually in my classes the top exams have missed maybe two, three, or more of the key issues: they developed the others with such depth and flare that these omissions are overwhelmed.

It is, of course, better to spot as many issues as you can.

-Read the question a couple of times, underlining or making notes in the margins.

-Read *aggressively*. Assume that *every fact in the problem is there for a reason.* Why is it that the defendant kicked the plaintiff's *ugly* dog? "Why is that fact there? Why not a cute dog? Why not a rabid dog who always wanted to be a good dog?" There is very little filler in law school exams.

Once you have spotted several issues, discuss them *all*, even if you believe that one would resolve the case.

Although the defendant has a very good chance of winning on the Statute of Frauds issue, there are two other defenses that should be considered.

Don't put all your eggs in one basket.

Sometimes students make up false issues, either because they expected them to be on the exam (they were, after all, on the checklist) or because they want to show the professor they learned something during the semester.

Had the plaintiff assumed the risk, then that would be a defense. The doctrine was first developed in the case of Jones v. Smith, and today the elements of "assumption of risk" are blah, blah, blah. Of course, because the plaintiff was at home, in bed, asleep, when the defendant's car smashed through the wall, it doesn't seem he assumed the risk, unless, of course, we are

> *talking Cosmic Assumption of Risk which leads us to what I wanted to talk about all along, Sartre and Boyle's Second Law of Thermodynamics.*

Discuss only issues that were *fairly raised* by the problem. If you are not *sure* whether an issue was fairly raised, err on the side of inclusion but don't spend much time developing your answer. Recall how Answer 2 in the last chapter dealt with the possible issue of intoxication:

> *If Bill had been drunk, that would be another defense.*

This gives you some protection against overlooking an issue but doesn't get you sidetracked on to long discussions that may lead nowhere.

Outlining

Exam questions will trigger a tidal wave of ideas: a towering mixture of issues, good points, and counter-arguments. You need to sort it all out or you will be awash. Make a rough outline. "Outline" suggests too much formality; on a separate piece of paper, jot down major categories and, below them, rough thoughts.

In the problem I discussed in the last chapter, there were three issues: Were the parties serious in making the contract? Did a letter withdrawing from an oral agreement satisfy the Statute of Frauds? Was the contract void for illegality? Jot, leaving spaces:

Serious?

Letter/Statute of Frauds

Illegal?

Now, as you turn things in your mind, jot down rough ideas to develop under each:

Serious?

   met in bar

   discussed details

This should not be a full-blown outline and should not be completed before you begin writing. It is designed merely to help you think through the problem and capture your initial ideas. You will continue to develop this list as you write your exam. Say you are writing on the seriousness issue and a point concerning illegality comes to mind. You don't want to forget it but you don't want to interrupt your flow. Jot down a couple of words on your list and then return to your answer.

Illegal

   not illegal on face—selling a house—

   why not enforce illegal Ks?

Some issues are more equal than others. It is probably best to start with the most difficult or challenging issues, as those will win the most points for good analysis. *Time is always a factor,* and you must keep track of it. If you run out, far better to miss the minor issues.

Don't spend time *not* making points. Long recitals of the facts and long conclusions where you essentially repeat what you have said just kill the clock.

Introductions and conclusions are great in most legal writing, since previews and repetitions help recall. However, the prof will be focused and hence these devices are not needed.

Be sure you are clear on the relationship between the issues. For example, must the defendant win *both* the seriousness issue *and* that of the Statute of Frauds or is one enough $(1+2$ or 1 or 2)? As I discussed previously, IRS transitions show these relationships. They introduce the next issue, relate it to the prior issue, and indicate its legal significance.

Thinking in terms of IRS transition will help you think through the problem. If you do so, good transitions will come naturally. Although I do not grade on style, looking back at the best papers, it strikes me how well they read. *Style follows understanding*.

"So what?" "Yes, but …"

The two common exams errors are the failure to be *explicit* and the failure to consider *both sides*. By failure to be explicit, I mean the failure to show how the facts you are discussing relate to the legal standard you are discussing. For example, out of the blue, a student may write:

"The two men met in a bar."

Without more, the reader is forced to ask, "What should I make of this interesting tidbit?" I like to think of these free-floating tidbits as *"free radi-*

cals.'' Their cure: ask yourself, as you merrily go along, *"So what?"*

"The two guys met at a bar." So what?

"Well, that might mean that they weren't serious in their negotiations." So what?

"If they weren't serious, that means, under a doctrine of contract law, that the contract is not enforceable."

Long discussions of law, not grounded in the specific facts of the case, are also *free radicals*.

The other common error is the failure is to consider both sides of the issue. Sometimes this is because the student has *taken sides* by concluding, early on, that the plaintiff or defendant should win. Being an advocate is not conducive to seeing both sides.

While there may not be two sides to every issue, unless there are, the issue isn't worth spending much time on. If it seems that one side has the much better argument concerning an issue, pause to consider whether you are overlooking anything. Here the mantra is, *"Yes.... but ..."* For every point, there is generally an answer.

Writing your exam, avoid the mistake of first considering all of the points for one side and then all of the points for the other side.

Plaintiff will argue:

As to the seriousness issue, blah, blah, blah.

> *As to the Statute of Frauds issue, blah, blah, blah.*

> As to the illegality issue, blah, blah, blah.

> *Defendant will argue:*

> *As to the seriousness issue, blah, blah, blah.*

> *As to the Statute of Frauds, blah.*

The format is confusing and wordy. More significantly, it doesn't produce sparks. The proper format is:

> *As to the seriousness issue, Plaintiff will argue . . . and defendant will respond.*

Only by running contention against contention will your analysis deepen.

Writing your answer you can avoid the "sing-song" of "plaintiff argues, defendant responds," by *writing down the middle.*

Instead of:

> *As to the seriousness issue, Plaintiff will argue . . . and defendant will respond.*

Try:

> *As to the seriousness issue, on the one hand . . . . on the other hand . . . . .*

Or:

> *As to the seriousness issue, even though . . . . it is true that . . . .*

Finally, to sharpen your analysis, do a pre-exam warm-up. Opera singers bellow a few notes before going out; ball players practice their mean stares (for opponents) and their innocent "What, me?" expressions (for refs). During your warm-up, repeat, and repeat, "So what?" and "Yes.... but...."

Multiple Choice Exams

Many state bar examinations devote one of their two or three days to the Multi–State Bar Exam, a multiple choice test covering basic first-year courses. Multiple choice exams are also becoming popular in law schools. They're tough.

They differ from essay exams in several ways. They don't test your ability to organize and write a compelling answer. Second, while it is difficult to write essay questions that cover all issues discussed in a course, objective questions can be comprehensive. To assure course coverage, some professors have been known to scurry back to their offices to write a multiple choice question after each class.

Most importantly multiple choice questions can focus on specific knowledge. While it is possible to bluff some on essay tests, with brilliant points concealing matters you didn't fully understand, bluffing is much more difficult on objective tests. In one sense, an essay test allows you to show what you *do* know, while an objective test exposes what you *don't*.

Some claim that these differences dictate different study strategies. Be leery of such claims. Both essay and objective exams require an understanding of the law, the ability to read carefully, to spot issues, and to analyze problems. This comes from immersing yourself in your studies, and I caution against distractions such as "This will be an multiple choice exam; should I be doing things differently?"

That said, law school multiple choice tests are not your mother's multiple choice exams, the ones you aced in high school. They're tough and they're sneaky. *Review old or model exams.* You don't want to first meet that strange beast on exam day. Further, at least in some areas of the law, there are only so many multiple choice questions that can be asked even though they can be repackaged.

As to taking multiple choice exams, two initial matters: First, be clear about whether or not there is a penalty for guessing and, second, be sure to keep track of your time. You will have so many minutes per question; try to get ahead of the time limits so you can revisit any questions that stump you.

To figure out how to take objective exams, put yourself in the shoes of the people who draft them. I hate to break it to you but, at this point in the course, those professors who you dearly love and respect are *not* your friends. They *want* you to check the *wrong* box. Otherwise, no curve. How can you protect yourself from their cunning?

Read carefully and don't jump at answers.

Multiple choice questions are drafted with great care. An ambiguity can ruin the question. Every word is chosen with a goal in mind: a weird fact may be trigger a specific aspect of a legal principle or may be included simply to confuse you. Rest assured, however, that everything is there for a purpose. Possible answers are carefully written so that all have initial appeal. Don't jump at the first one that seems right; most will seem right.

Questions are in three basic parts: facts, question, and choices. Dearly Beloved can lead you astray in all three.

Answer the question the *professor has asked*, not the one that you would have asked. Reading the facts it may *seem* like the question will focus on a particular legal issue or on the situation of a specific party but your adversary plays cruel tricks. Distracting information may throw you off or key legal phrases may mislead. Watch for *omissions*. A party may have had a bottle of vodka but, unless it says he was "drunk," don't assume so. On multiple choice exams, folks are notorious in being able to hold their liquor and in not dying simply *because* they were shot three times in the head.

Be aware that you may blow by facts or fill in omissions because you want the question to be easier or because you have decided that one side should win. Expect a tough question and don't take sides.

And don't be a smartass: if the question says the plaintiff was "driving," it is safe to assume we are talking about a car, not an ox team. Note that on an essay exam, if it might make a difference if it were an ox team, you could quickly raise the point and then move on. On multiple choice tests, you are stuck with the common sense of the problem.

As to the question, be sure to read carefully.

There is a bewildering range of possible questions. Some ask you to identify one correct answer out of four or five choices. Others ask you to identify, out of four or five good arguments, the "best" argument or, out of several significant facts, the "most significant." Note, in making your selection, that the "best" argument need not be a winning argument or even as good as ones you can think of; it is the best of those given.

Real cunning, however, comes in writing the choices. All will seem plausible; again, don't jump. Analyze. As Professor Rogelio Lasso points out, some of the baits include:

1. A correct statement of law that does not address the central issue raised by the problem.

2. An incorrect statement of law that is correct as far as it goes but doesn't include all of the required elements.

3. An inaccurate statement of the facts, either because it misstates the facts previously given or improperly fills in the blanks: "The defendant will lose because he was drunk," or "The defendant is guilty of murder because he killed the victim by shooting him three times in the head."

There will many, many other tempting "wrong" boxes. How to avoid them? Pause and consider how you would answer the question *before* reading the choices. This will give you some distance and help you sort out the alternative answers.

Frequently it will come down to eliminating answers. Despite Dearly Beloved's best efforts, some answers will be silly: "A police officer is standing in front of you in the middle of an intersection, telling you to stop. The light is green. You should proceed through the intersection." Admittedly I got that one wrong on my first driver's test, but you get my drift.

Often you will be able to eliminate all the choices but two, and those two, alas, are utterly indistinguishable. My colleague, Dan Dobbs, has some good advice. First, reread the facts and the question; you may pick up something, a fact or an omission, that you didn't previously notice. If that doesn't work, try to construct a hypothetical set of facts on which one of the contending answers would operate but not the other. This will show you that they are not the same and may point the way to the correct answer. As a last resort, skip the question and come back to it. Later questions my throw some light on it.

Bottom line: multiple choice questions are tricks, snares and delusions. Be very cautious; read carefully and don't jump too soon.

Learn from your experiences

After your first exam, before studying for the next, ask:

What did the exam teach me about the way I studied? Did I spend enough time analyzing the questions? Did I carefully consider the facts and address the important facts in the discussion? Did I develop both sides of the arguments? What did I do well? What should I do differently next my Torts exam Tuesday? Is it on Tuesday? Oh, no, it was yesterday!

CHAPTER 14

FEAR AND LOATHING IN THE FIRST YEAR

Visualize yourself a cute, lovable baby, lying in your crib, playing with a teddy. Next to you is another crib. You look over and are delighted. A friend! Someone to share the unfolding wonders.

"Hey, wait just a minute!" you suddenly realize, "That baby's standing! I can't do that. I can't even pull myself up. I'll never make it. I'll never walk! Hey, you, you're not so cute, you know. Pudgy in fact. Show-off. Stuck-up! . . . . Brat!"

If you don't get this story, you haven't started law school yet.

Not so long ago, a creative-writing professor from Stanford decided to go to law school. It would be a piece of cake, what with his academic record, what with his history of intellectual achievement. Not so.

Why was I afraid?

Imagine, is all that I can answer.

You have a stake. You have given up a job, a career, to do this. Or you have wanted to be a lawyer all your life.

You've studied hours on a case that is a half page long. You couldn't understand most of what you read at first, but you have turned the passage inside out, drawn diagrams, written briefs. You could not be more prepared.

And when you get to class that demigod who knows all the answers finds another student to say things you never could have. Clearer statements, more precise. And worse—far worse—notions, concepts, whole constellations of ideas that never turned inside your head.

Yes, there are achievements in the past. They're nice to bandage up your wounded self-esteem. But "I graduated college magna cum laude*" is not the proper answer when the professor has just posed a question and awaits your response with the 140 other persons in the class.*

The feeling aroused by all of that was something near to panic, a ferocious, grasping sense of uncertainty. . . . On many occasions I discovered that I didn't even understand what I didn't know until I was halfway through a class. Nor could I ever see how anyone else seemed to arrive at the right answer. Maybe they were all geniuses. Maybe I was the dumbest guy around.

The writer was Scott Turow. He went on to great things as a lawyer/novelist. Isn't it nice to know that someone whose books routinely appear on the *New York Times Best Sellers List* once sat where you sit, terrified?

Why is the first semester so scary?

Partly, it's the hype. Professor Kingsfield, dreaded Contracts Professor of *Paperchase*, bellows at his first-year class:

Your minds are filled with mush. You will teach yourself the law. I will teach you how to think!

Whatever that means, it doesn't seem to bode well to entering students.

Partly, it's that law school is a brand new game. Had you gone into other graduate programs— schools of education, philosophy, social work—you would have a fairly good idea what to expect, how to study, and how you would do.

And there is very little feedback. There are no term papers or midterms. You will sit in a large class (classes over 100 are not uncommon), awaiting the *one and only* test.

Why the lack of feedback? Economics. Legal education is graduate education on the cheap—one demigod handling a class of 140! Things are getting better. Some schools offer at least one small section in the first semester, and, in the second and third years, there will be seminars and clinical courses that have a lower student/faculty ratio and hence more feedback. With these exceptions, the general model holds: large classes followed by a single final.

In this chapter, I will look at the psychological tensions of the first year. In your darker moments, you will come to believe that "I'm the dumbest one here" and "Everyone here is viciously competitive, except me and my friends." And you will, most likely, assign a wildly inappropriate meaning to first year's grades. I will also cover the almost universal fear of being called on in class. I will explain why we teach the way we do, the so-called Socratic Method, and I will urge you to help us out, by raising your hand and volunteering.

"I'm the Dumbest One Here!"

Take heart! *Every* first year student believes this, even the smug guy from Princeton sitting next to you.

Flunking out is no longer much of an issue. In the old days, deans would welcome incoming students with,

"Look to the person to your right, look to the person at your left. Only one of you will be here second semester."

We now pre-flunk most of the class with high admission standards. Flunking out usually isn't a real threat. Nonetheless, the "ferocious, grasping sense of uncertainty" remains. Why?

The psychologist Carl Rogers wrote of our basic insecurity, that we know, deep down, that we really aren't all that "hot." We know that our prior successes have been lucky. Sure, we've been able to fool the others, but this is law school, and that "demigod" up front will expose us, once and for all, as the incompetents we really are.

The brilliant things your classmates will say feed this basic insecurity. Realize this. There are so many interesting and profound things to say. Student A and student B will both have interesting, insightful comments to make, comments which are, however, quite different. Student A recites; student B is dumbstruck—"I would never have thought of that; there are notions, concepts, whole constellations of ideas that never turn inside my head!"

If only B had talked first!

Insecurity, although understandable, can lead us to what will not be our finer moments. One is the pathetic posturing that occurs:

> *"I don't study more than an hour a day and understand everything."*

> *"Why did everyone in class have such a problem with Pennoyer v. Neff? I understood it immediately."*

One of my favorite stories involves an ex-professional football player who was, wittingly or not, something of a Zen Master. His friends would often tease him with the fact that others who played his position, defensive lineman, often sacked the quarterback while he seldom did. Would he bite? No.

> *"Did you ever consider that those guys were better players?"*

Concession often entails victory. To admit that you didn't understand *Pennoyer* will convince the braggart that you are, not only more secure and honest, but probably smarter and better-looking.

"Law Students Are Viciously Competitive"

Law students are aggressive, competitive, humorless and, worst of all, they study all the time. Now, of course, *I* wasn't that way as a law student, nor were my close friends. I am sure you and your friends aren't that way either. But we can agree that everyone else is.

One of my students wrote of her first day at law school. She met another woman and thought, "She's smarter than I am, better educated, better looking and, obviously, more stable." Instant hatred.

Don't reject people simply because they had the effrontery to come to law school.

Note a curious fact. Although you may feel a little like jelly, in fact *you* are that smart, educated, good looking and stable person everyone is afraid of. That sentence is worth rereading and pondering.

Competitiveness and aggressiveness are not just psychological projections. They are real. Your classmates are competitive, and so are you. It is important to confront and contain your aggressiveness and competitiveness. It will not do simply to deny these feelings, "Oh, I don't care what grades I get or how I do; I just want to get by!" Some students take denial to the extreme of not trying; they do a minimum amount of studying and miss class frequently. (If you refuse to try, then failure will be less painful. On the other hand, there is always the possibility of the ultimate seventh-grade fantasy— an "A" in Contracts and an "F" for Effort.)

You are competitive, or you wouldn't be in law school. You have achieved recognition and pleasure in competing successfully in the past. This is not shameful. Accept this part of yourself; however, do not let it consume you.

Scott Turow describes how he was almost consumed as a first year student. He found himself telling a friend, *"I don't give a damn about anybody else. I want to do better than them."*

My tone was ugly.... What had been suppressed all year was in the open now. All along there had been a tension between looking out for ourselves and helping each other; in the end, I did not expect anybody—not myself, either—to renounce a wish to prosper, to succeed. But I could not believe how extreme I had let things become, the kind of grasping creature I had been reduced to. I had not been talking about gentlemanly competition. There had been murder in my voice.

That night I sat in my study and counseled myself. It's a tough place, I told myself. Bad things are happening. Work hard. Do your best. Learn the law. But don't suffer, I thought. Don't fear. And for God's sake, don't give up your decency. (Another sentence worth rereading and pondering.)

The Socratic Method

Where there is understanding,

> *Let me sow confusion.*

Where there is light,

> *Darkness.*

No, although sometimes it may seem like it, law professors are not committed to a terrible misreading of the Prayer of Saint Francis.

The "Socratic Method" involves a professor randomly calling upon students to "state the case," and then to answer a series of follow-up questions, either directed at the coherence of the case itself or its future application. Critics argue that this method keeps students in terror and is designed to humiliate; that it teaches future lawyers that is it proper to abuse people. Other critics argue that the process of demanding justifications and meeting argument with counter-argument leads to extreme relativism. This is not a new fear.

Suppose the student is confronted by the question, "What does 'honorable' mean?" He gives the answer he has been taught, but he is argued out of his position. He is refuted again and again from many different points of view and at last is reduced to thinking that what he called honorable might just as well be called disgraceful. He comes to the same conclusion about justice, goodness, and all the things most revered. We shall see him renounce all morality and become a lawless rebel.

Plato, *The Republic*

When I was a student, when I was a target, these criticisms of the Socratic Method rang more true than they do now, now that I am a professor. Let me say a few nice things about it.

You are not learning legal rules in the classroom, you are learning how to "do law." By tearing apart the cases, testing their coherence and rejoicing in their ambiguities, your professors are showing you how.

The goal of the method is *not* to inculcate relativism; the goal is *not* to expose student ignorance; the goal is *not* to ridicule. The goal of the method is *to force students to justify their positions, to consider other points of view, and to realize that even the best of arguments suffer from "inconvenient facts."*

To illustrate, take a familiar case: a tenant is suing the landlord for negligently maintaining a common stairway. The landlord sets up as a defense a clause in the lease in which the tenant agreed not to sue the landlord for negligence. Is the clause valid?

Student: I don't think the tenant should be held to her promise not to sue if that promise was buried in the small print in the lease.

Professor: Why not?

Student: It just isn't fair.

Professor: Why not?

Here the student may feel that she is being attacked. Still worse, the student may feel that she is being argued out of her sense of fairness. This is not the professor's goal; rather it is to force the student to bedrock why she feels the way she does.

Student: Well, it seems to me that one reason we enforce promises is to protect free choices. If the

> *tenant didn't know what she was signing, then the whole justification for enforcing promises collapses.*

Behind our sense of justice often lie good sound reasons. For the professor to insist upon their verbalization is not to attack them.

> *Professor: Good. But what if the evidence showed she read the contract? Would you still think the agreement unfair?*

> *Student: Yes. The facts show that she was poor and probably not that well educated. She really didn't know that she was giving up valuable rights.*

> *Professor: Good. But isn't that a little paternalistic? If the law doesn't enforce her promise because she is poor and not well educated, aren't we saying that she is legally incompetent? That she doesn't have that most basic of rights, the right to mean what she says?*

The professor is not attacking the student, not trying to trip her up and humiliate her. Nor is the professor trying to argue her out of her position and turn her into a mouthpiece for landlords. The professor is attempting to force her to consider other points of view, to adopt the "yes.... but" form of reasoning. "*Yes*, my initial reaction is valid, *but* there are counter-considerations."

Max Weber, the great sociologist, wrote that the "primary task of a useful teacher is to teach his students to recognize *inconvenient facts*." The teacher should force students to understand what their opinions and arguments entail. Weber continues:

> *If you take such and such a stand, then you have to use such and such means in order to carry out your conviction. Now, these means are perhaps such that you believe you must reject them. Does the end "justify" the means? Or does it not? The teacher can confront you with the necessity of this choice.*

> *The teacher can force the individual, or at least we can help him, to give himself an account of the ultimate meaning of his own conduct. This appears to me as not so trifling a thing to do, even for one's own personal life. Again, I am tempted to say of a teacher who succeeds in this: he stands in the service of "moral" forces; he fulfills the duty of bringing about self-clarification and a sense of responsibility.*

Having made a very compelling argument why the tenant should be excused from her promise to pay, it is discomforting to have the professor point out that the argument entails paternalism and denies tenants the very basic right to "mean what they say." Again, in Weber's analysis, the professor is not suggesting that the promise should be enforced; the professor is forcing the student to realize the important values which would be sacrificed if the promise were not enforced. *"The teacher can confront you with the necessity of choice."*

Our goal is not to hurt feelings. Of course we screw up. Teaching law is not easy. We don't lecture from well-worn notes. All is movement, and you never know exactly what will happen next. No doubt in the hurly-burly of class we reject what the student believes is a valid point; undoubtedly, we are too abrupt with students who seem to be meandering; and, undoubtedly, the shock and dismay we occasionally experience shows. These are but inadvertent and unfortunate slights and insults caused by the intellectually challenging and unplanned nature of Socratic discourse.

When the Socratic Method Happens to You

You'll be in class one day, just sitting there, minding your own business, actually rather enjoying the discussion, when, without warning, you hear someone calling your name. The Professor! All eyes turn to you. There is total silence.

Relax! Take a deep breath, loosen your jaw. Shift your attention from "Oh, no, it's happening to me!" Focus on the question. If necessary, ask that it be repeated. While answering the question, remember that you are probably doing a whole lot better than you think you are. Just because *you* thought of something, just because *you* understood a point, that doesn't mean that it is so obvious it doesn't justify discussion. What you have to say might be terrific. Realize that you appear less nervous than you feel. When your classmates recite, they do not *appear* nervous even though they surely are. The guy sitting next to you, from Princeton? Jelly. It's just that you don't hear the pounding of his heart nor feel the quiver in his lips.

Confront, finally, the dreaded fear: You make a total fool of yourself. Your classmates laugh. You bumble, meander, and eventually give up. The professor moves on and asks the person behind you what has to be, and I'm not making things up here, the easiest question you have ever heard.

Shattered, you walk from class. You overhear smatterings of conversations and are greatly relieved.

> *"They're* **not** *talking about me and what a fool I was. They're talking about the cases and lunch. But wait! It's worse than I feared. They just don't* **care***!"*

Play the fool and the world continues to turn. This is a valuable lesson even if a disappointing one. The willingness to take risks is absolutely essential to effective lawyering. Who was foolish enough to first assert that separate means unequal? To argue that, despite tradition and practice, police must warn defendants of their right to remain silent? To suggest that manufacturers of goods could be held "strictly liable" for injuries their products cause?

Law demands creativity; creativity demands we try new things; creativity demands we play the fool.

Volunteering in Class

For a law school class to succeed, students must participate and share their insights, questions, and experiences. You can't sit on your hands and then complain that the class is boring. A good class is as much the doing of the students as it is of the professor.

Give me a good class that is on my side and is willing to take risks, I am pretty good. Give me a silent, resentful class, I stink.

Once I was discussing hard/soft metaphor and how it plays out in law study. Some courses are "soft"—family law, clinical courses, interviewing and negotiation; and some courses are "hard"— Antitrust, Federal Jurisdiction, Tax. And "hard" always trumps "soft." Admitted all of this wasn't Contracts but I was enthused: the metaphor guides many of our choices. But I noticed a student in the back, looking bored and resentful. "That student thinks this is a waste of time. Probably he's right." I caved. "Okay, let's get back to Contracts."

"Wait." My silent critic raised his hand. "Before we leave hard/soft, it's about masculine/feminine. When I was growing up, I liked books, and they are soft. My friends all liked sports, and it was very painful for me...." His voice trailed off.

The discussion he facilitated, the discussion he almost shut down, was wonderful.

You have a stake in your classes. You can make them *better*, and you can make them *worse*. Take part. Raise your hand. Ask a question. Stab at an answer.

Volunteering pays off. Even if it isn't counted towards your grade, volunteering gives you experience in trying out your ideas and thinking on your feet—important lawyering skills.

Don't volunteer all the time, as there is a definite drawback. Volunteering requires blocking out remarks of other students while you wait until you are called on. It is difficult to listen and retain what you want to say or ask. (Try jotting down a few words and then turn attention to the class). And, if you volunteer too much, other students will resent you.

Realize that in the first few weeks of law school you are making important choices about yourself. William Blake had a marvelous phrase, "mind-forged manacles." Don't forge: "I'm just not the kind of student who raises his hand!" Volunteer at least occasionally; otherwise, you'll lock yourself in a closet. There will come times, trust me, when you have something burning to say, but by then you aren't that kind of student.

Grades

Finally, you are *not* your first-semester grades. "Of course not," you laugh nervously.

Just wait.

You work really hard all semester. Suddenly it all comes crashing down into a letter or a number. "So that's it, huh. I'm a C."

No, you are not a C. You are whoever you were before you came to law school, the same person who, as a small child, took such good care of the puppy. Only you're different: you have a lot more knowledge and a lot more skills. You are well on your way to becoming a competent professional.

Remember why you came to law school. You didn't come to be a successful law student; you came to be a successful lawyer. Some students, disappointed in their grades, forget this and drop out in place. Keep working hard on your studies; you will know more law and will have better lawyer skills when you really need to, when another individual puts important matters into your hands. From now on, it's about your clients.

If you do well on your exams, more power to you. Feel good; celebrate. But don't fall victim to your own success. A good friend of mine, a regular Joe, did remarkably well his first semester and he suddenly became a character of Shakespearian dimension, walking the law school halls

". . . . dressed in an opinion

Of wisdom, gravity, profound conceit—

As who should say, 'I am Sir Oracle,

And when I ope my lips, let no dog bark!' "

Fast forward to a recent movie. An elderly man is asked advice by a younger person.

"Get to be my age, everyone thinks you know what you are talking about. But I'm the same old [expletive deleted] I have always been."

On your way to the Law Review office, just remember that you're the same kid who was always picked last.

———————

This chapter has been kind of a downer. It focused on the negatives. It started with Professor Kingsfield, who, I admit, is one of my heroes:

Your minds are filled with mush. I will teach you how to think.

He's right and you will come to know it. When you aren't complaining, you'll be talking law and loving it.

You are going to meet many wonderful people and make life-long friends. Expect bumps and moments of despair. You are mastering a new and difficult discipline. At first you will be doing it wrong; you will garble facts, misstate issues, and confuse holdings. After much hard work, you will do it right.

"Hey, look at me! I'm walking!"

PART THREE
LITIGATION

Perhaps nine-tenths of legal uncertainty is caused by uncertainty as to what court will find, on conflicting evidence, to be the facts of the case.

Jerome Frank

In your first year of law school *legal* uncertainty will be your daily bread.

> "In the case of *Globe*, involving a business contract and financial loss, the court held that a clause in a contract agreeing not to sue for negligence is valid. Would that holding apply in the next case, one involving a landlord/tenant relationship and personal injuries? Well, maybe."

But as Judge Frank points out, you ain't heard the half of it. Even if we figure out what legal rule to apply, the outcome is not certain, because of *factual* uncertainty. Assuming the injured tenant gets around *Globe* and the court throws out the agreement not to sue, to win her case she now must prove that the landlord was negligent. On the basis of conflicting evidence, will the jury find that he was?

Well, maybe.

In this part, we take a detailed look at the factual side of things, the litigation process. Now, you won't be trying lawsuits for years, so why four chapters devoted to this topic? As a first year student, your job is to master legal doctrine, not the art of cross-examination nor that of closing argument. The reason I walk you through the litigation process is that it will deepen your understanding of the legal doctrines you will study.

"How will this rule play out in the courtroom? If it were my case, how would I prove it?"

On a less grand and more immediate level, these chapters will be a great help in understanding the cases you read as judges throw around unfamiliar terms. What's a "motion to dismiss"? An "affirmative defense"? "Impermissible hearsay"? I will introduce you to these terms and show you how they fit into the bigger picture of a lawsuit.

This part will also put your Civil Procedure class in context.

There are no exams, and, again, you won't be going to court for a long time to come. (I hope.) Therefore, don't try to memorize the points I will make. Simply read along in order to get a sense of how lawyers try lawsuits.

Chapter 15 begins, naturally enough, with late-night lawyer advertising and then describes something of the lawyer/client relationship, including the important matter of fees. It then describes how lawyers plan and investigate cases, backwards, from potential jury instructions. Chapter 16 shows you how lawyers reduce the factual chaos of the world into Complaints and Answers and then describes how the law tests for the legal adequacy of those factual stories, in motions to dismiss. It will also cover the discovery process. The last two chapters show you how all of this comes together in trial.

Sit back, get a good light, and take a glimpse of what might be your future.

CHAPTER 15

CASE PLANNING: THE IN-TERPLAY OF LAW AND FACT—BACKWARDS

The Return of Ms. K

You remember Ms. K. She had tripped on a defective step in her apartment house. Recuperating, she watched a lot of T.V. Late one night, during the reruns, after the ad giving the 1–900 number for an authentic psychic, the lawyer C. Darrow appeared on the screen. Solemnly, indeed reluctantly, she broke the bad news:

"Insurance companies are sleaze! Physicians are murderers! Even, I hate to tell you, authentic psychics are frauds. I am your only friend." A warm, inviting smile:

"If you've been injured, been worrying you might get injured, or if the person who saved your life bruised your arm, hurry on down and we will see just how much money you get."

The next day, Ms. K hurried on down.

"Don't tell me what happened," instructed Darrow. "Just tell me how badly you were hurt."

Ms. K did. Her injuries were substantial.

"That bad, huh? You have a *great* case. Now tell me what happened."

Lawyer Fees and Retainers

Eventually, after much talk of sugar plums, it gets to the unpleasant part of the interview, fees. Rather than an *hourly fee* (used most often in business representation) or a *flat fee* (used often in criminal defense), they agree that Darrow will work on a *contingency fee* basis. If settled prior to trial, Darrow will receive 25% of the recovery, if litigated, 35%. If there is no recovery, Darrow gets nothing.

The idea behind the contingent fee is to assure access to the courts for folks who have been injured. If they don't win their case, they don't have to pay their attorney. Without a contingent fee arrangement, many people could not afford to hire a lawyer because of high hourly fees and hence could not get compensation for their injuries. Some argue that contingent fees are a bad idea because, first, they encourage lawyers to bring unmerited law suits and, second, with meritorious cases, they put too much of a successful plaintiff's recovery in the lawyer's pocket.

Contingent fees are permissible only for personal injury cases and not, for example, in criminal, divorce, or child-custody cases.

However, even personal injury plaintiffs do have to pay *costs*: filing fees, reporter's fees for depositions, juror fees, and expert witness fees. Depending on the complexity of the case and the extent of discovery, these costs can run into quite a bit. If Ms. K wins her case, however, most likely the defendant will be ordered to pay these costs. If not, she's stuck.

Two quick points about attorney fees and court costs. Usually a large amount of money can be saved by both parties if they settle prior to trial: litigation costs and attorney fees. In addition to uncertainty of outcome, the saving of pretrial costs is a major incentive for settlement.

Second, the tradition in this country is that each side pays its own lawyer, even if it wins. In many European countries, loser pays for both lawyers. The rule concerning attorney fees has tremendous impact. "Each side pays its own" prevents people with small claims from getting legal representation—"Sure, I can get you the $400 you spent on the refrigerator back, but my fee would be $2000." On the other hand, "loser pays" tends to discourage novel law suits, people thinking, "If I sue Big Tobacco and lose, I will be out the money I paid my lawyer plus the zillions they paid theirs."

After they settle the matter of fees, Darrow and Ms. K sign a *retainer agreement*. It spells out the fee arrangement and states what Darrow is to do. Does the fee include representation of any possible appeals? A major source of lawyer/client fights is misunderstanding the lawyer's commitment. (Another is the failure of the lawyer to keep the client informed as to what is happening with the case.)

Hands are shaken. Ms. K leaves. Darrow, left alone with her books, will start preparing for trial even though she knows the chances are high the case will be settled; without some trial preparation, she won't know how strong the case is and won't know what a fair settlement would be. Where does she start? At the very end of the trial. What will the jury be told?

Jury Instructions and Their Politics

After all the witnesses and all of the objections, the judge will instruct the jury as to the law. Lawyers prepare cases backwards. They begin with finding out what must be proven, by whom and by what standard. This is the stuff of jury instructions.

Visualize a warm courtroom, with jurors nodding off. The judge clears his throat and instructs:

*Ladies and Gentlemen of the Jury. I will now tell you the rules of law which you must follow to decide this case. (1) If you find that the defendant was **not** negligent **or** that the defendant's negligence did **not** cause plaintiff's injuries, your verdict must be for the defendant. (2) If you find that the defendant **was** negligent, **and** that his negligence caused the plaintiff's injuries, then your verdict must be for the plaintiff.*

Plaintiff claims that defendant was negligent.

Negligence is the failure to use reasonable care. Negligence may consist of action or inaction. A person is negligent if he fails to act as an ordinarily careful person would act under the circumstances.

Before you can find the defendant liable, you must find that the defendant's negligence caused the plaintiff's injury. Negligence causes an injury if it helps produce the injury, and if the injury would not have happened without the negligence.

If you decide for the plaintiff on the question of liability, you must then fix the amount of money which will reasonably and fairly compensate for any of the following damages proved by the evidence to have resulted from the defendant's negligence:

(1) The nature, extent and duration of the injury;

(2) The pain, discomfort, suffering, and anxiety experienced and to be experienced in the future as a result of the injury;

(3) Reasonable expenses of necessary medical care, treatment, and services rendered and reasonably probable to be incurred in the future; and

(4) Earnings which were lost by the plaintiff to date, and any decrease in earning power or capacity by the plaintiff in the future.

The plaintiff has the burden of proving by a preponderance of the evidence:

(1) That the defendant was negligent;

(2) That the plaintiff was injured;

(3) That the defendant's negligence was a cause of the injury to the plaintiff; and

(4) The amount of money that will compensate the plaintiff for her injury.

*I will now tell you the standard of proof in this case.
Preponderance of the evidence means such evidence
as, when weighed with that opposed to it, has more
convincing force and the greater probability of truth.
In the event that the evidence is evenly balanced, so
that you are unable to say that the evidence on either
side of an issue preponderates, then your finding
upon that issue must be against the party who had
the burden of proving it.*

Now that's a mouth full, and there is even more.
The judge will also instruct as to witness credibility
and the role of jurors.

"Where do jury instructions come from?" asks
the precocious child. Appellate cases and relevant
statutes. In most jurisdictions, you can find them in
form jury instruction books. While these instructions seem quite dull, they mask vibrant political
and legal battles.

Here the jury is instructed that Ms. K must prove
both neglect and injury (*"burden of proof"*) and she
must prove it by a "preponderance of the evidence"
(*"standard of proof"*). These are not neutral or self-
evident decisions; they turn on political assessments. Do we want to encourage or discourage
personal injury suits? Do we want to shift losses, or
do we wish to let them stay where they have fallen?

If we wanted to help people in Ms. K's position
(to shift losses to folks who might be better able to
absorb them or prevent them), we could put the
burden of proof on the defendant to prove he wasn't

negligent. As the judge has told us, if the evidence is balanced, he who has the burden *loses*.

On the other hand, if we wanted to further discourage people like Ms. K from bringing suit, we could increase the standard of proof required of her, from "preponderance of the evidence" to "clear and convincing evidence" or even, as in criminal cases, to "beyond a reasonable doubt."

"Pain and suffering" awards are a hotly debated element of recovery. The huge jury awards one reads about are mostly for "pain and suffering." Insurance companies argue that they threaten Western Civilization. Others argue that huge jury awards do not harm American business but rather assures that it will be conducted in a safe manner. Both sides can keep you awake with compelling war stories and can put you to sleep with statistics.

Consider the following instruction:

> *Ladies and Gentlemen of the Jury, you are to decide the facts of this case. I will tell you the law. It is your **duty** to follow the law as I give it to you even if you disagree with it.*

Again, this seems to be an unremarkable statement but, like so much of law, it masks great debates. Why not tell juries, "If you think the law is unjust, don't follow it"? This is known as *jury nullification* and, in the early days of our country, was a proud tradition: local juries protecting neighbors from the unjust edicts of the King.

We don't tell juries that they have the power to disregard the law, and in fact we tell them that they have to duty to apply it as the judge instructs. Woe to the lawyer who tries to argue to the jury, "The law in this case would be unjust. Don't follow it." She will find herself in contempt of court. I hope you have the opportunity to consider the issue of jury nullification sometime in your law school career. It turns on assessments of how much we trust legislatures to do the right thing, how much we fear juries will do the wrong thing, and how much we believe that general rules can capture the nuisances of justice, "If you think the law would be unjust in *this* case, don't follow it."

Investigating and Proving a Negligence Suit

From the jury instructions, Darrow knows she must prove:

(1) That the defendant was negligent;

(2) That the plaintiff was injured;

(3) That the defendant's negligence was a cause of the injury to the plaintiff; and

(4) That the amount of money suggested is needed to compensate the plaintiff for her injury.

Two and three look fairly easy and may be established by Ms. K's testimony, "Before my fall, my leg and back were fine but not afterwards." But how can Darrow convert physical injury into dollars?

Ms. K broke her leg, hurt her back, and incurred hospital and doctor's bills. She also missed 10 days of work. Darrow knows that it will be relatively easy to prove the amount of the "reasonable expenses of necessary medical care" by simply introducing the bills at trial. She can easily prove "lost earnings" by having Ms. K testify as to their amount. It will be more difficult to prove that the injuries will cause her lost income in the future, and it may be hard to convince the jury to put a high monetary value on the "pain, discomfort, suffering and anxiety experienced" by Ms. K.

The real problem for Darrow, however, is proving that "the defendant was negligent." Ms. K says she fell because the step at the top of the stairs was loose. Darrow and her photographer visit the scene and inspect the staircase. They will find that the top step, made of wood, is cracked so that, when one steps on its outside edge, it gives. But neither Darrow nor her photographer can tell how long the step has been cracked.

Does the mere existence of a cracked step prove, by a "preponderance of the evidence," that Landlord was neglectful? Without more, it seems pretty weak. If this is all she has, maybe Darrow won't even be able to get to the jury. If the judge thinks the evidence is so weak that no reasonable juror could find for the plaintiff, he can take it away from the jury after the plaintiff has presented her case, by granting a motion for a *directed verdict*, or even after the jury comes back with a judgment in favor of the plaintiff, by entering a *judgment notwithstanding the verdict—"a judgment n.o.v."*

Darrow needs more evidence of Larry's negligence. She would like to argue that Larry knew of the defective stair for months prior to Ms. K's accident, that he knew that many people used the stairs and that he was seen, beer in hand, laughing the villain's laugh, "Let them tumble!"

The odds are that Larry will deny knowing anything about the step's defective condition and will claim that he inspects them often (on his way to Temperance meetings), and that he has nothing but love for all his tenants, and that his heart goes out to Ms. K, but that, hey, it wasn't his fault.

In hopes of proving that Larry knew of the defect before the accident, Darrow will send an investigator to talk to other tenants. Did they ever report the condition to Larry? Were there other accidents on the stairs? Does Larry himself use the stairway, thus possibly having firsthand knowledge?

If Darrow can't prove Larry actually knew of the condition, what about arguing that, as a reasonable landlord, he should have inspected the stairs periodically? Darrow will do legal research in hopes of finding a statute or case imposing a duty of reasonable inspection on landlords. If she finds one, she can ask the judge to instruct the jury:

> *Ladies and Gentlemen, a landlord has a duty to make periodic inspections of common areas.*

If Darrow can get this instruction, she has saved herself a lot of work: now she must prove only that Larry didn't make the inspections, not that he should have.

Assuming Darrow can't get the instruction as a matter of *law* (because she can't find any statutes or cases), she can argue to the jury that, as a matter of *fact*, failure to inspect is negligence. It would strengthen that argument if she could call other landlords to testify that they always make inspections and think it would be unreasonable not to do so.

Now she has something else to research: would testimony of other landlords as to what they do be admissible evidence? As many trial lawyers have learned, everything you want to get before jury might not be allowed into evidence. She will likely write a *trial memorandum* to use at trial if the issue comes up. (Note that this research can help in negotiation: "Look, I will call three landlords who will testify your client should have made inspections, and that testimony is admissible.")

Darrow realizes, however, that even if she can establish a duty to inspect (either legally or factually), she still must show that the inspection would have disclosed the defect. She needs testimony that the stair was defective for a long time. She needs an *expert*. An expert need not have academic degrees nor even "book learnin'". An expert is simply someone who has special knowledge that will help the jury understand the facts of the case. Darrow will ask a carpenter to inspect the stairs and tell her, if he can, how long the step was broken.

Enter, stage left, *Quibble Weaver*.

While these investigations are going on, Larry has retained his own lawyer, Mr. Quibble Weaver. Of course, *Quibble Weaver* is a fictional name, but it isn't mine. It was the name given the lawyer in the first modern Italian novel, *The Betrothed,* written by Alessandro Manzoni. It was written in 1827. Even then and even there, lawyers take their shot. Quibble Weaver, indeed!

In any event, Darrow contacted Quibble looking for a possible settlement. Her initial overtures met sullen rejection:

"Larry Landlord wasn't negligent. Ms. K wasn't injured. Besides, there is a clause in the lease releasing the landlord from all liability."

"If that's the way it is going to be, see you in court."

Time to start drafting.

CHAPTER 16

COMPLAINTS, ANSWERS, PRETRIAL MOTIONS, AND DISCOVERY

Sometimes a case will settle before a lawsuit is filed. If one doesn't, it becomes time to rachet things up.

The Initial Court Papers

IN THE SUPERIOR COURT

IN AND FOR THE COUNTY OF KERN

STATE OF CONTENTION

Ms. K	.	**COMPLAINT FOR NEGLIGENCE**
Plaintiff	.	**AND STRICT LIABILITY**
vs.	.	
Larry Landlord	.	**Civil Action Number 1066**
Defendant	.	

. . . .

Comes now plaintiff and complains of the defendant as follows:

Count I

1. The court has jurisdiction of this matter as all events complained of occurred in this county, and both Ms. K and Larry Landlord are residents thereof.

2. At the times herein mentioned, defendant owned the Owl Apartment Building.

3. At the times herein mentioned, defendant retained control in the Owl Apartment Building of the halls, lobbies, and stairways used in common by all tenants of the building and others lawfully coming onto the premises.

4. Plaintiff was a tenant of defendant on or about November 17 last year.

5. On that date, while plaintiff was proceeding down the common stairway provided by defendant for the use of all tenants, plaintiff was tripped by a defective stair on the stairway, thrown violently down the stairway, and in falling broke her leg and sustained injuries to her back.

6. As a result of such injuries, plaintiff sustained damages in the amount of $300,000.

7. Defendant knew, or with the exercise of reasonable care should have known, of the defective condition of the stairway, but negligently failed to correct, remove, or repair such defective condition, and such negligence by defendant was a proximate cause of plaintiff's injuries and the damages incidental thereto.

Count II

1. Plaintiff realleges 1–6 of her first cause of action.

2. Defendant is strictly liable for defective conditions in the stairway, and said defective conditions were a direct cause of plaintiff's injuries.

THEREFORE, plaintiff prays judgment against the defendant for $300,000, for costs of suit, and for such other and further relief as the court deems proper.

C. Darrow
Attorney for Plaintiff

———————

Reread Count II. What is Darrow up to? Why a Count II at all? Isn't it the same as Count I? Compare #7 in Count I with #2 in Count II. Read carefully.

———————

The first thing a plaintiff must allege in his complaint is that the court has jurisdiction to decide the matter. As you will learn in your Civil Procedure class, whether a court has jurisdiction over a defendant can be hopelessly complicated. In the workaday world of lawyers, however, most defendants do not live out of state, and most do not commit obscure torts offshore that, as luck would have it, do harm in our town. Most defendants live next door and do their nasty deeds in place; usually jurisdiction is not at issue.

After the jurisdiction issue come the factual allegations that are needed to constitute a legal wrong. Note that *notice pleading* is all that is required. All you have to do is alert the defendant to your general factual contentions. It is, for example, enough to allege that the stair was "defective" and it is not necessary to say just how.

Returning now to the allegations in Count II, Darrow is asserting an alternative theory of liability. Unsure she can prove neglect, she is trying to avoid the problem by alleging that the landlord should be liable under the doctrine of strict liability. You will learn in Torts that, in cases involving very dangerous substances or activities, people can be liable for injuries they cause even if they were not negligent. This is true, for example, of people who store explosives. If the explosive goes off and injures someone, that person can recover without showing that the defendant was negligent: if you store explosives, and they go off, you are *strictly liable* for any injury caused. There is no need to show that you stored them in a negligent manner.

The law is always in a state of flux; Darrow hopes to convince a judge that the doctrine should apply to landlords and dangerous stairs. She does this by alleging that basis of liability. If Larry's lawyer is on his toes, he will file a motion saying that landlords are not strictly liable and then, as we are apt to say, the issue will be joined.

We'll see.

Proud of her work, Darrow takes it down to the County Courthouse, pays the County Clerk the filing fee, and files the complaint. The clerk gives it a case number, and we're off to the races. Darrow gives a copy of the complaint and a summons to a process server, who thereupon serves it on Larry Landlord.

Dismayed and no doubt quite fearful, Larry will take the compliant to his lawyer, Quibble Weaver, who now scurries to the law library. He has but twenty days to "answer."

IN THE SUPERIOR COURT

Ms. K	.	
Plaintiff	.	**ANSWER**
vs.	.	
Larry Landlord	.	**Civil Action Number 1066**
Defendant	.	

. . . .

Comes now defendant to answer plaintiff's complaint as follows:

1. *Admits allegations 1–4 inclusive.*

2. *Denies allegations 5, 6 and 7.*

3. *As to count two, denies all matters not admitted to in number 1 hereof.*

AFFIRMATIVE DEFENSE

As an affirmative defense to both counts, defendant alleges:

1. *That the lease between Ms. K and Larry Landlord, which Ms. K signed, provides: "The Landlord shall in no event be liable for any loss or damage which may occur to the Tenant."*

2. *Said clause bars plaintiff's suit.*

THEREFORE, defendant prays

1. *That plaintiff take nothing on her complaint.*

2. *That the court order plaintiff to pay defendant's costs of suit and order such other further relief as the court deems proper.*

> *Q. Weaver*
> *Lawyer for Defendant*

Weaver admits that the court has jurisdiction, that the defendant owned the apartment house and controlled common areas, and that the incident occurred on November 17. He denies the things he will contest at trial: the fall, the injuries, and the landlord's neglect. Ms. K, as plaintiff, will have the burden of proving them.

He also raises an *affirmative defense* concerning the lease provision protecting Larry from suits like this one.

Usually a plaintiff must prove all the elements of her case; sometimes, however, the law requires the defendant to bring up certain matters and then prove them. For example, the plaintiff must prove that the defendant was negligent; if the defendant claims that the plaintiff was *also* negligent (she was drunk) and this contributed to her injuries, the defendant must allege and prove it. Note, again, that these are political/legal decisions. One could, for example, require plaintiffs to prove not only that the defendant was negligent, but that they, the plaintiffs, were not.

You will spend time in your Civil Procedure class on how and why courts allocate issues between things the plaintiffs must prove and things the defense must prove (affirmative defenses).

As a matter of pretrial strategy, try to avoid getting into a situation where you must prove something. It is far better to have the burden of persuasion placed on the other side. This is because if the evidence is evenly balanced, the party with the burden of persuasion loses. The general rule is that, if you allege something, you must prove it, so the general advice is try not to allege it. Assume that you represent a defendant in a negligence action and the law is unclear whether the plaintiff's contributory negligence is an affirmative defense or whether "due care" on the part of the plaintiff is part of her case. Don't just allege, in your answer, that the plaintiff was negligent. Rather file a motion which challenges the sufficiency of the complaint, arguing that it must allege that the plaintiff was acting with "due care." That way, if you can convince the judge of your position, you put the burden of persuasion on your opponent.

Discovery

Trials used to be a whole lot more dramatic. Weaver could call surprise witnesses. "The defense calls Mrs. Ortelere."

At counsel table, Darrow would turn to Ms. K and anxiously whisper, "Mrs. Ortelere? Who is Mrs. Ortelere, and what does she know?"

"I dunno. She was my third grade teacher. My God, they're not going to bring *that* up?"

In 1938, the Federal Rules of Civil Procedure were adopted with the goal of taking the surprise out of litigation. The basic idea was that, if both sides of a lawsuit knew all of the evidence that would be introduced at trial, more cases would be settled, and, as to those that weren't, they would be decided on their merits rather than on lawyer gamesmanship.

To illustrate something of discovery, by way of *written interrogatories*, parties can ask each other questions:

1. *List all of the witnesses you intend to call at the trial and summarize what testimony you will elicit from each.*

If Weaver didn't list Mrs. Ortelere, she would not be allowed to testify, except in very rare circumstances.

In your Civil Procedure class you will learn all about the various *discovery* methods available to lawyers. They are quite extensive. One, for example, allows for opposing lawyers to inspect premises and another can compel a personal injury plaintiff to undergo physical examinations by doctors hired by the defense.

The most popular discovery device is the *deposition*. In a deposition, a lawyer is allowed to question opposing witnesses, under oath, in order to see what they will testify in court and to get a sense of whether they will make good witnesses. Just how much sympathy will Ms. K elicit in describing her injuries?

Weaver will *depose* Ms. K in his office. Darrow will be there, and, before things start, she and Weaver will engage in that easy banter that lawyers love and clients hate ("What's my lawyer doing being nice to that sleaze?"). Once things start, Darrow probably won't do much except sit and listen. There is generally not much to object to in a deposition; Weaver can ask pretty much any question that can *lead* to admissible evidence, and that gives him a lot of room to question Ms. K about a whole manner of things. For example, he can ask her, "Tell me everything you were told by the neighbors about the stairs." As this calls for hearsay, such a question would not be permissible at trial; however, as it might *lead* to admissible evidence (calling one of the neighbors to testify), it is a fine question during discovery.

A court reporter will transcribe the questions and answers. Ms. K will be sworn in, and Weaver will try to pin her down, both as to the cause of her accident and as to the extent of her injuries. If Ms.

K changes her story at trial, she can be *impeached* by these prior statements. Suppose, for example, she testifies *at trial* that she hurt her left arm during the fall. Weaver has her deposition and is ready to *cross-examine*.

Cross Examination by Quibble Weaver

Q: *Ms. K, you testified on direct that you injured your arm during the fall, is that correct?*

A: *Yes.*

Q: *Do you remember coming to my office for your deposition?*

A: *Yes.*

Q: *Wasn't your attorney with you?*

A: *Yes.*

Q: *And you were sworn to tell the truth on that occasion?*

A: *Yes.*

Q: *And I told you before we began not to answer any question you didn't understand, isn't that a fact?*

A: *Yes, I remember. You seemed like such a nice man at the time.*

Q: *During the deposition I asked you to describe your injuries. You told me of your back pains and your broken leg, isn't that right?*

A: *Yes, my back was quite painful. And my leg was really smashed up. It was terrible.*

> Q: *I appreciate your injuries. Please just answer my questions. Now, after you indicated your problems with your back and leg, didn't I ask you whether you were injured in any other way?*
>
> A: *Yes, you asked me that.*
>
> Q: *And didn't you tell me, "No, I had no other injuries." Weren't those your precise words?*
>
> A: *Yes, but . . . . .*
>
> Q: *(Cutting her off) Thank you, nothing further.*

If Ms. K has a good explanation for her inconsistency, Darrow can bring it out during redirect. In the jargon of the trial bar, this is known as *rehabilitation.*

Redirect by C. Darrow

> Q: *Before you were cut off, I believe you were about to explain your inconsistency.*
>
> A: *Yes. During the deposition, I was in pain. My back and leg hurt so much that I simply forgot about the injuries to my arm.*

Trial lawyers will tell you that some rehabilitation is better than others.

Despite the spirit of the discovery rules, lawyers, like kids, still love surprises. Unlike kids, however, they don't like to be surprised, they like to surprise. Lawyers resist full disclosure. For example, before a deposition, a party will be told by her lawyer:

"Just answer the questions. Don't volunteer any-thing. You will want to tell your side of the story. But remember that the lawyer asking you ques-tions will never be convinced by you, and it is his job to turn anything you say against you. But, don't be nervous!"

Before trial, Darrow will undoubtedly depose Lar-ry Landlord, hoping to find that he either knew of the condition or failed to make ordinary inspections of the stairs. Discovery is going per usual when suddenly Weaver makes a move designed *to end it all.*

Pretrial Motions Designed to Avoid Trial

IN THE SUPERIOR COURT

Ms. K   .

   Plaintiff   .

   vs.   .   **Civil Action Number 1066**

Larry Landlord   .

   Defendant   .

. . . .

DEFENDANT'S MOTION TO DISMISS COUNT 2 OF PLAINTIFF'S COMPLAINT

DEFENDANT'S MOTION FOR SUMMARY JUDGMENT

TAKE NOTICE THAT at 8:30 a.m. or as soon thereafter as the matter can be heard, on April 6 in

Courtroom 4 of the Superior Court of the County of Kern, defendant will move the court to dismiss Count 2 in plaintiff's complaint as it fails to state a claim upon which relief can be granted. DEFENDANT WILL FURTHER MOVE that summary judgment be granted it as to Count One, dealing with allegations of negligence, on the basis that there is no triable issue of fact in this case. As attested to in the attached affidavit of Larry Landlord, Ms. K signed a lease that provided she could not sue for negligence.

> Respectfully submitted,
> Quibble Weaver

If Weaver wins this motion, there will be no trial.

Why have a lengthy and expensive trial if it is clear that Ms. K will lose? Procedural law allows for various moves to abort cases without trial if there really isn't a true factual dispute.

A quick aside. *"Procedural law"* refers to the rules which govern the *method* by which disputes are resolved, such as rules governing which court should decide the controversy (jurisdiction), what issues may be joined in the same lawsuit, and how long one has to answer a complaint. *"Substantive law"* refers to rules which determine the *outcome* of the dispute, the rules of contract, property, and dog bite. Substantive law governs our daily lives and those of our dogs.

The two most common procedural devices to test the legal effect and sufficiency of fact are *motions to dismiss* and *motions for summary judgment.*

Motions to dismiss a pleading as insufficient as a matter of law

The plaintiff files a complaint making certain allegations. A motion to dismiss basically says "no soap"—what is alleged doesn't make it as a matter of substantive law.

In this case, defendant is moving to dismiss plaintiff's second count. Plaintiff alleged that the defendant landlord should be liable on a theory of strict liability, that he should be liable even though the plaintiff cannot prove that he was negligent in relation to the stairs. Darrow wanted a fallback position in the event she could not prove negligence. Clever idea. Defendant's motion to dismiss is saying, "Without showing negligence, there is no cause of action as a matter of law and hence the count should be dismissed. No need to have a trial on it."

Similar to a motion to dismiss, a motion to strike can be used to test the legal sufficiency of answers. Darrow could move to dismiss the affirmative defense, the one raising the exculpatory clause, by arguing that such clauses are void. If that motion was granted, then the defendant could not even introduce evidence of the clause at trial: *You can introduce evidence only in support of what you have alleged (or evidence which contradicts what your opponent has alleged).*

In olden days, days of grace and style, motions to dismiss were called "demurrers." You will find that term in some opinions you read. It is still used in our more romantic states, such as California.

Motions for Summary Judgment

A motion to dismiss is solely defensive in that it can only attack the sufficiency of the facts alleged by the opposition. But what if there is an important fact not alleged by the opposition that would abort the case? How can you get it before the court? By a Motion for Summary Judgment. Along with the Motion you file an affidavit by someone who swears that the fact is true. If the opposing party files an affidavit saying the fact is not true, then the matter will be set for trial. However, if the opposing party doesn't file an affidavit denying the fact, the court deems the fact admitted. Then the question becomes, with that fact admitted, should judgment be granted to one of the parties? The test, as you will learn, is whether there remains "a triable issue of fact". If there is, judgment will not be entered; if there is not, then it will be.

Now, in our case, Ms. K did not mention the exculpatory clause in her complaint. To get it before the court, Quibble files an affidavit attesting to it. K can't deny it. The issue is joined: does the clause, as a matter of law, bar her suit? Yes, if the clause is legally enforceable; no, if it is not. Thus we are thrown back to the first chapter of this book. Seamless web and all of that!

Come 8:30, April 6, Darrow and Weaver arrive in Courtroom 4. Most likely they have each previously submitted a *Memorandum of Points and Authorities,* which are legal briefs arguing their respective positions. Does the case law suggest it would be appropriate to impose strict liability on landlords? Do any cases or statutes address the issue of exculpatory clauses in apartment leases? At the hearing, both Darrow and Weaver will have the opportunity to quote precedent, argue policy, distinguish cases, wave their arms and predict doom. No doubt the judge will "take the matter under advisement." After a short interval the judge will enter judgment, in all likelihood striking the plaintiff's second count (nice try Darrow) and denying Weaver's motion for summary judgment, holding exculpatory clauses unenforceable.

The matter is set for trial of plaintiff's remaining count, the one alleging negligence. Can Darrow make it out *factually?*

Trial's set for tomorrow. Get some rest.

CHAPTER 17

TRIALS

A tree falls in the forest. No one is there to hear. Does it make a noise? Despite the mush you learned as as an undergraduate, the correct answer depends on the jurisdiction in which it fell. We'll see.

Jury trials go something like this:

1. Jury selection.

2. Opening statements.

3. Plaintiff's (or State's/People's) case-in-chief.

4. Motions, such as a *directed verdict* motion, designed to test whether, at this point in the trial, a reasonable jury *could* (but not necessarily *would)* find for the plaintiff. If such a motion is granted, that's that.

5. Defendant's case-in-chief.

6. Plaintiff's rebuttal (witnesses called to contradict new testimony given in the defendant's case).

7. Defendant's rebuttal (witnesses called to rebut plaintiff's rebuttal witnesses).

8. Closing arguments.

9. Jury instructions. In some jurisdictions, jury instructions are given before closing arguments.

10. Jury deliberation.

11. The joy of victory, the agony of defeat.

Let's take a closer look at some of these phrases.

Jury Selection (Voir Dire)

The goal is to get an impartial jury. In the old days, whenever *they* were, jurors were neighbors; who better to know who is lying? Who is malingering? In today's enlightened society, we seek an ignorant jury. We get it by asking prospective jurors questions. This is known as "voir dire."

"Do you know any of the parties to this action?"

"This case involves a suit for personal injuries growing out of an automobile accident. Have you been in such an accident yourself?"

"The plaintiff is asking for money damages to compensate her for the pain and suffering she suffered as a result of the accident. The law allows for such damages. If you believed the evidence warranted damages for pain and suffering, would you award them?" (Some people simply don't believe that these damages should be available.)

"This is a criminal case involving burglary. Have you been the victim of a crime? Do you have any relatives in law enforcement?"

"If you are instructed not to put any more weight on a police officer's testimony than that of

*any other witness, would you follow that instruc-
tion? If you were instructed not to consider what
will happen to the defendant if she is convicted,
will you follow that instruction?"*

In some jurisdictions, the lawyers conduct the
voir dire; in others, judges do. The reason that
judges are replacing lawyers is that lawyers used
the opportunity to "try their cases" by converting
what will become their closing argument into a
series of questions:

*"Now, if the evidence showed Ms. K suffered
permanent leg damage, you wouldn't hesitate to
compensate her fully for that injury, say in the
neighborhood of $300,000, would you?"*

After juror questioning comes juror selection. It is
really juror *rejection*—those still standing after the
rejections become the jury.

First come challenges *for cause,* and each side has
an unlimited number. Say a potential juror is married to one of the police officers who investigated
the crime. Defense counsel, no doubt insensitive to
the dynamics of married life, would challenge this
juror for cause. Of course the prosecutor, equally
blind to life's subtleties, would attempt to keep this
juror:

*"Now the fact that you're married to the investi-
gating officer would not mean that you would
believe your spouse more than any other witnesses,
would it?"*

It will be the judge's call. What about pretrial
publicity? Even if a juror has read about the case in
the newspaper, she will be kept if the judge feels
that she can put all that aside and render a verdict
upon the evidence presented at trial. In cases involving major media coverage, however, the case
may have to be moved for trial in another city.

In addition to challenges for cause, each side will
have a limited number of *peremptory* challenges.
Exercised when the lawyer feels, for whatever reason, that it would be best not to have the person on
the jury, peremptory challenges are the stuff of war
stories and crude stereotypes (in criminal cases, the
prosecution wants Germans, preferably Lutheran,
and ideally retired high school vice principals, while
the defense wants drunken fraternity boys of all
faiths and denominations). Peremptory challenges
have created the cottage industry of "juror consul-
tants" who, in high-profile cases, sit in the back of
the courtroom and watch ever so closely for telltale
body twitches.

As you will learn in your Constitutional Law
class, peremptory challenges cannot be used to systematically exclude individuals based on race or sex.

Opening Statements

Opening statements are often referred to as
"road maps" that help the jury fit the various
pieces of evidence into an overall story. "We will
call Dr. Dread to prove that Ms. K sustained serious
injuries. He is not a real doctor but plays one on
TV. He examined the plaintiff shortly after the

accident. He will testify as to her injuries and as to the great pain she was in."

During their opening statements, lawyers are not supposed to "argue" their cases. Argument is the drawing of factual inferences and legal conclusions from the raw facts presented at trial. However, the line between "road map" (stating the facts that will be proven, e.g., the stairs were in disrepair) and "argument" (drawing inferences from those facts, e.g., "This means the landlord was negligent") is often a fine one, and lawyers often cross over. However, grand pleas for justice, or for the need to send landlords "messages," are clearly argument and must be saved for closing, where the only limit, frequently ignored, is good taste.

Case-in-Chief: Hearsay and Examining Witnesses

In the plaintiff's case-in-chief, evidence must be presented to establish all of the elements of the plaintiff's case. In a typical personal injury case, they are:

a. That the defendant was negligent

b. That the negligence caused plaintiff's injuries

c. The extent of those injuries

The evidence can consist of *exhibits* (X-rays showing plaintiff's broken bones, photographs of the victim's injuries), *documents* (doctor bills) and, of course, *witnesses*, including *expert witnesses*.

Live witnesses are the most fun. A major limitation on what they can testify to is the *hearsay rule*. It basically prohibits a witness from testifying as to what others told him. Of course, in the real world, we love hearsay; our ears go on high alert when we hear the rich and promising phrase, "Guess what I just heard?"

The hearsay rule prohibits the introduction of "an out-of-court statement introduced to prove the truth of the matter asserted."

"Sam told me that he had tripped on the stair two weeks before Ms. K did."

As this would be introduced to prove the matter asserted, that Sam did indeed trip on the stair, it would be inadmissible hearsay. To admit it would be unfair to the other side. Sam isn't testifying, and hence there is no way for Landlord's attorney to cross-examine him as to his ability to recall and as to his possible motivation for lying.

Hearsay comes in many variations. Irving Younger, a professor of trial advocacy, would tell the following story:

From a distance, bystanders saw a man crawl out of a bedroom window. They were too far away to identify the man but watched as a dog began to chase him. Bystanders followed but were unable to keep the dog and man in vision at all times. A few minutes later they came upon the dog at the foot of a tree; in the tree was a man. Can the bystanders testify to this?

The hearsay problem doesn't jump out at you but, in essence, it is really as if the dog is testifying, "The guy in the tree is the same guy I chased from the house."

Younger would conclude, "It would seem that the testimony would be admissible because there really is no need to cross-examine the dog. We all know dogs never lie."

Younger would pause. "*But*, they have a great sense of humor!"

Like most legal rules, there are scores of exceptions to the hearsay rule, exceptions which will become the bane of your Evidence course. The two most common exceptions are *party admissions* and *prior inconsistent statements*.

Anything a party to a lawsuit said is admissible *against* that party. (A party is either the plaintiff or the defendant.)

"Now, you are a friend of Ms. K. Did she tell you what she was doing before she tripped on the stairs?"

"Yes. She said she was drinking beer and listening to Merle Haggart songs."

"How much beer?"

"She couldn't remember."

This testimony is being introduced to prove the matter asserted, that Ms. K was drinking (a lot) before she fell. But, because she's in the courtroom, she can take the stand and deny, or explain, her out-of-court statement.

A related rationale justifies the introduction of *prior inconsistent statements*. If a witness (any witness, not just a party) testifies one way at trial, the opposing lawyer can always bring up that witness's prior inconsistent out-of-court statement. This is why lawyers are fond of deposing opposing witnesses: if they change their story at trial, they can be *impeached* with their prior sworn deposition. This was illustrated in the last chapter.

In addition to the hearsay rule, the prohibition against *leading* witnesses on direct also helps ensure that the jury hears only what the witness has to say. When the lawyer calls his witnesses, he takes the witness on *direct* examination. Generally a lawyer cannot *lead* his own witness; that is, he cannot suggest the answer to him, as does the following:

> *Mr. Plaintiff, isn't it a fact that you received severe back injuries in the accident?*

Only a dumb (or honest) witness would answer, "No."

On direct, you must ask non-leading questions:

> *Mr. Plaintiff, please describe the injuries you received as a result of the accident.*

Leading questions are prohibited on direct because we want the witness to testify, not the lawyer. Leading on direct is permissible as to non-contested matters (where the witness lives) or in the case where the witness is having a hard time remembering.

After each witness, the opposing lawyer has the opportunity to *cross-examine*.

> *"Mr. Plaintiff, you testified on direct that you injured your back in the accident. Now, isn't it a fact that you had injured your back several weeks prior to the accident?"*

On cross-examination the lawyer can, and usually does, ask leading questions. They are a great way to control the witness and force answers on unpleasant matters.

My colleague Paul Bergman points out the ultimate irony. Inexperienced lawyers tend to ask leading questions on direct (because they know the answers) and non-leading questions on cross (because they don't).

Let's examine one piece of lawyer lore: "Never ask a question on cross you don't know the answer to." War stories are offered in support:

> *The defendant was charged with biting off the victim's nose. An eye-witness, called by the prosecution, had testified on direct that indeed the defendant had done this heinous deed. On cross, the defendant's lawyer established that this witness was not looking in the direction of the defendant and his victim until after he heard a scream, thus throwing grave doubt on the testimony that he saw the crime. Then came the dreaded question: "If you weren't looking at the time, how can you know the defendant bit off the victim's nose?"*

> *"Because I saw him spit it out."*

Great story. Troubling story. It suggests that lawyers should use their craft to hide the truth. That is a highly debatable proposition. Further, the story assumes that the prosecuting lawyer is incompetent. After cross-examination, there is always *redirect*.

> *"Now, on cross-examination, it was shown that you didn't see the fight. So how can you testify that the defendant bit off the victim's nose?"*

Cross-examination is a needed response to the human tendency to take sides and, once a partisan, to fudge their testimony: to recall a better look than they had and to fail to recall good points for their opponent. Wellman, in his classic book *The Art of Cross–Examination*, gives a striking example of witness partisanship. This is not a recent phenomenon. Wellman was writing at a time when folks traveled by ship. He wrote that when two ships collide, "almost invariably all the crew on one ship will testify in unison against the opposing crew, and, what is more significant, such passengers as happen to be on either ship will almost invariably be found corroborating the stories of their respective crews."

Cross-examination has been touted as the best known device for ferreting out truth (from weaseling witnesses). It usually doesn't work as well as it does on TV, but it can be quite powerful. Volunteer to play the role of a witness at a trial practice court. Feel the rush of combativeness and fear when the judge says, "You may cross-examine." It's only you and the lawyer, and you must answer the questions.

Gone are your jokes, your charm, your easy eva-
sions.

*"I didn't ask you that. Please answer my ques-
tion."*

Another limitation on witness testimony is that,
unless the witness is called as an expert, the witness cannot testify as to her *opinions* or *conclusions*. This is best illustrated by the cartoon
showing a rather smug dog on the stand, and the
frustrated lawyer shouting, "We're not interested
in what you think. We are only interested in what
you smelled."

Rebuttal

Once the defense finishes its case, it *rests*. Certain
things may come out during that case that plaintiff
feels he can prove wrong. Rebuttal is his opportunity. Suppose defendant calls a witness who testifies
he saw the accident. Plaintiff, during rebuttal, can
call witnesses who will put the defendant's witness,
at the time of the accident, in Nova Scotia. A
defendant's rebuttal is quite infrequent. Perhaps
witnesses could testify that plaintiff's rebuttal witnesses don't even know where Nova Scotia is.

Closing Argument

Once the evidence is in, and after (or in some
jurisdictions, before) the judge instructs the jurors
as to the law and their role as fact-finders, lawyers
are allowed to make closing arguments. Here they

"marshal" the evidence, wax poetic, and strut. We'll see this in the next chapter.

One criminal defense lawyer of the Civil War era used to call, as his only witnesses, his own small children.

"What would happen if Daddy were to die?"

They would mourn, cry, and ultimately have to be helped off the stand.

The lawyer's closing was short, focused, and effective.

"Ladies and Gentlemen of the Jury. If you convict my client, I am going to kill myself."

This is no longer considered good form.

Who argues first? The party with the overall burden of proof (the plaintiff in a civil action, the prosecution in a criminal action). Then it is the defense's turn. Finally, the opening party gets to rebut the defendant's argument. In theory, this can only be for rebuttal, and a lawyer should not bring up new matter; to do so would be unfair because her opponent would not have the opportunity to respond.

The two most common mistakes lawyers make in closing arguments is putting *their own credibility in issue* and *arguing evidence that is not in the record.* You put your credibility in issue by arguing, *"I know my client is telling the truth."* It is fine to argue, *"The evidence shows my client is telling the truth."* Subtle but important distinction.

The reason lawyers begin planning their closing argument as an almost first step, before even investigating the case, is because they know that unless they get the evidence in the record, through a document, exhibit, or witness testimony, they cannot argue it even if it is true. Good lawyers will make a list of the evidence they want to argue and, as the trial goes on, check off items that have been covered.

Legal planning begins at the end and looks backwards.

Finally what about the tree falling in the forest?

It's a question of *habit* evidence. Can you introduce evidence that someone has a "habit" of doing a particular thing as evidence that he probably did it at a particular time? In some jurisdictions you can; in others, you can't. Thus, as trees habitually make a noise when they fall, if they fall in a jurisdiction that admits habit evidence, they will make a noise even if no one is there to hear.

Of course, it may be that falling trees habitually make noise *only* when there is someone there to hear. It would make for a great law school exam question:

> *A tree, standing in a jurisdiction that admits habit evidence, falls into one that does not. It is in that jurisdiction that the person who wasn't there to hear would have been.*
>
> *Discuss.*

CHAPTER 18

K v. LANDLORD, **GREATEST HITS**

In this chapter we take a more detailed look at trial dynamics. As you are years away from your first trial, now is not the time to take notes or to try to memorize things. Just sit back and observe what a trial looks like. There will be a few jokes *and* you will learn the secret identity of Ms. K. Whose sister is she, anyway?

We will use the case of *K v. Landlord*. As you will recall, Ms. K is bringing suit for injuries she sustained when she tripped and fell on common stairs in her apartment house. Her basic claim is that Landlord failed in his duty to provide a safe place to live by failing to repair a defective step. Ms. K is represented by Ms. C. Darrow and Landlord by Mr. Quibble Weaver. In the last chapters, we went through their pretrial haggling.

Darrow, for the plaintiff, has the burden of proof and, therefore, goes first. She plans to call Ms. K to testify to her fall and injuries. She plans to call Dr. Dread to establish the extent of those injuries. To establish Larry Landlord's negligence, she will call Joe Ham, a tenant of the apartment house, who will testify that he complained of the loose stairs to

251

Larry Landlord two weeks before the unfortunate accident. Darrow will also call a carpenter, with the unlikely name of Woody Nails, who inspected the stairs shortly after the accident and concluded that they had been in a dangerous condition for at least two months.

Quibble Weaver, for the defense, will call Larry Landlord and Chuck Pile, a tenant who will testify that he takes out the garbage by way of the back stairs every week and has not once tumbled. Weaver will also call, to rebut the seriousness of Ms. K's injuries, a doctor who usually testifies for insurance companies, Dr. Polly Anna. Pursuant to a discovery order, Dr. Anna, hired by Weaver, gave Ms. K a complete physical. She think Ms. K is a malingerer. Or worse!

Waiting in the wings, for the defense, is Billy Knowles. When Weaver deposed plaintiff's witness Joe Ham, he learned just how devastating his testimony would be. Weaver decided he needed an *impeachment witness*. His investigator found Billy Knowles, who will testify that Ham hates Larry Landlord; Landlord has threatened to evict him and has called the police on his parties. Joe told Billy that he would get even with Landlord. When Weaver gets to cross-examine Joe during the trial, he plans to ask him about these matters. If Joe denies them, then Weaver, with great fanfare, will call Billy Knowles as part of the defense case.

Darrow can call her witnesses in any order she pleases. Trial lawyers will tell you that you should open and close with strong witnesses, putting the weaker one in the middle. People tend to remember best the first thing they hear and the last thing they hear, tending to fuzz over points in the middle. Knowing this, Darrow decides to put Dr. Dread on first and to put on Ms. K last. She wants to begin and end with a powerful presentation of her client's suffering. The weak part of her case, that of Larry's negligence, she plans to sandwich in between high points.

One reason she puts Ms. K last, rather than first, is that this will allow Ms. K to hear of the evidence before she testifies. There is nothing worse than having your client testify and then be contradicted by her own witnesses who testify after her. Witnesses in a case are usually prohibited from listening to other witnesses testify before they testify. This rule does not apply to *parties,* and, to allow them to hear what others have to say before they take the stand, they usually testify last.

As to each witness, Darrow knows she can develop the testimony in any order she selects. Chronological order is often the easiest to follow but, frankly, it lacks flair. Take the testimony of Ms. K. The chronology of it is:

1.   She trips.

2.   She goes to the hospital.

3.   She misses some work and loses some wages.

4.   The mail arrives, with the doctor bills.

To have Ms. K testify in this order would put even me to sleep, and I'm getting paid. Darrow first sits down and lists what points she wants to make with Ms. K.

First she plans to use Ms. K to prove up medical bills and loss of earnings. These matters are not controversial and lack emotional impact; they should go in the middle of the testimony. Second, Darrow wants Ms. K to testify as to the terror of the fall. She also wants to establish that Ms. K was being careful at the time of her fall. Darrow is concerned that during jury deliberations, a juror might remark, "If she had been looking where she was going, this never would have happened." Darrow wants to shut this down if she can. Third, Darrow wants to have Ms. K testify as to the pain and suffering she has experienced and continues to experience. Darrow decides on the following order:

1. Description of the accident and the fact that Ms. K was being careful.

2. The amount of her medical bills and the extent of her loss of earnings.

3. The pain and suffering; the fear she would never walk again.

There is no magical order, but a good trial lawyer should be able to answer the question, "Why did you present the testimony in the order you did?"

Of course, the first problem Darrow faces is getting Ms. K on the stand, making her comfortable, and, if possible, bringing in some interesting tidbits which will make her more human and compelling. Most judges will allow such tidbits although they are technically irrelevant. You wouldn't be allowed to go on and on about things: "OK, those are all the good and kind things you did in the third grade; now, turning your attention to the fourth. . . ."

It would be nice if Ms. K coached Little League or chaired the United Way Campaign at her job. Alas, you play the hand you get.

Q: *State your name and address for the record.*

A: *Ms. K., 1601 E. Kleindale.*

Q: *Are you nervous?*

A: *Yes. After what the judiciary did to my brother, Mr. K, you'd be nervous too. He woke up one morning and found himself accused of a heinous crime. No one ever told him what the crime was. He ended up, like, you know, killing himself.*

Q: *That's horrible. Do you have any other siblings?*

A: *Yes, another brother. He woke up one day and found himself turned into, like, you know, a giant cockroach.*

Pausing to wipe a tear, Darrow now turns to developing the notion that Ms. K did not contribute to her fall.

Q: *(by C. Darrow). Now, Ms. K, you weren't at fault in this, were you?*

Q: *(by Q. Weaver). Objection. Leading. You can't lead on direct. You know better!*

Q: *(by C. Darrow). Of course I do. This is an instructional book, and the author keeps making me do things that are wrong. Then he can come in and be a big hero. Sometimes I wish I were real!*

Cut and back to fiction:

Q: *(by C. Darrow) The afternoon of the accident, had you been drinking?*

A: *No.*

Q: *Were you tired or sick?*

A: *No, I was feeling fine.*

Q: *Now, prior to the accident, did you know the step was loose?*

A: *No, I seldom use the back stairs. I hadn't used them before my fall for at least two months.*

Q: *Now, as you approached the top of the stairs, were you distracted in any way?*

A: *No, I was looking where I was going.*

Q: *Then why did you step on a step that was loose?*

A: *Well, I did look down and nothing seemed out of the ordinary. I had no idea that the step was going to give way like it did.*

Note how Darrow develops the facts. It is far more effective to develop a conclusion than it is to simply come to it:

Q: *Were you careful?*

A: *Yes.*

Details convince.

Q: *After the accident, did you have occasion to inspect the top step?*

A: *Yes.*

Q: *Is it your opinion that Larry Landlord was negligent?*

Q: *(by Q. Weaver) Objection! That question is clearly improper as it calls for an opinion of a lay witness. Darrow knows better than that.*

Court: Sustained.

Yes, Darrow does know better than that. She knows that the question is improper. She also knows that it is *unethical* to ask an improper question in order to sneak impermissible material before the jury. You can't ask, *"When did you stop beating your spouse?"* unless you have a good faith belief that the witness did.

I forced Darrow to ask the impermissible question in order to be a hero (I'm not one at home) and to tell you about the *opinion evidence rule*. One statement of the rule is found in the Federal Rules of Evidence:

Opinion Testimony By Lay Witnesses

If the witness is not testifying as an expert, his testimony in the form of opinions or inferences is limited to those opinions or inferences which are

(a) rationally based on the perception of the witness and (b) helpful to a clear understanding of his testimony or the determination of a fact in issue.

The rule forces witnesses to testify about the raw data of experience: what they saw, heard, smelled, tasted, and felt, not what they concluded from those experiences. Drawing conclusions is the job of the jury. A witness cannot testify, "Landlord was negligent." That opinion is neither "rationally based on perception"—the witness didn't *see* the landlord being negligent—nor is it helpful to a "clear understanding of his testimony." A witness can testify:

"I stepped on the stair and felt *it give. I* looked *at the stair and found a crack about 6 inches long and a quarter of an inch wide. I told Landlord about it and* heard *him say, "That sounds dangerous. I will fix it immediately." A week later I* looked *at the stair and* saw *nothing had been done.*

From the facts witnesses testify to, the jury concludes whether the landlord was negligent.

Some witnesses can testify as to their opinions: experts. For example, the Federal Rules provide:

Testimony by Experts

If scientific, technical, or other specialized knowledge will assist the trier of fact to understand the evidence or to determine a fact in issue, a witness qualified as an expert by knowledge, skill, experience, training, or education may testify thereto in the form of an opinion or otherwise.

Darrow plans to call two experts. Dr. Dread, based on his training in medical school and his experiences as a physician, will testify as to the extent of Ms. K's injuries and as to her prognosis. Woody Nails, carpenter, will be the other expert. He will testify about the condition of the stairs. Let's pick up the trial with him.

Court: Call your next witness.

Darrow: Plaintiff calls Woody Nails.

Witness is sworn.

Q: *(by C. Darrow) State your name and address for the record.*

A: *Woody Nails.*

Q: *And you live at 5010 Randlett Drive?* (A leading question, but it is OK as it goes to preliminary matters.)

A: *Yes, that's right.*

Q: *What is your occupation?*

A: *Carpenter. I have been a carpenter for thirty years.*

Q: *Have you ever built staircases?*

A: *More than I can count.*

Q: *Do you ever have occasion to inspect staircases for safety?*

A: *Quite often. Several insurance agents ask me to inspect buildings before they insure them. I* pay particular attention to stairways, because, if they're not built proper, folks can get hurt real bad.

Q: What happens if you find a staircase that is dangerous?

Q: (by Q. Weaver) I object, Your Honor. This line of questioning isn't relevant to the issues of this case. What happens when this witness inspects other staircases is beside the point.

Q: (by C. Darrow) Your Honor, this line of questioning is relevant to show this man's expertise. That insurance agents rely on him is evidence that he knows what he is talking about.

Court: Objection overruled.

Q: Again, what happens when you find a staircase that you think is unsafe?

A: I'll tell the owner or the agent. They have me repair it.

Q: Do they ever go ahead and insure the building without insisting on having the stairs repaired?

A: Not that I know of. It would be real dumb.

Q: Did you have occasion to inspect the back staircase at the Owl Apartments?

A: Yes. I went over there about two days after Ms. K fell.

Q: What was the result of your inspection?

A: *The top stair was unsafe. It was loose and gave when you stepped on it. The problem was that it had a big crack in it, about 6 inches long and a quarter of an inch wide.*

Q: *Could you determine how long the crack had been there?*

Q: *(by Quibble Weaver) Objection, Your Honor. There is nothing about this witness that would make him an expert in this matter. I let his testimony about "unsafe" pass but not this. Without some showing that this witness has some expertise in knowing how long conditions have existed, I object to the testimony.*

Court: *I'm going to allow the question. I think carpenters can make these decisions. You can cross-examine Mr. Nails about how he came to his conclusion. How much weight to give his testimony will be up to the jury, but I will admit it.*

Note here the very important distinction between *admissibility* of evidence and its *weight*. The judge decides whether or not to *admit* the evidence; once it is admitted, the jury decides whether or not to *believe* it. The fact that Nails' conclusion will be admitted into evidence does not mean the jury will believe it. Weaver will still argue that carpenters really can't make that determination; this time he will argue to the jury rather than to the judge. On the other hand, if the judge refused to admit the testimony, the jury would never hear Nails' conclusion.

To exclude evidence on the basis that it is untrustworthy strikes me as problematic. For example, if Woody Nails really doesn't have the expertise to offer an opinion, why shouldn't the jury be allowed to hear his opinion and then, after cross-examination, reject it? A lot of rules of law you will study seem to come from a deep suspicion that jurors are, not to put too fine a point on it, dunces.

But I digress. Here the judge let the evidence in.

Q: *(Darrow, continuing) How long would you say the stair had been in that condition?*

A: *Well, from the dirt and grime embedded in the crack, I'd say a fairly long time.*

Q: *Could you be more specific?*

A: *At least a couple of months.*

Q: *Thank you, no further questions. You may cross-examine.*

Cross–Examination.

Q: *(by Q. Weaver) Now, isn't it a fact that life's a stage and we're but actors?*

A: *(nervously) Well ... er ... I guess you can say that.*

Q: *And isn't it true that your testimony has been sound and fury, signifying nothing?*

A: *(looking desperately at C. Darrow) I, I ... just don't know.*

Q: *Well, you know this, **Mister** Woody Nails. That isn't even your real name, is it!? And not even a very clever one, at that!?*

Note that leading questions are *not* questions. They are statements of fact disguised as questions. Note too that when you ask a question, your voice goes up at the end and this encourages an answer. When you make a statement of fact, your voice stays flat and does not invite long responses but, at most, an agreeing grunt. Try it! Cross-examining a witness, you don't want answers, you want agreeing grunts.

A: *(beginning to sob) I, I don't have a real name.*

Q: *Of course you don't. That's because you don't exist. You are not Prince Hamlet, nor were you meant to be. You're a bit player in an instructional manual. Your Honor, I move to strike his entire testimony! Your Honor? Where's the judge? What's happening in here?*

The rest is silence. Exeunt.

To illustrate something of cross-examination, let's take the testimony of Joe Ham who, on direct, stated that two weeks before the accident he had told Larry Landlord of the bad condition of the stair and that Larry had said, "That sounds dangerous. I will get it fixed immediately." What Larry said to Joe seems like inadmissible hearsay but it isn't. Note that, to be hearsay, the out-of-court statement must be introduced to prove the *truth* of the matter asserted, that the situation was "dangerous." Here it is being introduced to show Larry's "state of mind," that he knew of the condition. That he spoke those words, not whether they were "true," is the issue. Larry can, and probably will, get up and testify he never said those words.

If the statement was introduced to prove that the stair situation was dangerous, then it would be hearsay. While hearsay is generally not admitted, it is admitted if the statement was made by a party to the lawsuit. It would be admissible as a party admission. But of course you knew that from our discussion in the last chapter.

However, Larry has told his lawyer, Q. Weaver, that the conversation never happened. As this is not something Joe could merely be mistaken about (like an eyewitness identification), it must be that Joe is lying (or Larry is). The purpose of cross examination in such cases is to suggest possible motives for perjury. Note, however, that Weaver realizes that even hostile witnesses can be used to make needed points, here to throw doubt on the testimony of Woody Nails. Note too that the questions on cross are leading.

Cross-Examination of Joe Ham

Q: *(by Q. Weaver) It's true that you used those stairs on several occasions both before and after Ms. K's fall.* (Ed. note: the period, not a question mark, is correct. You want an agreeing grunt.)

A: (Grunting) *Yes.*

Q: *And you never noticed the defective condition before the time you reported it to Larry Landlord.*

A: *That's right.*

Q: *So, as far as you know, the condition was of fairly recent origin; isn't that right.*

A: *Well, I didn't notice it before.*

Q: *So as far as you know, the stairway was not cracked before the time you reported it?*

A: *Yes.*

Q: *And that was two weeks before Ms. K's fall, and not a couple of months.*

A: *Yes.*

Q: *Thank you. Now you never fell on those stairs, did you?*

A: *No.*

Q: *And you never heard of anyone else tripping on those stairs, isn't that right.*

Q: *(by C. Darrow) Objection, Your Honor. The question is not relevant.*

Q: *(by Q. Weaver) Your Honor, the lack of other accidents is relevant to the issue of whether the stairs were safe.*

Court: Objection overruled. You may answer the question.

Note: This might be an error on part of the judge. Maybe, under the law, the lack of other accidents cannot be used to show that the stairs were safe. If Ms. K loses, she can appeal and base her appeal on judicial error. But good luck if this is all she has, even if the judge was wrong. Appellate courts don't like to reverse cases and make the parties start all over again. Despite what you may have read in the local press, appellate judges are not vultures looking with sharp eyes for mere technicalities to reverse convictions and thus thwart justice. Appellate courts reverse only when the judge below really screws up. (One particularly flamboyant trial court judge used to brag, "I've overruled the Supreme Court many more times than it has overruled me.")

A: No, I never heard of anyone else falling.

Q: Thank you. Now, you are a very good friend of Ms. K's, isn't that right.

A: Yes.

Q: And you want her to win this lawsuit, don't you?

A: I think she should.

Q: Please answer the question. Do you want her to win this lawsuit or don't you?

A: I guess I do.

Q: Do you guess or do you?

A: I do.

Note how Weaver pursues the witness. Most witnesses will try to deflect the lawyer's questions; you must become something of a bulldog.

Q: And isn't it a fact that you don't like Larry Landlord?

A: Well, maybe not.

Q: Maybe not? Isn't it a fact that he has called the police on your wild parties?

A: Well. They weren't wild, but yes.

Q: And hasn't he threatened to evict you?

A: Yes.

Q: And didn't you tell Billy Knowles that you would get even with Landlord?

A: No, I didn't say that.

Bingo! Now, as part of his case, Weaver can call Billy Knowles to testify as to that conversation. It is admissible as a prior inconsistent statement.

During trial, lawyers make points to use in closing argument. Weaver's closing argument, as it relates to Joe, will run something like this:

Ladies and Gentlemen, there is one glaring contradiction in this case. You remember Joe, the tenant who testified that he told Larry of the faulty condition of the stairs a good two weeks before the accident. Not only did he tell him, but he told you Larry said, "That sounds dangerous. I'll get it fixed immediately."

Now that's quite convenient Larry said that. Note how well it fits into the plaintiff's theory. It shows not only that Larry knew of the condition, but also, that Larry knew it was quite dangerous. What better evidence could you ask for?

Larry testified he never had that conversation with Joe. You must decide who to believe. Some-

one is lying to you. How can you decide who is telling the truth? His Honor will instruct you that you can consider the "character and quality of the testimony" and the existence of any bias or interest.

Does Joe's testimony make sense? To believe that that conversation actually took place, you must believe that Larry knew that there was a very dangerous condition on the stairway but simply failed to do anything about it. Joe would have you believe that Larry was content to wait until someone tripped and fell, to wait until someone sued. Joe's story doesn't make sense. Further, Joe continued to use the stairs. Does it make sense to go on using a staircase after you have reported its dangerous condition to the landlord?

Joe's story just doesn't hold together. Had he told Larry of the condition, it is reasonable to assume Larry would have acted, not only to prevent someone's injury but also to avoid a lawsuit. Does Joe have a motive to make up his testimony? A motive to lie to you? You bet. He is a good friend of the plaintiff. He admitted that he wants her to win this case and obviously he knows his testimony is essential for her victory. And he dislikes Larry. He threatened to get even with Larry. Sure, he denies that, but Billy Knowles, who has no interest in this case, came in here, raised his right hand, and swore that he did.

Now you have two witnesses, Larry and Billy, against one.

No, Joe is not to be believed. He was simply lying about his conversation with Larry. Larry told you it never happened because it never did.

Closing Argument: Weaving Law and Fact

Effective closing argument relies on the primary lawyering skill, the ability to bring law and fact together. That's what you do when you write your exams. Here you'll do it in public.

The witnesses and the documents and the exhibits have put before the jury bits of information: that Joe was threatened with eviction, that the carpenter believes that the stairs had been in a state of bad repair for a long time, that Ms. K fell. At closing, the lawyer *marshals these bits of information into factual conclusions that have legal relevance.* To illustrate this, let's pick up part of Darrow's closing argument.

Closing Argument: C. Darrow

From the fact that Joe told Larry of the condition of the stairs and from the fact that they had been in disrepair for a long time, we can conclude that Larry knew or should have known that the stair was dangerous.

Next Darrow shows the jury what these factual conclusions mean in terms of law.

That Larry Landlord knew of the dangerous condition and yet did nothing about it means that he was not acting as would an ordinarily careful person under the circumstances. An ordinarily

> *careful person would have done something to pre-*
> *vent the accident. As the judge will instruct, if you*
> *find that Larry did not do as would an ordinarily*
> *careful person, you are to find him negligent.*

This mode of analysis is quite familiar. In an exam the bits of information in the question are turned into factual conclusions which are then turned into legal conclusions.

Closing arguments are, however, more, much more, than logic. They are emotion and power. In the hands of a good criminal defense lawyer, "reasonable doubt" becomes the finest and most delicate flower of Western Civilization, a flower about to be ground under the shiny black boot of the State. Listening to a good personal injury lawyer you experience the victim's anguish as he lies sleepless in a hospital bed thinking of what might have been.

When it comes your time to make a closing argument, there are few experiences so intense and immediate. When you start, there will be distractions. You will be nervous, you will be aware of the spectators, of the judge, and of your trembling hands.

Soon, however, you soar. Forgotten are your notes and gone is the judge; for awhile it is just you, your argument, and the jurors.

Just once makes three years of law school worthwhile.

Most law schools offer Trial Advocacy courses. I urge you to take one. As one of my students told me, "Now I know I don't want to be a trial lawyer."

There are several excellent books on trial advocacy. One of my favorites, by the way, is Hegland, *Trial and Practice Skills in a Nutshell*.

*

PART FOUR

LEGAL WRITING AND ORAL ADVOCACY

All writing is persuasive writing. You have to persuade the reader to keep going.

Kay Kavanagh

This Part deals with legal writing and oral argument. Both rest on your ability to do legal analysis. Instead of "Legal Writing," think "Written Legal Analysis," and instead of "Oral Argument," think "Oral Legal Analysis." Expect old friends, "Yes, but ..." and "So what?" and a plethora of "on the other hands."

We begin with some basics about writing: goals, getting better and getting started. Chapter 20 then discusses two common forms of legal writing, the office memo and the appellate brief. It gives examples and involves you in the analysis. Chapter 21 gives you some general writings tips, such as IRS transitions and avoiding common errors in legal prose. Chapter 22 gives you two exercises to hone your writing skills. Chapter 23 gives you an editing structure; no need to read it until you are actually editing one of your documents.

Chapter 24 is quite important. While it focuses on oral advocacy, it stresses the importance of Statements of Fact, how to tell effective stories and gives you an idea of the three concerns of judges: doing justice, following law, and creating good policy. This chapter should be read before you write an argumentative brief. The last Chapter in this Part deals with the mechanics of oral argument and draws on the insights of the acting profession. It need not be read until you are facing the task yourself, perhaps in a Moot Court Program, your opportunity to dress up and dazzle the judges with the depth of your knowledge and the sparkle of your wit.

CHAPTER 19

WRITTEN LEGAL ANALYSIS: GOALS, GETTING BETTER, AND GETTING STARTED

A lawyer's teenage daughter threw the gauntlet: "Dad, you can't write and I'm taking one of your briefs to my creative writing teacher to prove it!"

A week later, the verdict. Smugly. "I was right, Dad. My teacher says you can't write! He says your sentences are too short, your paragraphs are too short, and besides, anyone can understand it."

Is Legal Writing Dull? Exotic?

You may fear that legal writing is dull and unimaginative (who can say *anything* interesting, cleaver, or profound about widgets?). You may also fear that legal writing is unlike anything you have done before, that it is exotic, strange, and forbidding, replete with Latin phrases, weird constructions, ("party of the first part"), and white-powdered wigs. You're wrong. Legal writing is neither dull nor exotic.

True, stream of consciousness is out along with character development; as for symbolism, legal writing is pretty much about what it's about. True, legal writing is fairly structured, both in format (Facts, Issues, Analysis) and in story line: you are to apply given legal principles to given facts; you are not free to break out and posit laws from far galaxies nor small creatures who actually eat widgets. Tied down, can you be creative?

Structure focuses creativity. A friend teaches poetry to middle school children. Tell them to write a poem, and, in order not to impose on their creativity, leave them on their own. You get gibberish. If you tell them to write a sonnet, with its well defined structure and rules, and tell them the topic, a red pig perhaps, you get wonderful work. It is hard enough to write a good poem without also worrying about length, rhyme schemes and topics. ("My gosh, I have to write a beautiful poem." "No you don't; you have to write a sonnet about a pig.")

Writing law will take you to exciting depths. You will have insights you never thought you could, and then you will struggle to refine those insights and capture them in words. "That's close; that's almost it, but not quite." Expect to wake up in the middle of the night and shout, "That's it!"

If that's not creativity, who needs it?

As to exotic, legal writing demands something of a different vocabulary. But that's about it. Good legal writing is like all good non-fiction writing: clear and to the point. You've been writing good prose all your life, so you basically already know how to write law.

These two beliefs, legal writing is dull and exotically different, mislead. You don't have to write dull, unimaginative prose, and even an occasional metaphor works. More importantly, don't forget your own voice: write as you would talk and not as how you think some pompous, long-winded prig would write.

Rejoice to hear that "your sentences are too short, your paragraphs are too short, and besides, anyone can understand it."

Let's get started.

The Goal of Legal Writing

The goal of all legal writing is the same: to help someone make a difficult and important decision. You might be writing a client concerning whether to file a lawsuit, a senior partner concerning whether to advise a client to plead guilty, or a judge concerning whether a statute is constitutional. They all need your help in understanding the legal situation.

The goal of legal writing is *never* to impress the reader, to show off, to use big words, to write long sentences and never-ending paragraphs.

Bad legal writing is pretty much the same. It is not the overuse of adverbs, passive voice, unclear referents, or split infinitives; it is simply bad legal analysis. From this time and place, let our topic go forth no longer as "Legal Writing" but rather "Written Legal Analysis."

Good legal analysis, and hence good legal writing, focuses on the interplay of law and fact. It is always grounded in the here and now. It avoids long discussions of abstract law by always demanding an answer to "So what?" Good analysis always considers both sides of an issue, and to assure you do, keep "Yes ... but" in mind. Yes, that is a very strong point on behalf of the defendant, *but* what are the counter-arguments the plaintiff could make? *Yes,* that's a good counter-argument, *but* how would the defendant respond? Not only does this ping-pong process force you to consider both sides, but it also deepens your analysis: the real analysis begins when we get to the responses to the responses to the counter-arguments.

Let's turn to our most pressing questions: how to get better and how to get started.

Getting Better

Writing classes and books on writing will help, but practice is key. Stephen King, in his book *On Writing,* points out that he learned to write while washing motel sheets in Bangor, Maine, and that Faulkner learned while working in a post office in Oxford, Mississippi.

> *You learn best by reading a lot and writing a lot, and the most valuable lessons of all are those you teach yourself.*

Of course, he doesn't tell you this until *after* you buy his book, but no matter, neither did I. As to reading a lot, you will: appellate cases, statutes, uniform codes, law reviews, and legal texts. Pause, every now and then, to consider matters of style. Become a *student of legal expression*. If what you are reading is clear, how is the author pulling it off? If the writing is confused or if you are bored to tears, don't beat yourself up: what is it about the writing that contributes to your confusion?

As to writing a lot, take law courses that require papers and those that have essay exams, not multiple choice.

How to teach yourself? Easier said than done. It will take effort.

Have friends, not law students, read what you have written; remember, *anyone should be able to understand it.* The best thing you can hear is, "Hey, Dude, I thought law school was supposed to be hard. This stuff is simple." More likely, a mutter, "This is real good." Don't take their word for it. Ask them, gently, to explain your arguments. If they can't, see what you did wrong. It is *never* the reader's fault.

Wait a week to read your draft, now you will read it as a reader, not as the author. If you had a life-and-death decision to make, would this memo help you? Does it tell you what you need to know? Read aloud. If it doesn't sound like you, you have fallen victim to the myth that legal writing must be high-falutin'. If you gasp for breath, your sentences are too long and your paragraphs too dense. If it reads well, consider how you were able to do this.

This business about getting better by reading and writing a lot may suggest that writing is easy, that one just sits back and lets it come. Not so. Writing is hard work. Stephen King tells the following:

A friend came to visit James Joyce one day and found the great man sprawled across his writing desk in a posture of utter despair.

"James, what's wrong?" the friend asked. "Is it the work?"

Joyce indicated assent without even lifting his head to look at the friend. Of course it was the work; isn't it always?

"How many words did you get today?" the friend pursued.

Joyce (still in despair, still sprawled face down on his desk): "Seven."

"Seven? But James ... that's <u>good</u>, at least for you!"

"Yes," Joyce said, finally looking up. "I suppose it is ... but I don't know what <u>order</u> they go in!"

Okay, legal writing isn't that hard, but it is still hard. Start early; it will not simply flow. Anticipate frustration, anger, rethinking your life. Plan to revise and revise, and, with a cry of despair, hitting Delete and starting all over. If you find writing easy, you aren't doing it well.

Getting Started

"If you tell yourself you are going to be at your desk tomorrow, you are by that declaration asking your unconscious to prepare the material."

So advises Norman Mailer in his book, *The Spooky Art: Thoughts on Writing*. This makes sense to me. Don't just sit down one morning, look at the problem, and begin writing. Read the problem a day or so before and let it simmer. Talk with friends. Try out ideas. Dream on it. Think about it at dinner, even if it irritates those who want the salt.

Once you sit down, don't freeze up. Start.

Over the next chapters, I will discuss how to tell effective stories, how to present the law, how to improve transitions, how to achieve brevity and explicitness, and, surprisingly, how to avoid the lurking danger of adverbs. Don't freak. Don't try to make things perfect; you are writing only a draft.

Legal writing is stylized: facts first, then issues, then analysis. Don't freak. Writing is not a one-two-three affair. Don't try to get your statement of facts perfect before you turn to stating the issues. Don't try to get your issues just right before you start your analysis. Writing your analysis, you may see that you should have included something more in your statement of facts or that you should rewrite the issue. Some writers start with the analysis or with the issue and write the statement of facts last.

When you begin, forbidding legal issues that you don't understand will loom. Don't freak. You don't need to figure everything out before you start writing; indeed, writing helps you figure things out. Cross that bridge when you get to it.

Stephen King doesn't know where his books will take him.

The situation comes first. The characters—always flat and unfeatured, to begin with—come next. Once these things are fixed in my mind, I begin to narrate. I often have an idea of what the outcome may be, but I have never demanded of a set of characters that they do things my way. On the contrary, I want to do things their way. In some instances, the outcome is what I visualized. In most, however, it's something I never expected.

Approach your writing this way. Take the law and the facts and see how your analysis works out. You may have had an inkling of what you were going to say but don't be surprised if you are surprised.

Don't freak.

Finally, remember this. As you sit there struggling with your prose, cursing your fate, you are not primarily meeting a deadline nor even trying for a good grade. You are getting better!

CHAPTER 20

MEMOS AND BRIEFS

Two common forms of legal writing are office memos and appellate briefs. Office memos are neutral, with a goal helping senior lawyers come to a conclusion about a legal situation. Appellate briefs are argumentative, with a goal of convincing judges to arrive at a particular conclusion. I will walk you thorough an example of each, but first, some general points on Statements of Fact and Statements of Law.

Stating the Facts

Both office memos and appellate briefs open with a "Statement of Facts"; however, tone is markedly different in the two situations. *Neutrality* is the hallmark of an office memo. You are not an advocate. Your role is to analyze the situation objectively, much as you do on an exam. Taking sides will skew your analysis, leading you to overlook valid opposing arguments. Don't take sides in your analysis or in your statement of facts; never, not once, begin: "You're not going to believe what happened to our poor, innocent client!"

Writing an appellate brief, you are an advocate, and how you tell your story is vastly important. If the reader of your Statement of Facts is not left feeling sympathy for your client, you have failed. I will return to this topic in the chapter on legal argument.

Long statements create problems. While you will know why the facts are important, your reader may not because the convention is not to disclose the legal issues until after the factual statement. If your statement is too long and too confusing, your reader will be tempted to skim (Visualize a car hydroplaning on wet pavement). How to edit your facts?

Let's back up. Assume you interview the client. You write a *memo to the file*, erring on the side of over-inclusiveness: what appears trivial now may emerge as critical later. As to how to interview clients, try lawsuits, and be happy, see Hegland, *Trial and Practice Skills in a Nutshell*. (Has this man no shame?) Writing an *office memo*, which combines the facts with a legal analysis, you edit the facts to *operative facts,* those that matter in your legal analysis. The question is whether, if the facts were different or not present, the legal decision would have been different. Reducing a mass of facts to operative ones is part of your legal analysis. Of course, lawyers might argue about which facts are operative, but do the work. Except for some fluff facts to round out your story, don't include facts simply because they are there. Include them only if they will be used, downstream, in your legal analysis.

Even after reducing the raw facts into operative ones, you may still have a long Statement. While there is something to be said for presenting the reader with the entire story before beginning, consider two other approaches. In your initial Statement of Facts recount only enough to give a brief overview and to get your analysis started, adding the following: "Additional facts will be discussed later when they become relevant." The other alternative is to sketch briefly the legal issues first and then turn to the facts. That may improve understanding.

Stating the Law

Let's say a homeowner refuses to pay the last installment on his home-remodeling contract. The contractor bribed the Building Inspector to get her to expedite some of the paperwork, thus raising the possible defense of illegal performance of contract. As a statement of law, consider:

Cases have held that people cannot profit from their own wrong.

This would be an adequate statement of law on an exam because there is generally no need to cite specific cases or recount specific language. But if things really matter, as they do in the case of office memos and appellate briefs, how is the reader to know that you got the law right? Cite sources (cases or statutes) and quote language.

In the case of Riggs v. Palmer, *it was held that 'No one shall be permitted to profit from his own wrong.'*

This seems pretty strong language in support of the Homeowner. The Builder did wrong by bribing a government official and now is seeking to profit from it. But wait. Before applying that language to our case, what don't we know about *Riggs v. Palmer?*

The facts! Judicial language is spoken in the context of specific facts, and there is always the danger that the language, by itself, will be misleading. When you are citing language from a case, alert your reader to the context. You do not need detail, just the major facts. You can do so with an introductory sentence or with a parenthetic clause, to wit:

> *In the case of* Riggs v. Palmer, *it was held that 'No one shall be permitted to profit from his own wrong'* (murderer denied inheriting his victim's estate).

Now does this case seem such a strong precedent for Homeowner?

There are a couple of other common problems in discussions of law:

1. *Coming in the middle of the story.* Kids begin telling what happened in nursery school with "Then Pat said...." They assume that you know everything that they do, who Pat is, what was said before, and what they had for lunch. Even though your readers will be lawyers, you *will* know much more about the particular area of law than they do. If necessary, put the precise issue in an overall legal

context. Say your case turns on an interpretation of Section 8(b)(ii) of a Statute. Don't begin "Section 8(b)(ii) says...." without first telling the reader something about Section 8.

2. *Citing too much law.* Don't go overboard on this business of not starting in the middle. If your issue is whether a car search was unreasonable, discuss cases involving car searches; there is no need to discuss the Incorporation Doctrine, the Constitutional Convention, the American Revolution or, indeed, the Big Bang. Judges will not be amused. However, in law school, and as a learning device, err on the side of too much context (stop at the Incorporation Doctrine).

Just as you must reduce unruly facts to manageable bits, you must extract from the legal universe the precise controlling authority. A plethora of precedent doesn't impress anyone. Decisions turn on the meaning of a few key cases or statutes; instead of needles, we get haystacks.

Beware "cut and paste."

Beware "cut and paste."

Beware "cut and paste."

Pledge to copy, by hand or keyboard, the controlling law. That's work and you will only copy what you need. "Do I need that quote?" "Can I omit that subpart?" You are forced to analyze the law *now*, not at some date to be named later. Copying, one word at a time, will disclose otherwise hidden ambiguities and implications. "Wait a minute. I can interpret that word differently."

Let's now look at some examples of legal writing: the office memo and the appellate brief.

A Legal Memo

One acceptable format of the office legal memo is:

1. Caption

2. Facts

3. Issue

4. Statement of law

5. Conclusion

6. Analysis

As you read through my partial example, be active. What is good about it? What is lousy? Write comments in this book, not only to prevent resale, but also to get used to writing in law books. Writing slows the mind.

OFFICE MEMORANDUM

To: Senior Partner

From: Humble Associate

Re: Contract Claim of Charles Mills

Facts

Levi Wyman, 25 year-old son of the defendant, fell sick upon his return from a sea voyage. It is unclear what his actual disease was. The plaintiff,

Charles Mills, age 62, is a local resident who has recently retired from his printing business that he ran for several years. Mills was unable to contact the young man's family and cared for him for several weeks. Unfortunately, the young man died. The defendant is the father of the young man. It is not known how old he is, but it is known that he is divorced. Upon hearing of the kindness plaintiff bestowed on his son, the defendant wrote plaintiff, promising to pay the expenses the plaintiff incurred in boarding and nursing his son. The defendant now refuses to pay on his promise.

Issue

Is Mr. Wyman's promise, made in recognition of services rendered to Wyman's son, enforceable under Section 89a of the Restatement (Second) of Contracts?

Statement of Law

Section 89a of the Restatement of Contracts provides

(1) A promise made in recognition of a benefit previously received by the promisor is binding.

(2) A promise is not binding under Subsection (1)

    (a) if the promisee conferred the benefit as a gift . . . or

    (b) to the extent that its value is disproportionate to the benefit.

Conclusion

The Restatement enforces promises made "in recognition of a benefit" previously received. If the benefit must be a direct material one, then the father's promise is not enforceable because the services were rendered to the son. However, if the court interprets "benefit" to include the benefit of knowing one's child died in peace, then the promise is enforceable because the other requirements of the Restatement seem to be satisfied as it doesn't seem that the benefit was conferred as a "gift."

Analysis

[Omitted; only I can make such a move]

Have you done your own critique of this? You should have. Here's mine.

Analysis of Memo

The statement of facts begins:

Levi Wyman, 25 year-old son of the defendant, fell sick upon his return from a sea voyage....

This passes the "I really don't care" test. Unlike the Statement of Facts in an appellate brief, it is not skewed in favor of either party.

Does it seem cluttered? What of the operative facts? To analyze the case, one doesn't need to know that the disease is unknown, the age of the plaintiff, or what he did before retirement. Edit! Note that there is one important fact not mentioned: why did the Dad refuse to pay? If he is claiming, for example, he wrote the letter when he was drunk, then that changes the legal posture of the case.

This underscores two important points made in the last chapter. Write now, edit later. Don't try to make things perfect in your first draft. Second, legal writing is fluid. The importance of why Dad refused to pay may not strike you until you are writing your legal analysis. On an actual case, you would go back and reread your *memo to the file* and, if it's not there, call your client. If you don't have these options, *flag* the matter in your statement of facts: "It is unclear why the father is refusing to pay, and this is a matter we should discuss with our client."

Let's now look at the statement of the issue:

Is Mr. Wyman's promise, made in recognition of services rendered to Wyman's son, enforceable under Section 89a of the Restatement (Second) of Contracts?

Think about this for a minute. Do you see any problem with it? Do you know *why* we are even looking at Section 89a?

We've walked in at the middle of the story. Your readers are lawyers, but you know more about the particular area of law than they do. A funny thing happens after you have struggled and struggled with an area of law until it becomes clear: it now seems obvious, something everyone knows. This is the Teacher's Dilemma: you don't want to bore people by stating the obvious, but you no longer know what's obvious. Err on the side of boring, rather than confusing, your reader, to wit:

Issue: Common law doctrine requires that promises, in order to be enforced, received consideration, something in return. Here Mr. Wyman got nothing for his promise, to pay for services already rendered; thus it would be unenforceable as a gift promise. However, in some circumstances, a promise for a past benefit is enforceable. Those circumstances are given in Section 89a of the Restatement (Second) of Contracts. Is Mr. Wyman's promise enforceable under that section?

Turning now to the statement of law:

Section 89a of the Restatement of Contracts provides

   (1) A promise made in recognition of a benefit previously received by the promisor is binding. . . .

   (2) A promise is not binding under Subsection (1)

      (a) if the promisee conferred the benefit as a gift . . . or

      (b) to the extent that its value is disproportionate to the benefit.

Here the Restatement section is copied verbatim. Like the thought of being hanged, copying key language focuses the mind. Copying also puts the reader squarely in contact with the source material. Once you get into your analysis, keep the reader in contact with it by highlighting key words.

   Compare: *Was the promise made in recognition of a benefit previously received?*

With: *Was the promise "made in recognition of a benefit previously received"?*

In the first example, the reader may think that this "benefit" matter is just an interesting twist you came up with. In the second, because of the highlighting, the reader is reminded that this is indeed a legal requirement.

When copying controlling authority, edit out parts that do not apply. Show their omission with " ... " (three dots for mid-sentence omission, four for end-of-sentence) and, if the quote is still too long (say 50 words), indent and single space.

Note that here we are dealing with what I call a *Type 2* legal problem: *how* to apply a given legal principle (here the Restatement) to a fact pattern. A *Type 1* legal problem is where you must decide *what* legal principle to apply. The clearest example of *Type 1* is a case of first impression; recall the First Case in the World: no court anywhere has addressed the issue of whether, and under what circumstances, promises to pay for prior good deeds should be enforced.

The more common example of *Type 1* is where the issue has been litigated elsewhere but there is no controlling authority in *your* jurisdiction. Assume that your research discloses a case from another state holding that, if the promise to pay for a prior good deed was *in writing*, it would be enforced. In our case, because of the father's promise was in writing, it would be best if our court followed that case, thus avoiding the complicated analysis under the Restatement.

Type 1 issues raise policy concerns that a court would evaluate in adopting a new rule: does the rule make sense in terms of justice, community expectations, and ease of application? Decisions from other states might be helpful: what have the most recent cases held? Is there a clear majority rule? Once you have discussed this, then you would return to *Type 2* analysis, applying the two tests to the facts at hand.

Finally, what of the memo's conclusion? We don't want to learn, after 300 pages, that the butler did it. If the butler did it, tell the reader up front; that way the reader can check your analysis as you go along. (How many times do we suspect that Agatha had written herself into a corner and the butler had the misfortune to walk by at that *very* moment!)

In legal writing, *conclusions* become *introductions*. At the top of your memo or brief, tell the reader what you conclude and quite briefly why (what clues you will be relying on). ''The butler did it; as we will see he had the motive, the opportunity and the phoney upper-class accent.'' This allows your readers to check your reasoning. The memo's conclusion does a good job with this.

Note: I haven't recopied the memo's conclusion. I have forced you to go back and find it. If you don't go back, and you probably won't, there is no way for you to check to see if my assessment of it is correct. Never force your reader to go back; it is not nice.

Argumentative Briefs

Argumentative writing directed at an appellate court is known as a *"Brief"*; if it is directed at a trial court judge, it is known as a *"Memorandum of Points and Authorities."* Who knows why?

Local court rules will dictate their precise format. Usually, up front, you will be required to list all of the cases, statutes, law review articles, and other authorities you discuss to allow the judge (more likely her clerk) to gather them before reading your prose.

A traditional format:

1. Caption
2. Table of Authorities
3. Procedural Status (What happened in the court below)
4. Statement of Facts
5. Summary of Argument
6. Argument

Court of Appeals

Appellant's Opening Brief

Mills,

  Plaintiff/Appellant

  versus

Wyman,

  Defendant/Respondent

Table of Authorities

Restatement (Second) of Contracts, Section 89a

Webb v. McGowin, 27 Ala.App. 2, 168 So. 196 (1935)

Statement of Facts (Omitted)

Procedural History

The trial court granted summary judgment to the defendant on the basis that his promise is not enforceable because it neither was supported by current consideration nor fell within the provisions of Restatement Section 89a. Plaintiff appeals this decision.

Summary of Argument

The defendant's promise to reimburse the plaintiff for the sums expended by the plaintiff in caring for the defendant's son, although not supported by consideration, is enforceable under the theory of past benefit conferred as provided in Restatement (Second) of Contracts 89a. That section provides:

(1) A promise made in recognition of a benefit previously received by the promisor is binding. . . .

(2) A promise is not binding under Subsection (1)

    (a) if the promisee conferred the benefit as a gift . . . or

(b) to the extent that its value is disproportionate to the benefit.

*A. The defendant received a "benefit" from the
kindness shown by the plaintiff to the defendant's
son in that he knows that his son died, not on the
street, but well cared for; it is noted that the Restatement, no doubt carefully drafted, does not explicitly
require that the 'benefit' be material and to so hold
would unduly restrict the application of that section;*

*B. The plaintiff did not confer that benefit as a
"gift" even though he did not expect payment for it;
to define any act done without expectation of payment as a "gift" would mean that no one could ever
recover under Section 89a;*

*C. The value of the promise made by the defen-
dant, to pay plaintiff's out-of-pocket costs, is not
"disproportionate" to the benefit he received.*

Two quick matters. What was discussed as a
neutral matter in your office memorandum ("Was
there a 'benefit'?") becomes an assertion in your
brief ("sure was"). Conclusions are central to argumentative writing. Note too the effective use of
highlighting the key words in the Summary: "benefit," "gift," and "disproportionate." This device re-
minds the reader that we are talking about legal
requirements, not just interesting tidbits.

In the analysis portion of your brief, you will use
the above captions (A, B, and C) to introduce each

section. If yours is the *opening* brief or memorandum, you can choose the order in which you make your points. Here, the order simply tracks the order as set out in the Restatement. But you have a *choice*. Some research shows that the best positions are first and last, suggesting that you might begin with strongest argument and end with your next best. Sometimes logic dictates a different order. Think. Don't start off with the first thing that comes to mind.

If you are *replying* to an opening brief or memorandum, track the same order as your opponent so the judge can easily turn to both positions on each point. You will rewrite the headings to state to your positions:

A.   The defendant did not receive a "benefit" from the plaintiff; any benefit was received by his son. To interpret "benefit" as including 'feeling good about what happened' would mean that a total stranger, learning of the event and being pleased with it, could be bound.

In appellate briefs should you raise weaknesses in your position? You must in office memos to help your supervisor think through the problem. However, students are reluctant to do so in their briefs, hoping, I assume, that their opponent is a dunce. Not likely. Besides, your role is not to win at any cost; your role is to win under the law, after the court has considered all the arguments.

Here Good Sam, the plaintiff, has two major problems. He did not bestow a *material* benefit on the father, and a court might conclude that his act was a *gift*. Note how our example deals brings up these problems and answers them:

It is noted that the Restatement, no doubt carefully drafted, does not explicitly require that the "benefit" be material and to so hold would unduly restrict the application of that section.

The plaintiff did not confer that benefit as a "gift" even though he did not expect payment for it; to define any act done without expectation of payment as a "gift" would mean that no one could ever recover under Section 89a.

Note that the argument concerning *gift* is what I have previously called an *Eats Pittsburgh* type of argument: one that interprets one element of a statute in such a way that it will always be met (and hence has no function in the statute) or in a way that it will never be met (and hence means that the entire statute will probably never apply). What kind of an argument is the one the follows?

To interpret "benefit" as including "feeling good about what happened" would mean that a total stranger, learning of the event and being pleased with it, could be bound.

Bring up weaknesses and deal with them. What if you can't? What if you have no response? Should you just make your argument and keep your fingers crossed, hoping your opponent won't see the winning rebuttal? No. If you have no response to the rebuttal, it means that your argument is flawed.

You should not be making it; you should not be trying to pull a fast one on the court.

But not to worry. There are very few perfect arguments. The late philosopher Robert Noznick defined the perfect philosophical argument as one that, if your opponents did not concede to it, would set off vibrations in their brains, leading to a quick and painful death.

That gives you a good idea of the *format* of legal briefs. As for *substance*, briefs should address the three main concerns of the judge:

a. *To do justice between the parties:* This will turn on an effective statement of facts

b. *To follow the law:* Cases are rules of law announced in a particular factual context and justified by a certain rationale. Both context and rationale can be used to distinguish a case or to argue that it applies by analogy. Statutes often appear as simple declarations, without legislative rationale. You will have to posit purposes and goals in order to interpret ambiguities.

c. *To create good precedent for future cases:* This involves arguing policies, slippery slopes, and floodgates.

I devote Chapter 24 to these concerns. Read it before writing a brief.

This has been a long chapter. Take a break.

CHAPTER 21

WRITING TIPS

Here are some basic tips:

- *Don't force your reader to stop and puzzle*

- *Use IRS Transitions*

- *Consider Both Sides (Ask, "Yes, but?")*

- *Be Explicit (Ask, "So What?")*

1. Don't force your reader to stop and puzzle

(1) A promise made in recognition of a benefit previously received by the promisor is binding. . . .

(2) A promise is not binding under Subsection (1)

(a) if the promisee conferred the benefit as a gift . . . or

(b) to the extent that its value is disproportionate to the benefit.

What a tangle! Writing like this forces your reader to continually stop and ask "What benefit? What promise? Who's the promisee? Who's on first?" How can you help your reader through the morass?

(1) A promise (*to pay Good Sam's expenses*) made in recognition of a benefit (*caring for the son*)

previously received by the promisor (*the fa-ther*) is binding....

   (2) A promise is not binding under Subsection (1)

      (a) if the promisee (*Good Sam*) conferred the benefit as a gift ... or

      (b) to the extent that its value *(the promise's)* is disproportionate to the benefit *(caring for son)*.

Sloppy legal writing is hard on the reader. When I read "the defendant will argue," I must stop and think, "Now which one was the defendant?" Why not, "the defendant, the *father*, will argue"? When I read "Section (2)(b) should not apply...." I must stop and go back and reread that section; why not "Section (2)(b), *dealing with 'disproportionate' benefits*, should not apply...." And "the latter argument" stops me cold every time.

Be reader friendly: make abstract terms concrete. Realize that abstract terms include, not only "Justice" and "Beauty" but also "Plaintiff," "Respondent," "Section 182," and "As I previously argued."

2. Use IRS Transitions

Good transitions help. Transitions can be more than topic sentences: in addition to introducing the topic of the paragraph, they can *tie that topic* to the previous material and can *explicitly state the legal significance* of that topic. After a paragraph discussing whether psychic benefits can count, the next paragraph begins:

The next issue is whether the promisee conferred the benefit as a "gift."

This introduces the paragraph, but what is the relationship of this issue to the one discussed in the last paragraph?

<u>If the court interprets "benefit" to include the kind of benefit the father received,</u> the next issue is whether the promisee conferred the benefit as a "gift."

Well and good. This tells the reader the *relationship between the issues.* The relationship between issues can be "and" or "or." For example, a given legal rule may state two elements: A and B. To prevail, must a plaintiff establish A *and* B or is it enough to establish A *or* B? Here the transition indicates that the plaintiff must clear both the "benefit" and "gift" hurdles.

But why does it matter whether it was conferred as a gift?

If the court interprets "benefit" to include the kind of benefit the father received, the next issue is whether the promisee conferred the benefit as a "gift," <u>because if it was a gift, then the promise is not enforceable</u>.

Now your readers know exactly where you are: you are not just rooting around trying to figure out what a "gift" is. You know how that element relates to others and why it matters. I call these transitions with everyone's favorite government agency in mind: *IRS transitions.*

I: They introduce the topic;

R: They relate that topic to the prior topic; and

S: They shown the significance of the topic.

Unlike the IRS, IRS transitions are flexible.

To enforce the promise (significance), *the court must not only hold that the benefit can be a psychic, non-material benefit* (relate), *it also must find that the benefit was not conferred as a gift* (introduce).

Like hitting a fast ball or playing the piano, IRS transitions are easy to understand but hard to do. In the next chapter, I'll give you an exercise.

3.   Consider Both Sides (Ask, "Yes, but?")

Thrust: Here we have a benefit, albeit a psychic, non-material one.

Response: Yes, but if those benefits count, then almost everyone who ever makes such a promise will have "benefitted" or they wouldn't have promised. Thus you are reading "benefit" out of the Restatement.

Response: Yes, that is a danger, but we can limit psychic, non-material benefits to family members of those who received the material benefit.

Something wonderful happens when you consider both sides: your analysis goes deeper. You are not simply arguing that non-material benefits should count but also addressing how such a reading can be limited.

4. Be Explicit (Ask, "So What?")

A common yet glaring failure in legal writing is the failure to make explicit the relationship between law and fact. Compare the following:

1. *Good Sam cared for the son voluntarily.* (That's an interesting fact, but so what?)

2. *Good Sam cared for the son voluntarily, and thus it may be said that his action was a gift.* (So what?)

3. *Good Sam cared for the son voluntarily, and thus it may be said that his action was a gift. If so, then under the Restatement of Contracts, the father's promise to pay for the services would not be enforceable.*

Facts only matter if they relate to legal principles; legal principles only matter if they relate to the facts. Sloppy writing simply points to facts or to principles and forces the reader to tie them together. I have previously labeled such free-standing statements "free radicals." To ground them, your little voice should chant, "*So what? So what?*" When you are discussing facts, "*So what?*" will force you to be explicit as to how those facts relate to the law, and, when you are discussing propositions of law, "*So what?*" will force you to articulate just how and in what ways that law relates to the facts of the case you are discussing. Once you figure out the relationship, be sure to tell your reader what it is.

A spiffy slogan might help:

Every fact you write,

Every law you cite,

Before the final dot,

Ask *"So what?"*

Well, maybe not.

CHAPTER 22

WRITING EXERCISES

Here is an opportunity to apply some of the skills we have been discussing. In the first exercise, I ask you to critique an office memo. My analysis will follow at the end of the chapter. The second exercise allows you to practice your IRS transitions. Don't leave home without them!

Exercise One: Critiquing a Memo

Critique the following memo. The question addressed is whether the defendant committed "Residential Burglary." A family build a new home and had moved most of their belongings inside. However, they were not yet living in it, in the sense that they were sleeping elsewhere, awaiting new bedroom sets. On the day in question, the family had left the house around 4 p.m. Sometime thereafter, Larry Durbin stole several items from the home, having gained entry by crawling through an open window.

Office Memo

To: Senior Prosecutor

From: Junior Associate

Re: State v. Durbin

Statement of Facts

(Omitted)

Statement of Law

The state Criminal Code provides:

Section 1: Residential Burglary in the first degree is:

A.   Any armed robbery of a residence in which a person is threatened. An armed robbery is committed with the use of a gun, knife, bat, or any other object capable of inflicting injury.

B.   Any robbery of a residence that (i) occurs at night and (ii) in which entry was accomplished by force.

Section 2: Upon conviction of residential burglary in the first degree, the defendant shall be sentenced to not less than 5 years nor more than 15 years in the State Prison. An individual who has been convicted of a prior felony or who was convicted under Section 1(A) shall not be eligible for probation.

Conclusion

The defendant is guilty of first degree residential burglary.

Analysis

The house is a residence even though the family had yet to spend the night. They had moved most of their belongings in, and they clearly intended to make it their home.

Crawling through an open window requires force. The Supreme Court of a sister state interpreted a similar statute and held that a great deal of force is not needed, only a slight amount. *State v. Stiggall (citation omitted)*. Here we have a slight amount for sure.

The only problem I see with this case involves Section 1 (B) (i). This is because the family left the house around 4, and it is usually light until 6 or so.

My take on this memo follows the next exercise; consult it only after you have done your own.

Exercise Two: IRS Transitions

IRS transitions are easy to understand but hard to do. They Introduce the new issue, they Relate it to the previous issue or discussion, and they show its legal Significance. Take the statute we used in the first exercise that defines "Residential Burglary" as

A.   Any armed robbery of a residence in which a person is threatened.

B.   Any robbery of a residence that (i) occurs at night and (ii) in which entry was accomplished by force.

We can rewrite:

*A.   Armed robbery **and** residence **and** person threatened **equals** guilt*

or

B.   Robbery **and** residence **and** night **and** forced entry **equals** guilt

Assume you want to discuss the "forced entry" and whether crawling through an open window is sufficient. You can simply introduce the issue (*The next issue is whether there was a "forced entry."*), but you can do much more:

> *Even if it is shown that a "robbery" occurred in a "residence," the defendant is not guilty unless it is also shown that there was a forced entry.*

While every new topic may not need an IRS transition, you should be able to write them easily; this will take practice, not just understanding. Take ten or fifteen minutes rewriting this IRS transition. Sometimes start with "Significance": *"The defendant will be guilty only if, in addition to finding a 'robbery' occurred in a 'residence,' it is found that a forced entry occurred."* Sometimes start with Introducing the topic: *"The next issue is whether a forced entry occurred, because, if it didn't, the defendant would not be guilty, despite the fact that a robbery may have occurred in a residence."*

Not only play with the order, also play with different words. Here are some possibilities:

Words of Contrast

despite	even though	nevertheless	but
conversely	instead	though	although
notwithstanding	on the other hand	even so	however

Words of Addition

in addition	also	further	moreover
besides	too	and	more importantly

Words of conclusion

therefore	consequently	hence	as a result
thus	accordingly		

My Analysis of Durbin Memo

As to the Statement of Law, by copying, not summarizing the law, the author put the reader in direct contact. However, don't copy everything. Because the question doesn't involve punishment, Section 2 can be dropped; as there is no suggestion of armed robbery, Section 1(A) can be omitted. Consider:

Section 1: *Residential Burglary in the first degree is:*

> *A. (Dealing with armed robbery—omitted)*
>
> *B. Any robbery of a residence that (i) occurs at night and (ii) in which entry was accomplished by force.*

Now we have needles, not haystacks.

Perhaps, however, we need a few more needles. If Durbin isn't guilty of this crime, perhaps because the house wasn't yet a residence, of what crime would he be guilty? Putting the Residential Burglary statute in the context of other theft statutes *might* help the reader interpret that statute.

The "Conclusion" isn't helpful. The goal of this memo is to help "Senior Prosecutor" evaluate the case; Junior's bare conclusion doesn't help. Had Junior stated the conclusion and briefly noted its basis, that would help because the reader could test the conclusion by reading the analysis portion.

There are a lot of problems with the "Analysis."

The house is a residence even though the family had yet to spend the night. They had moved most of their belongings in, and they clearly intended to make it their home.

The word "residence" should be highlighted, thus reminding the reader that this is a key part of the law. "So what?" isn't answered: so what if it was or wasn't a residence? Finally, "yes ... but" was not considered: couldn't Durbin argue that, before people spend the night, the house is more of a storage shed? When you consider opposing arguments, your analysis goes deeper: what is meant by "residence"? Why did the Legislature make robbing a residence a more serious crime than robbing a storage shed? We can get a better sense of what was meant by "residence" if we know that purpose.

Crawling through an open window requires force. The Supreme Court of a sister state interpreted a similar statute and held that a great deal of force is not needed, only a slight amount. State v. Stiggall (citation omitted). Here we have a slight amount for sure.

Yucky transition: how does 'force' relate to the first topic, 'residence' and what difference does it make whether or not force was used? Again we see a failure to develop opposing arguments: if crawling requires force, then so too walking, which would mean that the force requirement would always be met and Pittsburgh would be gone. Often a failure to develop opposing arguments stems from becoming an advocate as opposed to impartial evaluator: once one declares "The defendant is guilty," one has an interest in defending that conclusion.

As to the *Stiggall* case, it would be far more effective to quote specific language from that case (thus assuring the reader you are not misreading it) and far better to give a brief indication of the context in which those words were uttered ("The defendant drove a truck through the doggie door.") Finally, because *Stiggall* comes from a sister state and is not controlling authority, a Type 1 problem arises: Should our court follow *Stiggall*?

The only problem I see with this case involves Section 1 (B) (i). This is because the family left the house around 4, and it is usually light until 6.

Where can one begin? "Section 1(B)(i)" forces the reader either to stop and go back to the statute to see what it says or, as is more likely, skip the whole thing. Be helpful: "Section1(b)(i), which requires the crime to be committed at night." The argument is entirely implicit, forcing the reader to go from the fact (that it might have been light) to the conclusion (the crime might not have occurred at night) to the legal conclusion (then it ain't Residential Burglary).

Other than that, nice job!

CHAPTER 23

EDITING

"God and I both knew what it meant once. Now God alone knows."

Robert Browning on an early poem.

Editing requires distance and heartlessness. Pretend it's someone else's.

Put your draft aside for a week or so (if it's a Nutshell, a few years). You will then approach it as a *reader*, not as author. You will spot phrases, sentences, and even paragraphs ready for rewriting. Or the chopping block. Cutting is essential, yet hard. Intended victims will scream, "No, not me; I'm the crux of the whole thing. Look at that paragraph over there! Why, it's nothing but fluff. Cut it. Leave me. In fact, *expand me!*"

Read your draft out loud, *slowly*. If a sentence cannot be read easily, it's not well written. If it cannot be read without gasping for air, it is too long. *Write as you talk*. If it doesn't sound like you, you're in trouble. Few of us are instinctively pompous or verbose. We write that way because we think the law is pompous, verbose, and confusing, or because we mistake our goal: it is never to impress the reader; it is to communicate your understandings. The simpler, the better.

I recommend a three-step edit. Edit, at least initially, a hard copy. Hard copy allows you to get a sense of the entire document and allows scribbles. First, skim for structure—the statement of the issues, law, and transitions. Second, focus on analysis, is it explicit and does it consider both sides? Third, reread for style and zap offenders.

Edit for Structure

First step back and look at the overall memo. Do you cover all the issues you should? Have you included some you don't need? I have, after much heartache and self doubt, cut sentences, sections, and even *chapters* (and you're the better for it.)

Highlight your issues, legal authorities, and the first sentence of each paragraph. Reread the highlights. Does you draft hold together? Make sense? Check the order in which your points are made. You have considerable choice; just don't begin at the beginning and push through to the bitter end. The first and last points you make are the most likely to be remembered. Put important points either first or last; points in the middle tend to be overlooked and forgotten.

As to your *issues,* can you state them more clearly? More concisely? As to *legal authorities*, do you put the reader in direct contact with the law, do you begin the middle of the story, or do you lose your needles in haystacks? As to your *topic sentences,* are they IRS transitions, ones which not only introduce the new topic but also relate it to prior discussions and also show its legal significance? It's OK not to have IRS transitions, but only if you have a reason not to.

Edit for Content

Once you have considered the overall structure of your draft, reread for substance. Read as either a slow judge ("Say what?") or as a vicious opponent ("Gotcha!").

Explicitness. There is no room for interesting facts, standing alone; there is no room for brilliant legal analysis, standing alone. Reading your draft, is it clear how each fact you discuss relates to the controlling law and how each legal principle you discuss relates to the facts of the case? Ask *"So what?"*

Both sides. Even when you are writing an argumentative brief, you must consider, and respond to, your opponent's arguments. Here the saying is, *"Yes,* that's true, *but...."* Stop after each point you make and ask, "How could I respond to that?"

Edit for Style

You are probably getting a little sick of your draft by now, having read it once for general structure and once again for content. But the third edit is the most fun of all: it is of a search and destroy mission, much like a video game, except here your targets are pretentious diction, vague abstractions, and excess verbiage.

As to each sentence, ask, "Do I have any big words where shorter ones can do?" "Can I say this in fewer words?" "Can I make it more concrete?" "Can I make it more punchy?"

Find pretentious phrases, zap them with simple words:

At the present time	*zap*	*now*
In the event	*zap*	*if*
In the majority of instances	*zap*	*usually*
With the exception that	*zap*	*except*
For the reason that	*zap*	*because*
In my considered opinion	*zap*	*I think*

Find intensifiers, adjectives and adverbs, zap them with facts:

"The lecture was boring."	*zap*	*"It put me to sleep."*
"The defendant lacked ethics."	*zap*	*"She stole $1,257,876.24."*
"It is very important to note"	*zap*	*"Note"*

Not only are you making your prose more spiffy and hard-hitting, but you are also reducing clutter and making it shorter. Short is good. We aren't paid by the word. Picking up a long brief, a judge will be tempted to skim; short ones are read. "Omit needless words," preached Strunk and White, the authors of the classic *Elements of Style*. Omitting needless words does not mean omitting detail or treating subjects in outline form. It means that *each word must tell*.

Your goal? Cutting 10%. Stephen King's first rejection slip read: *"Not bad, but puffy. You need to revise for length. Formula: 2nd draft = 1st draft—10%."* If 10% works for him, it should work for us.

Passive verbs can trigger excess verbiage. The *active* voice is generally quicker than the passive:

The case was reversed *by the Supreme Court.* Passive voice: eight words.

The Supreme Court reversed *the case.* Active voice: six words.

Verb derivatives create problems:

He made a decision.

He decided.

They took action.

They acted.

Any sentence with *more than one verb* is a target. Clauses (a group of words with a subject and a verb) can often become phrases (a group of words without a verb).

"When the lawyer was conducting her cross-examination, the witness got up and left." 14 words.

"During cross-examination, the witness got up and left." 9 words.

Zapping is one activity in the third stage. Another is asking yourself, "Is it clear what, or whom, I am talking about?" To use a previous example:

"The promisee will argue that he did not confer the benefit as a gift.

"Who is the promisee here, Mills or Wyman?"

"The promisee, Mr. Mills, will argue ..."

"Is Mills the father or the guy who helped the son?

"The promisee, Mr. Mills, the man who aided the son, will argue that he did not confer the benefit as a gift."

Avoid constructions that stop the reader cold:

As to the former argument, the plaintiff would argue . . . .

Under Subsection 2a of the Restatement, the promise would not be enforceable.

These constructions *stop* the reader. "Which was the *former* argument?" "What did Subsection 2a provide?" These interruptions are irksome and can be avoided easily. You need not repeat the *entire* former argument; you can usually identify it in two or three words. The same is true in identifying particular subsections.

Under Subsection 2a of the Restatement, dealing with benefits conferred as gifts, the promise would not be enforceable.

Along these lines, don't begin a paragraph or sentence with a citation (the lawyer's sin). "In the case of Cat v. Dog, *42 P.2d 443, 182 Cal.Rptr. 123 (2003), rehearing denied, 43 P.2d. 18, 184 Cal.Rptr. 456 (2004), the Court held . . . .*" If you really want readers to know what the court held, tell them first and then follow with the citation.

Finally, as your last step, step back from the draft and ask, "Is there any way to make this more visually inviting?" There is nothing worse than turning a page and seeing nothing but type, type, type. White space tells the reader, "Hey, this isn't going to be that bad." Break up long paragraphs. There is nothing better than an occasional paragraph of one or two sentences.

'Tis.

CHAPTER 24

ORAL ARGUMENT: SUBSTANCE

*"No, Mommy, please don't send me to my room.
I didn't mean to spill it. It slipped. When Ben
knocked over his soup, he didn't have to go to
his room. Send me to my room only if I'm really
bad."*

There you have it: the big three, instinctively.
Arguing spilt milk in the kitchen or free speech in
the Supreme Court, all you have are *facts* (it was an
accident), *precedent* (Ben walked), and *policy* (save
the Big One).

Mom will have a different take on things. She'll
distinguish Ben's case ("He's younger") and, as to
policy, she might argue that, unless small infractions are penalized, worse things will happen (a
child-care version of the "broken windows" theory).
And, as to what happened, did she experience it the
same way as her child?

The major emphasis of this chapter is on the
importance of the Statement of Facts. At the end,
I'll review arguing precedent and policy.

Stating Facts: Arguing Justice

The statement of facts is not merely part of the argument, it is more often than not the argument itself.

John W. Davis

Judges want to correctly apply the law and create good precedent. But they also want to do justice, to do the *right* thing for the litigants. In stating the facts of your case, your goal is to get the judges to feel that justice is on your side and to leave them feeling, perhaps without realizing it, "You know, it just seems fair that she win. Let's see if the law allows it and, if it does, whether that would create a good precedent."

Read your statement of facts to a ten year old and then ask, "Who is in the right?" If it isn't your client, rewrite.

Let's practice. The facts:

- Defendant Paul is a local Chief of Police.

- Plaintiff Davis is a photographer for a local newspaper.

- Defendant, to help local merchants protect against shoplifting during the Christmas season, distributed a flyer showing the pictures of "Active Shoplifters."

- Plaintiff had been arrested for shoplifting but was never convicted.

- Plaintiff's picture was in the five page flyer, on page two.

- Plaintiff has sued defendant for violating his civil rights.

Spend a few minutes. If you were representing the defendant, how would you tell this story to a ten year old? What facts would you stress? If you were representing the plaintiff? Jot!

Here are a couple of stories of the case, the first told by the United States Supreme Court:

Defendant Paul is the Chief of Police of Louisville, Kentucky. For the purpose of alerting local area merchants to possible shoplifters who might be operating during the Christmas season, he distributed to approximately 800 merchants in the Louisville metropolitan area a "flyer" of active shoplifters. The flyer consisted of five pages of "mug shot" photos, arranged alphabetically. In approximately the center of page 2 there appeared photos and the name of the plaintiff, Edward Charles Davis. Paul v. Davis, 424 U.S. 693

You get a very different sense from reading a law review description.

Plaintiff Edward Charles Davis, a photographer for the Louisville Courier–Journal and Times, was arrested in Louisville, Kentucky on a charge of shoplifting. He pled not guilty. The charge was "filed away with leave [to reinstate]," but he was never called upon to face that charge in court. With the onset of the Christmas season defendant

Paul, the Chief of police for Louisville, prepared a five-page flyer containing the names and mug shots of "Active Shoplifters." Copies of this bulletin were distributed to merchants warning them of possible shoplifters. In fact, the flyer was composed not only of persons actually convicted of shoplifting, but included persons who had been merely arrested. Plaintiff's name and mug shot were included in the flyer.

Lawyers tell a lot of stories, to opposing counsel during negotiations, to juries during trials, and to judges during appellate arguments. One becomes a good storyteller by trying to figure out how they work. How does the Supreme Court's story create sympathy for the defendant while the law reviews leads one to root for the plaintiff? Reread them.

As readers we tend to be sympathetic with the first person we meet, at least if they are presented in a favorable light. The Supreme Court first introduces us to the defendant and immediately tells us some nice things about him: he is the Chief of Police and was trying to protect local merchants from shoplifting. The law review story starts with the plaintiff and immediately tells us some nice things about him: he has a responsible job and, while he was arrested, he was never convicted.

Not only are we sympathetic to the first person we meet, but their viewpoint is also apt to become ours. It is very important to realize that neither the Justice who wrote *Davis* nor the law student writer were *consciously* slanting their statement of facts.

The slanting occurred unconsciously once they, for whatever reason, became sympathetic to one of the parties. When we takes sides, the facts (and eventually the law) *tend* to line up in support; some facts jump out, others retreat.

In the Supreme Court's version, for example, we learn that the flyer was fairly long, 5 pages, and that the plaintiff was not singled out. Indeed his "photo" appeared on page 2. In the law review version, we are reminded that it was his "mug shot" and, for all we know, it could have been featured on a one-page flyer. Merchants were only "alerted" in the Supreme Court's version, while they were "warned" in that of the law review. Finally, while the law review leads with the fact that the defendant had never been convicted of any crime, the Supreme Court's version has yet to mention it.

This tendency for facts and law to line up to support one's side is the root of the whole matter. It is the reason why John W. Davis, the leading appellate lawyer of his day, would write: "A case well stated is far more than half argued.

The Supreme Court presents us with an image of a well-meaning cop at risk, while the law review presents the image of an innocent man seeking compensation. Which is the correct image? Both! There is a famous gestalt drawing that includes the images of both a young woman and an elderly woman. Some see one, some see the other. *Both are there.* Stating your case, bring your woman to the fore.

Dealing with Inconvenient Facts

You are a trial attorney and are about to call your client to the stand who will testify as to the horrible, permanent, harm inflicted on her by the defendant's negligence. "By the way," she whispers to you, "I had a great game of tennis yesterday." What do you do?

Don't do what immediately comes to mind: *"Shut up about that!"* One alternative is to ignore the issue in questioning your client, hoping that your opponent doesn't stumble upon it. Very risky. If your opponent does, the jury will conclude, (rightly), that you were trying to put one over, and your *entire* case crashes. The other alternative is for you to raise the issue. Among trial lawyers, this is known as "drawing the sting," the theory being that the jury will conclude, if you brought it up, it can't be that bad. Plus you can put spin on it.

Question: You have recently played tennis?

Answer: Yes. It is part of my physical therapy. I am working so hard trying to recover.

Some lawyers, however, draw so much sting there's nothing left but inconvenient facts and weak apologies. In trial, and in argument, you need not bring up every inconvenient fact. My test is this: *if your opponent brings up what you omitted, will the court feel betrayed?* Had I read the Supreme Court version and concluded that the defendant was my guy, I would feel betrayed if I later learned that Davis had never been convicted. "Hey, they were trying to put one over on me." You never, never once, want a judge to conclude that you are up to no good: your *entire* case will suffer, not to mention your career.

So tell your story from the viewpoint of your client and, as to inconvenient facts, be candid but not too candid. How to make it more spiffy?

The Importance of Opening Lines

"It was the best of times, it was the worst of times."

"Mrs. Dalloway said she would buy the flowers herself."

"All happy families resemble one another; every unhappy family is unhappy in its own way."

"It is a truth universally acknowledged, that a single man in possession of a good fortune must be in want of a wife."

Novelists work hard on their opening line. They only have one. They want to grab interest, state a theme, get things moving. They would never, ever, open: "This is a story about the French Revolution," or "So let's take a close look at Mrs. Dalloway's day," or "This is an appeal from the Superior Court in Toledo."

Begin with pizzazz. State your basic theme.

"This case is about a hard working police offi-cer who was doing his best to protect small

> *business owners from shoplifting. He mistaken-*
> *ly put a man's photo in the middle of a flyer*
> *showing shoplifters. Now he's being sued....*
>
> *This is an appeal from the Superior Court in*
> *Toledo."*
>
> . . .
>
> *"Mr. Davis, a photographer for a local newspa-*
> *per, awoke to find himself falsely accused of*
> *being a shoplifter. He found find his 'mug shot'*
> *posted all over town.... This is an appeal from*
> *the Superior Court in Toledo."*

Think long and hard about your opening lines, both in writing your Statement of Facts and in preparing your oral argument. Like most introductions, your opening lines will probably be written last. Most cases come down to very simple propositions: "One man, one vote," "Our Constitution is color blind," "No one should profit from his own fraud." What is the essence of your case?

The Power of Language

What if "mental illness" was called "mental exhaustion"? What if a "mug shot" was called a "photo"?

Jerome Frank noted the hypnotic power of words. Why were early common law courts hostile to arbitration clauses? Because an early judge labeled them an attempt to *"oust"* the jurisdiction of the courts. Well, no one is going to put up with that. Of course, arbitration clauses could have been characterized as *"parties freely choosing an alternative forum"* and, had they been, the emotional charge would flow in the other direction.

Can you state your argument more forcefully? Can you use words that might tip the scale?

Specifics, not Abstractions

One of the nice things about writing a book is that I can share instances of wonderful writing. In *The Merchant of Venice*, Shylock comes to claim his "pound of flesh." Asked why he would have Antonio's flesh rather than his money, Shylock responds

> *He hath disgraced me, and hindered me*
> *half a million; laughed at my losses,*
> *mocked my gains, scorned my nation,*
> *thwarted my bargains, cooled my friends,*
> *heated mine enemies, and what's his reason?*
> *I am a Jew.*
>
> *Hath not a Jew eyes? Hath not a Jew hands,*
> *organs, dimensions, senses, affections,*
> *passions? Fed with the same food, hurt with*
> *the same weapons, subject to the same diseases,*
> *healed by the same means, warmed and cooled*
> *by the same winter and summer,*
> *as a Christian is? If you prick us,*
> *do we not bleed? If you tickle us, do we not*
> *laugh? If you poison us, do we not die?*

Textbooks on writing often give examples of bad writing and ask you to rewrite. I think the opposite approach would work too. Rewriting something good to make it bad might help you understand what was good about it in the first place. Here's my rewrite of Shylock:

The man's a bigot. He has treated me very unfairly, simply because I'm Jewish. But being Jewish is no different than being anyone else. Like, I have feelings too.

Forget the rhythm of the language; we ain't Shakespeare. But note Shylock's specifics: losses, gains, friends, enemies, eyes, hands, organs, dimensions, senses, affections, passions, food, weapons, diseases, healing, warmed, cooled, bleed, laugh and die. We don't have to have anyone tell us that Antonio was a bigot; we know he was because we know what he *did*.

Telling your story, stress specifics, not abstractions; talk nouns and verbs, not adjectives and adverbs. If justice is really on your side, your proclaiming it in a grand sweeping manner won't convince the court. Facts will. Again, review the two statements in *Davis*. Neither statement resorted to adjectives or pleas, and yet each convinced the reader of very different positions.

A compelling factual statement motivates the court to rule in your favor; now you must establish a rationale that permits it to do so. You must discuss both the past (precedent) and the future (policy).

Arguing Precedent: The Past Shouldn't Be Dead

"The Statute of Frauds requires this kind of contract to be in writing. This one wasn't. It may be a stupid law, and it may be quite unfair in this case, but there you have it. I win!"

The common law is littered with remains. A lawyer, thinking the law squarely behind him, policy and fairness be damned, smugly sat down only to have the court come up with an exception, perhaps an estoppel, perhaps an implied promise, perhaps a new duty. All cases can be distinguished or, if not, overturned, and all statutes are ambiguous or, if not, many can be found unconstitutional. *You are never safe, and you should never be safe.*

Oliver Wendell Holmes, in his classic article, *The Path of the Law* (1896), argued that courts should not follow precedent blindly and that "it is revolting to have no better reason for a rule of law than it was laid down in the time of Henry IV." He argued a deliberate reconsideration of the worth of the rules.

When you get the dragon out of his cave on to the plain and in the daylight, you can count his teeth and claws, and see just what his strength. But to get him out is only the first step. The next is either to kill him, or to tame him and make his a useful animal.

Never trust dragons. Always tell the court why your reading of the cases or of the statutes comports with good policy and how it helps achieve justice between the parties.

By the time you get to writing legal argument, you will have a good feel of how to argue cases and policy. To briefly review, courts must follow the rules of law announced in prior controlling decisions (those of higher courts in the jurisdiction) unless (1) those decisions are distinguishable or (2) the court is willing to overrule those prior decisions, something courts are loath to do. The rule of law announced in a case (its holding or black letter) is announced in a specific factual context and is justified by a particular rationale. To distinguish a case (so the rule of law would not apply in the case at hand), you can argue either that the facts are essentially different or that the rationale does not apply. Conversely, you can argue that a case should apply by analogy by pointing out that, even though the facts are essentially different, the rationale of the case would apply.

If a case cannot be distinguished, it can always be overruled. Given that courts generally like to decide cases on narrow grounds, they will more likely distinguish a case than overrule it. A stock argument against overruling is, first, people may have relied on the rule of the case and, second, any overruling creates uncertainty in the legal order.

Occasionally a court will be caught between a rock and a hard place. It cannot with intellectual honestly distinguish prior cases but does not want to follow them where they lead. Rather than overrule the cases and create uncertainty, it will "read" them in a way that allows it to go where it wants. One illustration is a case we have considered previously, *Lucy, Lady Duff Gordon,* where Justice Cardozo essentially abolished the doctrine of mutuality of obligation without overruling any of the cases requiring it. I like to think he had a "What, Me Worry?" grin on his face.

A good lawyer, sensing the court may be in this position, will point the court toward a middle ground by suggesting a way out: an implied promise, a new duty, a new defense.

When dealing with a statute, the first choice is to argue that it can be interpreted so as to support your position. Only as a last resort should you argue that a statute be declared unconstitutional. This is for many of the same reasons that your last choice is to argue that a prior case be overruled.

Be sensitive to "Eats Pittsburgh" arguments: those which would interpret one element of a statute so that the statute will never apply or will always apply. Say a burglary statute requires a "forced entry." The defendant crawled through an open window. The prosecution would like the court to hold that a "forced entry" would occur simply by walking into a home: to walk takes force. However, to define the element that way means that it will always be met and, therefore, no longer an element. The defense would have "force" mean that accomplished by dynamite or a tank: that would also sideline the element because it would almost never apply.

Arguing Policy: Creating Good Law

Under the doctrine of *stare decisis*, whatever your court decides will become precedent. If it adopts your reading of the cases and statutes or your new theory of liability or defense, will that produce justice for not only the current litigants but also future ones? By now you have had your fill of policy arguments, so I will flag only a couple of concerns.

First, how will the decision play on the street? Many intellectually grand solutions have created chaos in the real world. How will the decision specifically impact the lives of those it will affect? Will governmental officials be able to apply it? Juries understand it? Citizens rely on it?

Second, be aware of *slippery slope* arguments. Many legal arguments focus not so much on the merits of the particular dispute but on where it might lead.

> *"If we invalidate this lease clause that exculpates the landlord from liability for negligence, the next thing you know we'll have all kinds of tenants in here demanding that we rewrite their leases, even the amount of rent."*

There are *three* responses to all slippery slope arguments. Write them out. They will be on the final. (Yeah, but if *they* are on the final, then *everything* will be on the final.)

1. All slippery slope arguments are reversible.

"If you refuse to invalidate this clause, then you will never invalidate a clause, even one involving forfeitures of first-borns in the event of late rent.

2.   Slopes have dumps and holdings can be limited.

"Your Honor, this exculpatory clause is unique in that it relieves the landlord from liability for personal injury. There is a strong policy to encourage landowners to take reasonable steps to avoid such injury. No such policy is involved in other lease terms, surely not the amount of rent."

3.   Some slopes may be worth the ride.

"Your Honor, now that you mention it, that would not be such a bad idea."

I recently saw a wonderful response to a slippery slope argument. The judge asked something like, "Counselor, if we do what you would like us to do in this case, in our next case, won't you come in here on the behalf of Acme Corporation arguing that we have already committed ourselves to the destruction of Western Civilization?"

"No, your Honor, I won't. I don't represent Acme."

I'm not sure if I would use this one.

CHAPTER 25

ORAL ARGUMENT: THE METHOD

"A sincere and single desire to be helpful to the Court."

Judges have heavy responsibilities to the parties before them and to litigants perhaps unborn. Any case worth its salt will be a close one. You and your opponent are experts on the facts, on the law, and on the policy implications of the case. Judges need your help in understanding the complexities, and they need to try out their reactions and to discuss their ideas. A good oral argument is a good conversation.

Vigorous adversarial argument is the method, not the goal. Hang tough, make strong arguments, don't cave in, but don't get confused. Oral argument isn't about taking no prisoners, bullying the judges into finding for you, using smoke and mirrors, doing the old razzle-dazzle. John W. Davis, who argued frequently before the Supreme Court, saw his job as simply being "helpful to the Court."

Being Helpful

You are helpful if you are candid, if you go for the jugular, and if you encourage questions.

Candor

Cases are close and none are perfect. Admit what hurts.

> *"Yes, my opponent is correct, the case did hold that. However, we believe that it is distinguishable."*

> *"It is true, Your Honor, if you were to hold for my client certain expectations may be upset, but we believe that they may not be as extensive as feared because of the following limiting features."*

> *"I wish the cases were more clear in this area, but they are not. A fair reading of them, I submit, supports my position."*

> *"That is a really good question, Your Honor, one I haven't even considered. Rather than try to come up with an answer on the spot, I would be happy to file a supplemental brief on it."*

> *"The record doesn't support that theory of our case. However, we believe that there are sufficient facts to support our alternative theory."*

Being candid means citing authority that goes against you even if your opponent failed to do so. The Rules of Professional Conduct require citation of adverse "controlling authority." Go further. If you were making the decision, what would you want to know of the case or statute? As an officer of the court, you don't want to mislead the court by silence.

Should you argue points you don't believe? This is a tough issue. If you do, your lack of belief may show and undermine your credibility ("This lawyer doesn't want to help me; this lawyer wants to fool me"). Further, as time is limited, it's best to stick with your winners. On the other hand, I have seen courts buy arguments that I thought were weak. If an argument is in the ballpark, I wouldn't drop it because I was not 100% convinced. Perhaps the judge will see more in it than you do. (That is why, by the way, you always include such arguments in your office memos; your supervisor may see more in them than you do.)

Never, however, argue stupid points with great vigor. If you do, the judge will conclude that you don't know what you're doing, or that you are trying to bully him, or that you are showing off. Losing the judge's trust will hurt, not only your current client, but future clients as well.

A caveat on criminal defense. In order to protect the rights of the accused, criminal defense lawyers are allowed, often required, to advance arguments that stink. "Your Honor, my client is charged with violating a statute that prohibits 'obtaining money by false pretenses.' I move for a directed verdict as the state has only proved *one* pretense." Enough said.

The Jugular

Beginners want to cover everything they did in their briefs. "That point in footnote twenty-three sparkles!" Keeping their heads down, talking fast and dreading interruption, they sprint towards footnote twenty-three!

Most cases turn on two, maybe three, main points. Figure out what they are and stick with them. But are you sure they are jugular to the judges? Arguing a particular point, realize:

1. The judges are not convinced of your position and *never* will be; thus you are wasting your time.

2. The judges are *already* convinced of your position; thus you are wasting your time.

3. The judges are *undecided* about your point and *need* further guidance.

How can you make sure it is 3, not 1 or 2?

In an ideal world you could simply stop and ask, "Well, Your Honors, have I convinced you on that one yet? If not, do I have a prayer?" But oral argument is highly stylized, and you can't make this move. Rather, you will have to get the judges asking you questions so that you can address their concerns.

Questions

Answering questions will enable you to address the judges' concerns *and* improve your performance. Watch oral arguments. Lawyers are almost always better responding to questions than giving speeches. There is movement, creation, engagement. Some judges will pepper you with questions.

Others are reticent, too shy to interrupt, too unsure to voice their concerns. How do you draw them out?

Want questions. To get questions, *want* questions. Judges are people too, and human interaction is a subtle thing. If you fear questions, likely you won't get many. If you rejoice in them, they will come.

Don't assume questions are hostile. Don't immediately answer "No." Some questions will be friendly, trying to help you out. Others will be concealed arguments directed at other judges. Even those that flag weaknesses in your position are not necessarily hostile. The judge may be troubled by the point and wants your help in thinking it through. "Yes" is often better than "No."

Invite interruption.

> "I'll discuss the following three issues in the following order. But first, does the Court have any questions?"

> "That finishes my discussion of the duty issue. Are there any questions before I go on?"

Never tell the judge to shut up.

> "Your Honor, I will answer your question in a few minutes. Right now I would like to keep talking about what I want to talk about."

> "I covered that in my brief."

The fear is that if you get off your point you will never get back. But that's OK. Give up the notion that your job is to convince the judges; your job is to help them think things through. A good argument is a conversation, not a lecture.

Additional Pointers

Have fun and don't be yourself.

At big championship games, the coach is always quoted as saying, "I just told my team to go out and have fun." Sitting on the edge of my seat, biting my nails, this has always struck me as somewhat fanciful. Then I thought about it. For the fans, the championship game may be terribly serious but for the players, that's what they've worked long and hard to get to. They didn't work long and hard for grim. They have earned fun. So have you. Maybe it was the appeal of jury argument that brought you to law school, but appellate argument is pretty close. Soon it will be simply you, the judges, and the argument: no more jitters, no more audience, no more thoughts of dinner. It's just you, the judges, and the argument; you soar.

Mark Twain pointed out that *'Be yourself'* is the worst advice you can give some people. At this stage in your career, don't be yourself because you don't know who you are. "I'm shy, self-effacing, quiet. I could never get up there and be bold, lively or enthusiastic." William Blake had a wonderful phrase, "mind-forged manacles." You will have a lot of role-playing opportunities in law school: making appellate arguments, trying lawsuits, negotiating cases. Use them to try out different personas, particularly those you *know* you aren't. Pretend you're

Clarence Darrow. It will be great fun and who knows?

Practice and warming up

To think "I will then argue X" is much different than actually arguing it. Like writing, speaking slows the mind and, practicing before the bathroom mirror, you will get a much better sense of your argument and how to express it. Practice answering the questions you are likely to get.

In live theater, before they begin seating the audience, the cast is on stage, warming up, doing voice exercises, getting flexible, repeating snippets of dialogue. Courthouses (and law schools) aren't set up for this, but you might try finding an empty room. Do some riffs; get your voice limber.

Expect chaos

An ideal oral argument is a *conversation* between you and the judges on a difficult legal matter. Like all good conversations, they cannot be charted in advance. New insights and new arguments will be triggered in the exchange. Sure you have prepared, but remember that preparation is death. Don't insist on things going the way you planned; they won't, and this is the way it should be. Embrace the moment.

Nervousness

You will do better than you think. The universal reaction of law students watching the video tape of their arguments is "I don't look as nervous as I felt." When you are living a performance, you feel the pound of your heart and the tremor of your lip; watching your performance, like the rest of us, you are somewhat distracted. Not only do you appear more calm than you feel, but your confident, cocky opponent is, underneath, jello.

Nervousness is caused by self-focus: "This is going to be terrible. I will forget everything. I will make a fool of myself. Why didn't I listen to Aunt Margaret and move to a commune?" Refocus your attention. This is easier when you go second. While you are sitting there, waiting your turn, you can concentrate on your opponent's argument and listen to what the judges ask. I tell my students when they are responding, either initially or in rebuttal, that their first point must be a specific response to something their opponent just argued. This forces them to focus on those arguments and assures that their own argument will be spontaneous, a boxer coming off the canvas and throwing the knockout blow.

Finally, remember to breathe. Nervousness often leads to shallow breathing, which leads to oxygen deficiency, which leads to more nervousness, which leads to death (or worse.... embarrassment). Don't breathe at the top of your lungs; breathe with your stomach. (Put your hand on your stomach; it should be pushed out as you inhale.)

Maintain eye contact and don't read your notes

Reading is simply out. You will discourage questions from the bench (it's hard to interrupt someone looking down), and you will get no sense of how you are doing. Maintaining eye contact you, will know if a judge has a question and you can sense whether you are being understood. I am less sure that you can sense whether your argument is being accepted or rejected. A frown may mean the judge is thinking hard about your argument, not necessarily rejecting it.

Don't take a script; take a crib sheet. Preparing your argument, script. Writing slows the mind. But then reduce it to a short, one-page outline, flagging your two or three jugular issues, with a word or two under each that would remind you of your arguments. Dollars to donuts, you won't even need it, but, in case there is a sudden loss of pressure....

Themes and Exit Strategies

Reduce your argument to a basic theme, one that can be stated in a few sentences. It can focus on facts or on higher goals. From our last chapter:

"Mr. Davis, a photographer for a local newspaper, awoke to find himself falsely accused of being a shoplifter. He found his 'mug shot' posted all over town. We ask this court to reverse the lower court and hold that he has a cause of action under the Civil Rights Act."

"This case involves a very simple proposition: Our Constitution is color blind."

Begin and end your argument with your theme. While spontaneity is the hallmark of great arguments, don't count on it to get you off stage. Some advocates, not knowing how to close and hence repeating and repeating snippets of arguments, just fade away. Others simply say, "That's it." Memorize your closing.

Stating the Facts

An effective Statement of Facts motivates judges to rule in your favor and hence look at the law from the standpoint of wanting to do so. Never throw away this opportunity by too easily agreeing when the judge says "You can dispense with the statement of facts." Far too often the facts are recited in a boring, let's-get-through-this tone. Get excited. Tell an engaging story. The facts are not just part of the argument; they are often the *argument itself*.

What You Want Done

Tell the court what you want it *to do*. Do you want the court to remand the case to the trial court and order a new trial? Do you want an order for some particular relief? It is surprising how often lawyers, about to conclude their argument, cannot answer, "Assuming we agree with your position on the law, what do you want us to do? Let's assume you've won. What should the last paragraph of our opinion say?"

Silence, pauses and beats

If you ever get the chance, play the part of judge. You will learn just how iffy verbal communication is. Reading something, you can reread what you haven't understood; you can take a break when you are getting tired. How can you improve your chances of being understood during argument?

Repetition, again, is no sin. Talk slow. Nervousness causes us to speak too quickly. When you first get up, don't immediately launch into your remarks; pause a few seconds, look at the judges, and take a deep breathe. Then launch.

During your argument, take pains that it doesn't become a blur. Actors are taught the concept of "beat," a physical action that underscores a natural break in their dialogue. After a strong line, an actor may take a drink or walk across the stage to give the audience time to think. While we can't leave the podium, consider some physical act to mark transitions, perhaps looking down at your notes, adjusting your glasses, or a slight gesture. Variations in volume help too. We generally raise our voices to make important points; try lowering your voice and watch everyone lean forward.

Pauses can be very helpful. There is a difference, however, between suddenly stopping and an effective pause. Pauses should be motivated: why are you stopping? To trigger a question? To allow a point to sink in? To gather your own thoughts? On stage, this is known as "using silence."

Getting comfortable with *silence* is critical. When people are expecting you to speak, seconds feel like hours (but they seem like seconds to the people). If you are uncomfortable with silence, during a client interview, you will ask another question instead of letting your client think about how to answer your first. During negotiation, you will make another offer rather than keep pressure on your opponent. During oral argument, you will blurt out an answer to a judge's question without thinking about it. When asked a question, *don't* immediately reply. Think about your answer. Occasionally, "That's a very good question that I hadn't considered. Let me think a few moments."

Quotes

Don't read long quotes to the court. If you quote specific language, refer to the page in your brief where you quote the language so that the judges can sing along. If specific language is key, for example, in a case interpreting a statute for example, put it on a large chart that can be displayed on an easel during argument.

Being there

When your opponent is arguing, the judges can still see you. Pay attention and be respectful. You can feign this by taking phantom notes. Never be bush: shaking your head, raising your eyebrows, or, indeed, picking your nose. (Sorry, it happens and I don't want you coming back and yelling, "You never said anything about not picking my nose!")

When judges decide

Judges seldom decide on the spot. After arguments, they go to a safe room, take off their robes, and deliberate. Knowing this, how might it impact your argument? It might mean that you shift from trying to convince all of the judges of your position to supplying those judges who are on your side with good arguments, which can help them to convince the others or to resist assaults on their own position. Jury argument is often about supplying good arguments for allies to use during deliberations. Even when there is only one judge, if it seems unrealistic to convince her during argument, at least raise some troubling points that will follow her into her office.

Post Game Show

After the argument, jot down some things you learned from the experience. What have you learned about oral argument? About preparation and delivery? About getting judges to ask you questions? About the adversary process? About yourself? About chaos theory?

A variation on this theme is to list, before your argument, the criteria by which you will evaluate yourself. This will force you to do some serious thinking about the process of argument rather than the substance of your argument.

This is general advice. We all talk about teaching ourselves, but we seldom do anything about it. After your first law school exam, after your first client interview, after your first Supreme Court argument, after you have captured every electoral vote but Maine's, sit down and ask yourself: "What went well and why?" "What went badly and why?"

Intention

Actors know their lines: "Dost thou think, because thou art virtuous, there shall be no more cake and ale?" But much more is involved in acting. Stanislavsky (1863–1938), the father of Method Acting, spoke in terms of the character's "intention." What does Sir Toby intend by these lines? Is he defensive of his life style? Is he angry? Dismissive?

You will know your points. But what do you intend by them? Your oral argument is not about getting it over with, not about not appearing to be a fool, and not even about being brilliant. Beginners can get caught up in questions of whether they should gesture, what they should do with their hands, what facial expressions to have. The basic notion is that, if you know your intention, all of that will take care of itself.

So repeat, just before your begin:

My intention is to help these judges understand the plight of my client and how the law supports my position. My intention is to engage judges in conversation and to have them ask me questions. My intention is to have fun and not be that poor, pathetic, colorless person I really am.

CHAPTER 26

AN EXAMPLE OF ORAL ARGUMENT

If you are going first, you have a little more work to do. This overview will be from that perspective.

1. **Introduce yourself and the client you represent.**

"May it please the court, my name is C. Darrow and I represent Allprovidence Insurance, the defendant in the action below and petitioner here."

2. **State the nature of the case** (contract, tort, criminal) **and briefly describe its procedural history**.

"This is a suit on a life insurance policy on the life of Mr. Humpty Dumpty, brought by his widow. Our defense is that suit was barred by a suicide clause. At trial, it was our contention that Humpty did not have a 'great fall,' but rather that he took a 'great leap.' After a jury trial, judgment was for the plaintiff. We appeal on the basis that the judge improperly applied the 'plain meaning rule' and improperly excluded the testimony of one of the King's men concerning Humpty's dying declaration."

350

3. *State the facts of the case*.

"In order to protect the widows and orphans, the true owners of Allprovidence, and in order to discourage suicide, the Allprovidence Insurance Company routinely includes a suicide clause in its policy, which bars recovery if the decedent took his own life. In this case . . . ."

In stating the facts, remember that the judges have read your brief and thus don't need all the facts recounted. Keep it short and succinct, focusing on the important and determinative facts. Even then, the court may cut you off with, "We are familiar with the facts, proceed with argument." But, given the importance of the statement of facts, don't go up there expecting the court to cut you off or inviting it to: "Does the court want to hear the facts?" Walk to the podium expecting to tell your story.

4. *State the legal issues and preview the points you intend to argue*. A clear introduction to your legal argument is critical. Otherwise the judges may not follow it.

"It is our contention that the court below erred in applying the Plain Meaning Rule to Nursery Rhymes, thus preventing our argument that 'had a great fall' can be read as meaning 'took a great leap.' Unfortunately, the Yokel below is unfamiliar with Critical Legal Studies and trendy French Literary Criticism which suggests that texts can be read any way one wants.

*"Further, and as an **independent justification for reversal**, we assert the court below improper-*

ly excluded, as hearsay, Humpty's remark to one of the King's men, 'Being an egg I never got any respect. I'll make an omelet.' Although hearsay, we submit that it should have been admitted either as a dying declaration or as state of mind. Which issue do you wish me to address first?"

It is always a good idea to invite the judges to participate and always good to address their concerns, not yours.

5. **Argue the case**. As with your written work, your oral argument will be improved by the effective use of transitions.

> Not: *"The next issue concerns the admissibility of Humpty's dying declaration."*

> But: *"That concludes my discussion of the Plain Meaning Rule. Unless there are any questions, I would like to now address the matter of Humpty's dying declaration. **Even if** this court decides that the court properly applied the Plain Meaning Rule, **it must reverse** this case if it finds that the testimony was improperly excluded."*

IRS transitions are best: they introduce the new topic, they relate it to the previous one, and they show its legal significance. The more *explicit* your argument, the more you *tie law and fact* together, and the more *concrete examples* you use, the clearer your argument will be.

6. **Rejoice** if the court asks you questions.

7. *Conclude and sit down*.

You will be allotted a certain amount of time. There is no requirement that you use it all. If you are done, sit down. Many first-year students do brilliantly until the end. Then, not having not thought of a spiffy ending line, they thrash about aimlessly, repeating bits of prior arguments. Write and rehearse your last line. What do you want to leave the court with?

> *"Yes, Humpty was a good egg. But courts should not reward despair. Tell despondent eggs that their widows will not profit from their suicide; tell despondent eggs to stop exposing the incompetence of all the King's men!"*

Responding

If you are the person going second, after introducing yourself, unless there are factual matters you want to clear up, you can jump right into your argument. Before giving the overview of your argument, consider going after a specific point your opponent made during her presentation. This will assure spontaneity and zip.

Appellate arguments require clear introductions, clear transitions and clear summaries. This means repetition. Repetition is a virtue. As listeners, we can't go back to see how the arguments fit together. Often our minds wander. "What's for lunch?" Repetition is needed. Realize, too, that the judges, no matter how prepared, will not have the same familiarity with the law as you do. Give them a break and don't jump to the heart of your argument, which may turn on a rather fine point of law. Put that argument in context. As with legal writing, *begin with the basics*: "The Plain Meaning Rule basically provides that...." rather than "The Plain Meaning Rule shouldn't apply here because...." The latter construction forces the judges to go back and think, "What is the Plain Meaning Rule?" There is simply no need for them to have to do this. By the way, what is the "latter" construction and what's the problem with the word "latter"?

PART FIVE

FINISHING SCHOOL AND BEGINNING A CAREER

There are accidental law students, those who, hearing and fearing the rush of on-coming reality, have scurried back for another three years of academic safety. As to what lawyers do, and as to what they want to do when they graduate, they don't have a clue. Then there are those who come to law school with specific career goals in mind. More than often, however, career goals will change in the rough and tumble of law school.

Read this part at your leisure but read it in your first year. Critical choices lie ahead. I will give you a lot to think about in terms of the kind of career you want to pursue. You have vastly more choices than you might think and there are variables that you might not appreciate. Choosing a career is much more than choosing a job; in some ways, you will be choosing the kind of person you will become.

Of course, before you get to your career, you have to finish law school. The first chapter in this part is about the courses and activities in your second and third years. My main point is that law school offers rich opportunities that will not pass your way again: a talented faculty, interested and interesting classmates, and issues that matter. My advice is somewhat biblical: time to put away childish things. For a long time you studied hard to advance yourself, to get into a good college, to get into a good law school. From now on, it is not about you, it is about your clients, folks who will rely on you in times of their great need.

CHAPTER 27

THE SECOND AND THIRD YEARS

This chapter is written for *first-year* students. There is no rush to read it but it will give you some idea of what lies in store. I'll talk about course selection and extra-curricular activities such as law review, clerking and *pro bono* work. Along the way I'll tell you something of the history of American Legal Education—you are still living it. I'll close with some of the distortions legal education can cause.

The main point I want to make is that you should push yourself during your last two years. I will make that point by telling a story that, well, frankly, makes me look pretty good. But that's okay; I'll close the chapter with one that make me look rather foolish.

On Theoretical Legal Education

It was the 1960s in the small town of Americus, Georgia. Congress had recently passed the Voting Rights Act, and it was to have an immediate impact. Americus was holding an election for Justice of the Peace and, for the first time since Reconstruction, black citizens were going to vote. In fact, a black woman had decided to run for the office herself.

On the momentous day, when she arrived at the voting place, there were two lines, one marked "Colored." She stood in the "White" line. The deputy sheriff who arrested her was incredulous at being asked why he had done so. He testified, "I ain't completely color blind, you know." I'll never forget that; sitting in the courtroom, I remembered reading in a Supreme Court case, "Our Constitution is color blind."

Between my second and third year in law school, I worked as a summer intern for C.B. King of Albany, Georgia, who was then one of the two black lawyers in the state. C.B. wanted me to research the law to see if we could get a court to throw out the election and make them do it over; make them do it right. I looked up the cases on election irregularities and election fraud (mostly from Chicago).

"C.B., we've had it. You can't challenge the election. The law is clear. Unless the illegalities affected the result, it stands. Given the fact that the incumbent got 83 of the 95 votes, we can't allege that."

C.B. simply sat and stared. Didn't say a word.

I went back to my desk and went into a funk. "Why had I gone to law school? A monkey could have looked up those cases and reported the bad news to C.B. Why had I sat in class for two years, struggling, if I couldn't even try to use the law to do the right thing?"

I went back to the cases. Maybe they could be distinguished. Indeed, maybe there would be language in those cases suggesting that if the controversy wasn't simply about dead people voting, the rule might be different.

I sat and thought and read and reread. And yes, eventually I was able to distinguish those cases and, yes, I even found language to support our position.

I went back to C.B. This time he smiled.

A year later, under federal court order, the small town of Americus had another election. The same guy won, but this time: one line.

———————

Sitting where you are sitting, I thought I was learning the law, and I was often confused and resentful. But I now know I wasn't sitting there to learn the law; I was there to get ready for that hot summer in Georgia.

Push yourself in law school. Take hard courses. Enjoy the challenge. Don't run away from tough profs, and don't tune out those "nice" theoretical discussions. They won't be easy, and you won't understand them all. Stay awake. Down the road you'll have your own hot summers.

Course Selection

So many courses; so little time.

After a rigid first-year curriculum, most law schools leave the second and third years up to you.

You will have a dazzling menu. First, realize that your legal education does not end with law school. After graduation there will be Continuing Legal Education (CLE) courses and scads and scads of on-the-job training. Ask yourself: "What can I get in law school that I can't in practice?" I think it comes down to great professors, challenging courses, and meaningful clinical work.

Professors

Every school has a group of truly remarkable teachers. I would make them my first choice, not only for their knowledge but also for their style. Some stick closely to the "black letter," while others spin off into the realms of philosophy, economics, and social theory; with some, classes are like boot camp, and, with others, like encounter groups. Sitting there, you are learning more than "Federal Jurisdiction" or "UCC." You are learning how one lawyer approaches and solves problems, uses and communicates knowledge, treats and reacts to people. You'll need models.

Take professors you disagree with, the fascists or communists on your faculty. You know who they are. If you take only professors you agree with, you won't be prepared for the ill winds that will surely blow.

Courses

Many students forfeit the opportunities that law schools offer by focusing on "bar" courses or those they "know" they will need in practice. Realize that there will be *bar review courses* after graduation that cover the required subjects and that it is foolish to over-specialize during law school. Career interests can and often do change.

There are substantive courses that every "well-rounded" law student should take, if for no other reason than to hold your own at cocktail parties (if there are such things anymore). Friends read the paper, and they will ask you basic questions dealing with *Evidence, Corporations, Federal Tax,* and *Constitutional Law.*

Writing courses are important. The more you write, the better you will write. Take at least one course requiring *extensive research and writing* even if (particularly if) you dread it. *Seminars and problem courses* are a refreshing break from the traditional three-cases-and-you're-out courses. They also give you a real sense of lawyering: lawyers don't learn the law, they use the law. *Skills courses* such as trial advocacy, client interviewing, and negotiation are helpful. Trial advocacy is almost a must. Trying a lawsuit gives you a different and more profound understanding of law, an understanding particularly important if you have vowed never to enter a courtroom as a lawyer.

Clinics

Many states have "student practice rules" that you allow students to represent clients in court under the supervision of a practicing lawyer. Most law schools take advantage of these rules by having clinical programs. There is a no better opportunity to learn ethics and problem-solving than in the clinical setting.

If you take a clinic, consider the role of an anthropologist living with the natives. During the day, do your job, work the pots. At night, sneak off to your tent and get out your pencil:

> *Are lawyers happy? Are they bitterly adverse or is law practice something of a country club affair? Why are some witnesses more credible than others? Some legal arguments more compelling? What are the most important skills for a lawyer to have?*

In addition to class work, there are a host of activities in the second and third years. If your law school is part of a university, there will be a variety of cultural events to remind you that the question of life's meaning is as important as who gets the decedent's stuff. And some of you will write for the law review, others will earn money clerking for law firms, and still others will do *pro bono* work, perhaps helping out at legal aid, teaching law-related courses in high schools, or delivering meals-on-wheels to the elderly.

The Curious Institution of Law Review

Most law schools publish law reviews, some more than one. It is an honor to be asked to write for law review. Membership is based on good grades or on a writing competition. It is hard work but quite worthwhile. As a second year student, you will be asked to write a note or comment, either on a recent case or on recent trends in a particular area of law. You will be involved in the law's development. Lawyers and judges read student notes, and your work may influence actual decisions. Your work will be extensively edited (by a student editor), and you will come away with a feeling of how hard it is (and how satisfying) to produce good work. And, of course, having written for the review helps come interview time.

Law reviews present a mind-boggling affront. Law students write articles criticizing (or praising) judges. Do second year medical students crowd around operation tables and then fault the procedures of heart-transplant teams? Do budding young scientists trash Einstein? That beginners can play on the same field as veterans is one of the curious facts about the law. Whether this is a good or bad thing I'll leave to you. It does, however, tend to put the lie to Holmes' famous dictum:

The life of the law is not logic, it is experience.

This routine critique of the judiciary by law review students may be seen as playing an important institutional role. Confronted with the argument that judges can do whatever they like, some academics have defended the judiciary by saying that the fact that judges must write opinions justifying their decisions keeps them intellectually honest. Law reviews are the only institution we have that routinely critiques the work of courts.

There is another institutional role that law reviews play that is more problematic. We all know (some of us better than others) that in the academic world, it is publish or perish. While most academics (English profs) publish in journals refereed by experts in their field (English profs), law professors publish mostly in law reviews. Who decides what gets published? Student editors. Are these editors qualified to pass on the quality and importance of legal scholarship (and hence decide, at least in some measure, who gets tenure and who doesn't)? Absolutely! They did well in Contracts!

The style of law reviews deserves comment. In 1936, Yale Law Professor Fred Rodell wrote a delightful essay, *"Goodbye to Law Reviews."*

There are two things wrong with almost all legal writing. One is style. The other is content. It seems to be a cardinal principle of law review writing and editing that nothing may be said forcefully and nothing may be said amusingly.... Even in the comparatively rare instances when people read to be informed, they like a dash of pepper or a dash of salt along with their information. They won't get any seasoning if the law reviews can help it. The law reviews would rather be dignified and ignored.

If you ever get to be a law review editor, first, my congratulations. Second, lighten up. Otherwise I'll never get published. (One of my early mentors once advised me, "Never change your style, even if it means getting published.")

But I digress.

Don't make too much about law review. If you don't make it, realize that most famous lawyers didn't either and that, once you get out, you will find that lawyers will judge you by your ethics and hard work, not by whether you made law review (or where you went to law school, for that matter). Further, freed of the time commitments of law review, you'll have time to actually do some good.

Pro Bono Activities

Every lawyer, regardless of professional prominence or work load, has a responsibility to provide legal services to those unable to pay, and personal involvement in the problems of the disadvantaged can be one of the most rewarding experiences in the life of a lawyer.

—American Bar Association, Model Rules of Professional Conduct

The American Bar Association urges, but does not attempt to require, lawyers to devote fifty hours a year to providing free legal services to the disadvantaged. Do you think this should be mandatory? Why lawyers and not, say, plumbers?

Lawyers have a monopoly on the legal system and the notion is that those with monopoly powers have special public service obligations. This is not to say that *pro bono* activities should be mandatory. Indeed, most lawyers probably devote more that fifty hours a year to such activities. Making those activities mandatory tends to diminish their value.

Consider *pro bono* activities. They are a terrific way to experience your own uniqueness, recognize your own competence, and give something back to a community that has given you so much.

Often volunteer work is legal work: at Legal Aid, women's shelters, AIDS clinics, or public interest firms. But a lot of law students volunteer in non-legal capacities. In Washington D.C., law students help prisoners learn to read by tutoring them as they read story books to their children. Elsewhere, law students tutor elementary students as part of "Lawyers for Literacy" programs. Still others deliver "Meals-on-Wheels" to the elderly.

Most law schools have *pro bono* programs. If yours doesn't, don't curse the darkness. Light a candle. Some web sites that might help: *www.probono.net; www.pslawnet.org; www.aals.org*.

One of my favorite *pro bono* activities is teaching in local high schools. Lawyers spend a lot of time addressing groups and a lot of time explaining the law to non-lawyers. High school teaching programs allow you to do both. We have had a program here for years and years, and almost every student who has taken part has said that it was one of his or her best law school experiences. The experience can be rewarding and moving.

Two students once presented the program in a custodial institution for juvenile delinquents. At first the law students were greeted with, "Pigs!" They stayed with it. Ten weeks later, I got letters from the "inmates": "I always thought all the police and lawyers were pigs, out to get me. Now I know that some might actually understand me and help me."

One sociologist studied attitudes toward the law. He found that a major predictor of whether people respected the law and its various institutions was whether their first contacts with the law were positive or negative. Growing up next door to a loud and drunken lawyer tends to poison one's attitude toward the Supreme Court. Teaching in high schools, particularly inner city high schools, you may be the first "lawyer" your students will ever meet. In a very real sense, you become a "drum major" for law.

One great aspect of these programs is that you get to discuss law with people other than law students, law teachers, and bored and resentful companions at cocktail parties.

If you want information on starting such a program, contact "Street Law" at (www.streetlaw.org). It can provide you with materials and information on how to set up a program.

But what if you need money?

Clerking

Many students clerk for lawyers during school. Generally this involves legal research. Some professors advise against clerking, as it will surely compete with class work. I think it's fine. Many students need the money, and a good clerkship, just like a good clinical experience, can be quite educational.

If you are going to clerk, consider negotiating a meaningful clerking experience. Most lawyers like spunk. Ideally you get feedback, and the tasks are varied: not *always* arcane memos, sometimes interviewing witnesses and sometimes observing trials, and depositions.

So what else is there to say about clerking? Not much, except to say that the debate about its propriety reflects a very important division in thinking about legal education: is it better to learn law from books or from working in the vineyards? This debate continues today over the role of clinical legal education. The remainder of this section puts that debate in its historical context.

A Short History of Legal Education

In the old days, there was *only* clerking; there were no law schools and no LSAT. See, generally, Milton, *Paradise Lost*.

After working several years as an apprentice, the novice took the bar and that was that. When the first law schools were started, they *supplemented* apprenticeship; apprentices worked in law offices in the daytime and gathered at night to hear lectures on legal principles. Slowly law schools took over more turf. Eventually they became *alternatives* to apprenticeship, and novices became eligible to take the bar by either route.

The key year in legal education is 1870. Christopher Columbus Langdell became dean of the Harvard Law School. Langdell faced a real problem: how to make law school academically respectable. A lot of traditional academics (English profs) thought that law school did not belong in a university. It was a trade school devoted to *practical* knowledge (*yuck!*). It merely prepared people to make a living. Nothing theoretical about it. The economist Thorston Veblen once remarked something to the effect, "Law schools belong in the university no more than schools of dance."

That hurt.

How to make law academically respectable? Lawyers may not be cultured, but they're bright. Call law a science. Langdell wrote:

> *[L]aw is a science [and] all the available materials of that science are contained in books.... [T]he library is the proper workshop of professors and students alike; it is to us all that the laboratories of the university are to the chemists and physicists, all that the museum of natural history is to the geologists, all that the botanical garden is to the botanists.*

With law a science, not a grubby trade, who could keep us out of the tower?

The Harvard model of legal education became the rage. Casebooks (and Langdell wrote the very first one) replaced lectures. Why is your law school *three* years? The correct answer is "c"—because Christopher Columbus Langdell set his up that way.

With law schools safely established in universities and recognized as an alternative to apprenticeship, two more steps had to be taken to establish today's law school. The first was to kill off the competition: apprenticeship. After years of struggle, in a vast majority of states, law school, not apprenticeship, became the *only* way to become a lawyer. The second step was to raise law school admission standards. At first, some college was required, then college graduation, and now, as you are painfully aware, very good grades and a high LSAT score.

Consider the result. Without good academic credentials, you can't attend law school; without graduating from law school, you can't take the bar. The circle closes.

Law professors, in their assault on apprenticeships, marched under the banner of the "public good." Learning law by reading cases, they argued, made for better lawyers than learning law by working with lawyers. Well, perhaps. Cynics smile, seeing simply the imperatives of expansionism.

In any event, the "practical training" of law students was routed. Law school became almost entirely academic. Very few professors ever practiced law. They were hired because they had excelled in academic law schools and then clerked for an appellate court for a year or two.

Beginning in the 1970s, the "practical wing" of legal education counterattacked, marching under the banner of "clinical education." Clinicians today have a solid beach head in the hollowed halls:

clinical education is an accepted part of modern legal education, although just how big a part remains open to dispute.

The Distortions of Legal Education

Admittedly I have been something of a drum major for legal education. Realize, however, that it can distort your view of people and can rob you of your common sense.

I gave my contracts students a hypothetical. *Seller* is continually late in making his deliveries. *Buyer*, after pleas and much patience, finally cancels the contract. After stating the problem, I asked:

"If you were *Seller*, what would you say?"

I was looking for a discussion of the various legal theories that throw *Buyer* into breach for canceling the contract, legal arguments that would allow *Seller* to crush *Buyer*.

I looked around the room. As is so often the case with first year students, they were all writing in their notebooks or inspecting their shoes. There was, however, one eager face: that of the eight year-old son of one of my students. He had been biding his time, drawing pictures. Suddenly he raised his hand. Such behavior, even from an eight-year old, must be rewarded.

"Okay," I said, "What would you say if you were *Seller*?"

"I'd say, 'I'm sorry'."

Professor William Simon cautions that legal education presents a caricature of human existence. Plaintiffs always want more money and prosecutors always want more time; civil defendants want to escape all liability and criminal defendants simply want to escape. In the hundreds and hundreds of cases you will read, there are very few heroes.

Holmes once wrote that law students should study the law from the perspective of the "bad man"—the class bully who has no regard for morality and is only interested in what he can get away with. No doubt this is a great learning strategy. But don't confuse either the caricature or the bad man with life.

One of my first clients came to me with a consumer problem. After some research, I triumphantly advised:

"You don't have to pay any more on this bill! I have found several legal violations. We can get your money back, you can keep what you bought, and we can sue the store for punitive damages!"

My client looked at me. "But I bought it and I owe the money. I just want you to help work out a payment schedule."

One of our chores is to help people say, "I'm sorry."

———

As well as getting the distorted view that people always want to win no matter what, we may also forget our common sense and come to believe that everything is about cleaver legal argument.

My first job was with a state-wide program that provided free legal services for the poor. I worked in the Los Angeles office, where my first assignment was to find out whether, if the program opened an office in Delano, California, a business license would be required. Of course my pricey and demanding legal education gave me no clue about how to even begin to answer that question. Fortunately, a friendly librarian in the county law library got a copy of the City Code of Delano and found the applicable section.

The answer to the question was, "Yes, we'll need a license and it costs $20." In my memo to the boss, did I write, "Yes, we'll need a license and it costs $20"? No. What I did write, after three or four days of intense research, was, "Yes, a license is required and it costs $20. However, that City Ordinance is unconstitutional as a violation of Free Speech, Equal Protection, and Due Process because...." and I continued for about twenty pages. Pretty spiffy stuff.

Gary Bellow, my boss, was not nearly as impressed as I was. "Do that again, you're fired."

CHAPTER 28

CAREER CHOICES

I started with a girl with some flowers in her hand walking in a room in a country house. Sentences simply grew into paragraphs, and paragraphs became a chapter. I knew I had started a novel but I didn't know what novel it was.

Ian McEwan on writing a novel

What a marvelous image. I'll steal it.

Three years from now, to the applause of friends and family, you will walk across a stage, a diploma in your hand. You will have started a career but you won't know what career it will be.

Among other worries plaguing beginning law students is "What kind of law should I practice?" Not to worry; it is too early to decide and, even if you do, probably things will not work out the way you plan. Stephen King, discussing writing, tells us:

I distrust plots for two reasons: first, because our lives are largely plotless, even when you add in all our reasonable precautions and careful planning; and second, because I believe plotting and the spontaneity of real creation aren't compatible.

At this stage, avoid the anguish and effort of reasonable precautions and careful planning; your career will happen and, while being prepared may make things more efficient, it might make them dull. First a cautionary tale:

Once upon a time, a student sought a reference. His quest: the large, prestigious law firm of Blah, Blah, and Blah in Gotham City. I asked, "Looking forward to Gotham?"

"No, I hate Gotham. Nothing but traffic and strangers. I would rather go back home to Hicksville."

"Well, you must like the kind of law they practice at Blah and Blah."

"No, it's mostly corporate. I'd rather work with kids. That's what I did before law school, and that's why I came to law school. I worked at Blah last summer, and I hated it. As I told another summer intern, 'Terence, this is stupid stuff, yet I do my research fast enough.'"

"Then why do you want the job?"

"Because everyone tells me it's a very good one."

While you should be green and golden, singing in your chains like the sea, you'll hear rumors: you won't get a job unless you are in the top 10% of your class. This rumor starts from the fact that usually only large business firms interview students at the law school. Only these firms can project their needs over the next several years, and often they restrict their hiring to the top of the class. However, smaller firms and most governmental agencies hire lawyers only after they graduate and, frequently, only after they have passed the Bar. Let's turn to some little known facts:

Approximately 50% of lawyers were in the bottom 50% of their class.

While it is true that great law school success opens the door to certain kinds of law practice, large firm practice and law teaching, once one gets out in the real world *no one cares how well you did in Contracts* or even where you went to school. In practice, success in not measured in Bluebooks; it is measured the old-fashioned way: hard work, honesty, and common sense.

70% of lawyers are in private practice, the vast majority in firms of five or less or on their own. Only 5% are in large firms. (By way of comparison, 8.3% of Hollywood actors play lawyers on T.V.)

Only 5% of lawyers defend and prosecute criminals.

It is unlikely that the first job you take after graduation will be your last. Most lawyers change law jobs at least once after law school; some leave law altogether: to govern nations, to make revolutions, or to broadcast the Dodgers.

Studies suggest an inverse relationship between money and job satisfaction. Lawyers with large urban law firms report bigger bucks but less job satisfaction than do lawyers working for the government and public interest firms.

Very few "hired guns" exist. Most lawyers are convinced they are doing "the Lord's work," be they personal injury lawyers or insurance defense lawyers, prosecutors or criminal defenders, business lawyers or public interest lawyers.

This chapter will not offer any tips on resume preparation (except don't come off too pompous, as in "Why your firm needs me") nor tips on interview technique (except to appear to *really want* the job that is being offered: enthusiasm routs doubt every time). Rather, I will first discuss influences that can distort your quest, then discuss job attributes that you may want to consider, and, finally, offer some ideas as to what you can do in law school to test your alternatives. But first, we need a goal.

Once I asked a college basketball coach, "Are basketball coaches happy?"

"I don't know about all coaches," he told me. "All I know is that I wake up at 4 o'clock in the morning and realize, 'Great, I get to go to work today.'"

Frankly, I don't know a whole lot of lawyers (or law professors) that feel that way. But why not? Let us, you and me, shoot for the National Championship.

Mulling Things Over

Getting a job is more than getting a job: more than resumes, dressing up, and remaining calm during the interview.

In choosing a job, you are, at least to some degree, choosing what kind of person you will become.

I went to school in Berkeley. One of my radical friends was hired by a commercial firm in Santa Barbara. They told him he would be a Republican in a year. I saw him about a year later.

"They couldn't have been more wrong. It took six months."

George Orwell had a marvelous insight. When we get a job, we want to conform and hence put on a professional mask. As time wears on, however, our face grows to fit the mask. After twenty years prosecuting criminals, what world view will you have? After a career of advising business, defending insurance companies, or teaching law, whom will you know? What books will you read? Who will you be?

> *In this life we prepare for things, for moments and events and situations. We worry about things, think about injustices, read what Tolstoy has to say. Then, all of a sudden, the issue is not whether we agree with what we have heard and read and studied. This issue is **us**, and what we have become.*

> Robert Coles

Around "interview time," classmates will begin getting jobs. You will feel an incredible amount of pressure to land one. It doesn't help when friends and family ask, "Well?"

The danger is that you might take a job simply because "it's there."

I recommend that you take an hour or so now to write about the kind of job you want. Put the letter aside and reread it around "interview time." Writing now might help you sort things out. Rereading it then might help you remain calm until you get the job that wakes you at four o'clock in the morning . . .

Distorting Influences

A brilliant law school career might not be all it's cracked up to be.

Many students (maybe you) come to law school for idealistic reasons: to work with business in improving the environment, to work with abused children, or to return to their community to help those less fortunate. Many of these end up with Blah, Blah, and Blah, fighting traffic in Gotham City.

Why?

Many change career goals in law school for good reasons: learning more about themselves and more about their options, they realize that they will be happier doing something they hadn't previously considered. Some of my best friends work for Blah, Blah, and Blah and love it. More power to them.

However, some change goals because they get caught up in law school hype.

Tom Wolfe, in *The Right Stuff*, writes that America's astronauts were not motivated by money, fame, or challenge; they just wanted to get chosen for the most competitive program at the time; they just wanted to prove they were the "right stuff."

There is nothing wrong with this, as long as the "right stuff" is *your* stuff.

In law school, the "right stuff" is working with ideas rather than with people. This is the implicit lesson. Law school goodies are passed out on the basis of academic performance. Compassion, common sense, and, alas, humor can't be graded and hence don't count for much.

To prove that they are the "right stuff," the "best" students go to large firms. This career path rests on two assumptions, first, that all the "smart lawyers" end up in such firms and, second, that all the interesting legal work is done in them. Both assumptions are false. The two smartest lawyers I have known worked for poor people at Legal Aid. As to engaging legal work, when I was a trial lawyer, doing misdemeanors, I woke up at night to jot notes to myself. When I was an appellate lawyer, doing "law reform" and arguing cases of great moment, I slept soundly.

Getting caught up in law school hype is one danger to avoid. Another is selling yourself too short. We fear success as well as failure. The psychologist Abraham Maslow calls it "fear of one's own greatness" and "running away from one's own best talents." He asks his students:

"Which of you in this class hopes to write the great American novel, or to be a Senator, or Governor, or President? Or a great composer? Or a Saint?"

His students giggle, blush, and squirm, until he asks, "If not you, then who else?"

I am not saying that you should crave fame or fortune; I suggest that you should not run away from your dreams because you fear boldness, because you fear your own best talents.

"Mind-forged manacles"—a phrase of William Blake. "I could *never* do trial work." "I could *never* get a job in Washington." "I could *never* make a living in Hicksville representing kids."

How do you know?

Career Choices

Punt

It is OK to be indecisive. At least, I think it is. After law school, you can take a job that lasts, by definition, only a year or two. This is a good option. These jobs are usually exciting and are of a "once in a lifetime" variety. They provide valuable training and effectively silence those who ask, "Well?"

A *judicial clerkship* is a good choice. Most appellate judges and many trial court judges hire recent graduates as clerks. You get to sit in on either appellate arguments or trials, do legal research, discuss legal matters with your judge, and maybe even get to write an opinion or two. You will learn a great deal about how cases are decided, and most legal employers think a clerkship is a real plus.

Additionally, there are numerous *internships* offered by governmental agencies, public interest groups, and even some law schools.

Clerkships are highly competitive, and the race starts second year. See your Placement Director. Also, you will need recommendations from professors, so best to begin to get to know them now.

Of course, you can stay in school. Some law schools offer advanced law degrees in such things as tax. Or you may wish to get another degree in a field that you plan to use in conjunction with law, such as business, finance, real estate, counseling, or ventriloquism.

The hardest part of the "stay-in-school" option, and one that might prove insurmountable, is telling your family.

Non-Legal Careers

Kafka went to law school. He hated it. In fact, it has recently come to light that the first line of his classic, *The Metamorphosis*, has been incorrectly translated. The inaccurate translation reads:

Gregor Samsa awoke one morning and found that he had turned into a gigantic cockroach.

The corrected translation reads:

Gregor Samsa woke up one morning and found that he had turned into a rather rotund tax lawyer.

A surprising number of disgruntled lawyers become novelists (and, no doubt, disgruntled novelists swell our ranks). Others go into business (Kafka wouldn't have liked that either), teaching, politics, and the media. A good friend of mine went into "development" (fund raising), using his legal knowledge of wills and tax law. Another wanted to get into producing movies. She went to Hollywood, rented an apartment, hung out at the studios; after several months, she got a law job, and now, after several years, is producing her own movies.

Karen Waterman, a law school placement specialist, advises that routine want ads can be rich sources of ideas. "Would this job involve the use of legal skills?" Many jobs involve legal skills (such as risk management and compliance work) but traditionally have been filled with non-lawyers.

Show up and surprise everyone.

Of course, it is easier to get a traditional law job. However, maybe the rest of your life is worth a little effort, a little imagination, a little gumption.

Traditional Law Jobs

Your choices are vastly more than big firms versus small firms, prosecuting versus defending.

Public Interest Law, Legal Aid

Law reporting (print or TV)

Teaching (in law schools or colleges or community colleges)

Risk management; contract compliance

In-house legal counsel

Legislative counsel, lobbying

Government work (from Washington to Hicksville)

Law librarian (law schools and large firms), law publishing (writing ALR articles)

Law enforcement (FBI)

Military justice

Circus law

Your Placement Office will have tons and tons of information.

Let me alert you to two "hot" substantive areas of the law: *Intellectual Property* and *Elder Law*. Intellectual Property covers the traditional areas of copyright, patent, and trademark, but the field has taken on a new dimension in cyberspace. Things are booming, and there is no end in sight. Elder Law is a relatively new speciality but will also be in great demand as Baby Boomers reach retirement. For a general look at elder law, see Hegland and Bogutz, *Fifty and Beyond: The Law You and Your Parents Need to Know.*

In weighing your alternatives, what factors should you consider?

Ideas versus people. Some people prefer working with ideas, others with people. Some law practices involve mostly legal research and drafting. These jobs offer "nice" theoretical problems, the luxury of extended research and reflection, and the satisfaction that comes in drafting a well-written and thorough legal document. Large firms traditionally offer this kind of employment, but so too do many smaller "specialized" law firms, public interest firms, and "appellate departments" of the public defender and of the district attorney.

Law jobs that involve working closely with people are at the other end of the continuum. Great satisfaction can come in helping people solve real-life problems: helping work out a sensible child custody arrangement, helping two friends set up a partnership, helping a client understand a bureaucratic maze. As a general matter, smaller firms and some government agencies offer greater opportunities to work with people.

Responsibility. The larger the firm or agency, the less responsibility you likely will have. Your work will be constantly reviewed. You will work on parts of elephants.

Other jobs throw you directly into the heat of battle. In some small firms and legal aid offices, you interview clients the first day; in some district attorney and defender offices, you try cases your first week.

Responsibility can be exhilarating; after all those years of studying about the real world, you are suddenly part of it. Your decisions count.

Responsibility can be terrifying. Law is quite complex, and, as a beginner, you know so little. Add to that the elusive criteria of good practice: "Have I worked hard enough?" "Have I raised all the points?" "Has my client been well represented?"

Training. It is essential to develop your professional skills. Larger firms and agencies generally offer good training. Your work is almost always reviewed. This is the other side of "lack of responsibility." Generally you will be given time to "do it right," and the standards of the practice will be quite high.

Many smaller firms and smaller public agencies also insist on the highest professional standards. Don't take a job that allows for sloppy work habits.

An aside on solo practice. Some "hang out their own shingle" upon graduation. But times, since Lincoln, have changed.

Without someone to show you the ropes and discuss your cases with, you will teeter on the edge of malpractice. The most common cause of legal malpractice is missing deadlines. Once you get three or four cases, it gets very difficult to keep track of things. Working with an established firm or lawyer, you will learn the various retrieval systems. Going out on your own, you may not.

Two pieces of advice, assuming you ignore the implicit advice in the last paragraph. First, keep your overhead low. Second, don't take "dog cases," even if it is just to put some short-term bones on the table. In every community, there are folks who were drugged by the CIA and brainwashed by the F.B.I. (Now we know where our tax dollars go.)

These unfortunate folks flutter, like moths, around new shingles. They never go away.

Contentiousness. Even if you restrict your practice to adoption law, business planning, elder law, or some other form of "happy law," there will be some days when another lawyer will be yelling at you. In other law jobs, such as trying lawsuits, there is constant contentiousness.

Another area of contentiousness is with one's clients. It is said that, in criminal practice, you deal with bad people at their best and, in family practice, with good people at their worst. Interviewing, ask lawyers not only about how they get along with adverse lawyers but with their own clients.

"Alternative Dispute Resolution" is a movement to introduce kinder and gentler methods into our adversary system. Perhaps mediation can replace litigation and problem-solving the zero-sum game (those in which what one side wins, the other must lose). Brave lawyers are entering traditional combative fields with these goals. If you are repelled by the adversary system, consider this route. Even in traditionally combative law jobs, it may be possible to do something other than "chase each other around the table," where the "good" solution leaves both sides sullen but not mutinous.

Income and security. Larger firms start associates at higher salaries; partners in large firms do exceedingly, embarrassingly well. Some lawyers in smaller firms undoubtedly overtake their fat-cat brethren and occasionally make "megabucks" by getting into business ventures with their clients. Personal injury lawyers can almost retire if they get "the big one" (but, with TV advertising, the chances of getting "the big one" are about the same as winning the lottery).

Lawyers making a career in governmental agencies often do quite nicely. Gone, of course, the dream of vast wealth, but some government lawyers earn salaries higher than many lawyers in their area, with better benefits and job security.

Travel, adventure. It's possible.

Esprit de corps. Some law jobs involve a strong sense of shared purpose. One of the things I most value about my own days in practice was my relationship with the other lawyers in the office. We knew about each others' cases, we talked about them, argued about them, and shared the moments of joy and despair.

I found this sense of shared purpose and involvement in both legal aid and public defending. I am sure it exists in most prosecuting offices, in most government jobs, and, I am told, in most small law offices. The larger the firm or agency, the less likely the feeling. This lack of *esprit de corps* will not bother some, those who prefer to work alone (perhaps writing Nutshells) and those who simply want a job and will look for a sense of community elsewhere.

Weighing Careers During Law School

A sports agent was discussing how difficult it is for players to readjust after their playing days are over. "I tell them to keep a diary when they are still playing. What do they enjoy doing in their off hours? What are they good at? That way, when the time comes, they will have some idea of what kind of job they may like."

Keep track of what you like and what you do well. Do you enjoy the conflict of Moot Court or Trial Practice? Do you find the verbal encounter in the classroom exciting? Do you love research? Do you rush to your computer to get your thoughts on paper? Do you like close supervision? Do you like working with classmates?

Although law practice is much different from law school, many facets are the same: reading cases and statutes, making arguments, advising on how the law would play out in a given situation. Once you have given law school a fair run, at least a year, and you find you don't like the law, find it too nit-picky, too confining, too boring, consider getting out. Kafka went on to achieve modest success. So did Harry Truman, who had a year of law school. So too Vince Lombardi, who had a semester.

Course Selection

If you are considering a legal specialty, obviously take the courses in it. Consider that there may be courses in other departments of the university that will expose you to the "nuts and bolts" of a particular career. For example, if you are considering something in the media, check the catalogue of the Journalism Department. Better yet, go over and chat with the people there. Another obvious exam-

ple is Business School. However, *as career goals
often change*, it is a mistake to focus too exclusively
in the area of law you think you'll practice.

Most law schools offer courses in *trial practice*
and have *clinics*. Clinics involve representing real
clients either in a law school clinic or in a field
placement. These courses are very important, particularly if you are shying away from them. It may
be a matter of breaking out of "mind-forged manacles." You may find that you enjoy the hurly-burly
of trial and that you find deep satisfaction in helping people solve real life problems. Or you may
conclude "Never again." Either way: you win.

Clinical courses are needed by those students
planning to work for small firms or on their own.
There is the danger of developing sloppy work habits. Law school courses will instill a sense of excel-
lence in practice.

Work for Lawyers

A good way to experience practice is to work for a
lawyer. Doing the research, hanging out at the
office, and talking to attorneys and staff can give
you a good feel for that particular kind of law
practice.

If you are to work for a lawyer, what kind of
lawyer? Should you take a job with the kind of firm
or agency you "think" you would like to eventually
work for? Or should you take a job with one of
those "I-could-never-work-with-them" firms? There
are pros and cons for each. Some students find
permanent employment through their clerking. On

the other hand, much can be said for testing as many alternatives as possible. Even if you confirm your suspicion that you could never do insurance defense, having clerked with such a firm will make you a better personal injury lawyer.

Ask Lawyers and Professors

Most of us like to give advice (I, apparently, more than others). If you are considering prosecuting, why not go to the prosecutor's office and ask to see one of the attorneys?

I'm not here looking for a job. I'm here because I want some advice. I am thinking about prosecuting when I graduate, but I really don't know much about it. Perhaps you can tell me about it; perhaps I could sit in and watch what you do.

Note: This can be turned into a very clever job-getting ploy.

Now, Ms. Banker, I'm not looking for a job working in your legal department. I realize you are probably full. What I would like is some advice on how to go about getting a job in the legal department of a bank.

Of course *I* would never be bold enough simply to show up at a law office, unannounced. The problem is meeting lawyers. One possibility is to get together with some classmates, ask a friendly professor for some names of recent graduates, and throw a party.

We're first year students, and we want to meet some lawyers so we can get some feel for what it's like. Want to come to a party?

You can also infiltrate sections of your local Bar Association; many have student memberships. Another way to meet lawyers is to attend Continuing Legal Education (CLE) programs and go to Bar conventions.

Try to get your professors talking about their practice experiences. Most likely they will be more interesting than the Rule in Shelley's Case.

Go to Court

It takes absolutely no courage to walk quietly into the back of a courtroom and sit through a trial. Again, this experience is probably most needed by those who will "never" step into a courtroom—who knows, perhaps they'll never leave.

Read Books

There are several books about law practice. I recommend, as openers:

The Associates, Jay Osborne (author of *Paper Chase*), deals with life in a Wall Street firm.

Trial and Error, D. Michael Tomkins, is the story of a young lawyer starting off in solo practice.

Confessions of a Criminal Lawyer, Seymour Wishman, presents a criminal defense lawyer reflecting on several years of practice.

These books are relatively short, quite candid, and at places, humorous. They are excellent introductions to various kinds of practice. Ask your professors for other titles.

A Final Word

What does your future hold? Perhaps you will argue cases that shape your times, or perhaps you will be the trusted advisor of powerful groups, huge corporations, or even Presidents. Or perhaps you will never make the front page and will be simply another lawyer in the yellow pages, helping people with everyday problems. There is greatness in that as well.

Don't make too much of your ambition. It's OK if you don't get your fifteen minutes of fame. In Robert Bolt's play, *A Man for All Seasons*, Sir Thomas More is discussing careers with the politically ambitious Richard Rich.

More: Why not be a teacher? You'd be a fine teacher. Perhaps even a great one.

Rich: And if I was, who would know of it?

More: You, your pupils, your friends, God. Not a bad public that.

Comforting thought. Write if you get work. Hegland@law.arizona.edu.

CHAPTER 29

LAWYERS ON LAWYERING

The lawyers you will meet here are friends, not statistical abstracts. I selected them because they are reflective and insightful. I selected lawyers doing different kinds of law jobs, but made no attempt for balance either in terms of type of practice, age of practitioner, or geography. I prescribed no format; I simply told them that I was writing a book for first-year law students, students who knew little about various legal careers and who knew little about what lawyers actually do. Write, I advised, what you think might prove useful.

STEPHEN GOLDEN

Law Clerk

Law school was wonderfully challenging. But nothing in law school quite prepared me for the real world of law. (Or, should that be "the world of real law?") Part of the unpreparedness may lie with the continually repeated maxim that there are no wrong answers. Law school is an intellectual exercise. The practice of law is filled with intellectual rigor, but with nothing "exercise" about it. Judicial clerking is a wonderful way to bridge the gap between law school's "no wrong answers" and practice's "sorry, wrong answer."

I know the precise time when I became a lawyer. In the first week of my clerkship I was asked to research a particular point. It was like many law school exams where I had been given facts, had identified issues and had presented conclusions. I was finishing a memo when a bolt of understanding struck me. THIS MATTERS. For the first time I was *doing*. I was no longer just *learning*. I became a lawyer in that instant.

Cases have several life stages in an appellate court. First, the justices must decide if they will accept the case. A law clerk will prepare a bench memorandum, reading the briefs prepared by the lawyers and a memo from one of the staff attorneys working for the court, doing some research, and then writing a clear and concise summary of the issues. My justice (always "my justice" or "my judge," but never, "the judge I work for"—this is all very personal) always had a strong grasp of the issues and he wanted depth on what he felt was the nub. "Deep in the law and deep in the facts," he once said, "That's what makes good analysis."

Here is where I felt well served by the demanding professors and rigorous debate I encountered in law school. Except that unlike law school you take nothing for granted. You MUST check the cases cited in the briefs to see if the cases actually stand for what was claimed and whether they are still good law.

You will be surprised how often I found mistakes, even substantive mistakes.

When a case is accepted for review the initial research needs to be augmented because there is now a sharper, clearer vision of what the case represents. The justices will have agreed to consider one or two, or rarely three, precise issues and no matter what else the case may involve it is only those issues that now matter.

After a few months of exposure to the case you have a sense of what the outcome should be. But there is a good argument for a different outcome or the case wouldn't be in the appellate court and it is a clerk's job to be sure both sides are properly presented as simply and clearly as possible. Then, if you're lucky, there is a chance to express your own views if you support them with solid argument.

After argument, I would get more assignments if my justice was writing the opinion. Sometimes I did more research. Sometimes I did some editing. Sometimes I did some drafting. Sometimes a draft went back and forth in an iterative process.

I learned about brief writing, about framing legal arguments, about oral argument and about persuasive written and spoken speech. I learned how judges and justices think about issues and what kinds of arguments are more likely to succeed than others. I learned the importance of clarity and brevity. And, if you clerk, you will learn those thing as well. And, like me, you will put your stamp on the final opinion and one day you will be able to pull a law reporter off the library shelf, open it up, look down at a case and beam. "I helped make law. I clarified issues, I had ideas, and I played a part. I made a difference. That was me." (Or, if you took advanced legal writing, "That was I.")

GRACE McILVAIN

Mid–Size Firm

When I decided to become a lawyer, it was not because I thought the law would be exciting. I thought it would be boring. I did not expect to like the law, let alone love it the way one is supposed to. I wanted a job that would give me responsibility, a chance to use my brain, a good salary, and a chance to advance, none of which I had as a secretary. Those were my sole reasons for applying to law school.

It is amusing to recall what I expected the practice of law to be like when I was in law school. I expected it to be boring and tedious, so tedious that the hours in the office would drag by. Nothing could be further from the truth. I enjoy at least 90% of the things I must do. Filling out time sheets and preparing bills to send to clients are no fun at all, but litigation is very interesting. I think about my cases all my waking hours and often most of the night. I even dream about them.

The responsibilities and time pressures are, however, very stressful. The matters one handles are extremely important to the clients, and they place a great deal of trust in you. Because of that, and for many other more selfish reasons, there is great pressure to achieve an excellent result in every single case which is, of course, impossible. There is never enough time to be as thoroughly prepared as you would like to be. No matter how well organized and self-disciplined you are, every day is a struggle against time. There are never enough hours in the day. In that respect, law school is good preparation for the practice. But the time pressures in practicing law are much greater than time pressures in law school.

There is so much emphasis on legal theories in law school that you begin to believe that legal knowledge and analytical skill are all you need to be a good attorney. Law school doesn't prepare you for the psychological aspects of practicing law. You must build a good relationship with your client and make him or her have confidence in you. You must make the opposing attorney at least respect you, and it is to your advantage to convince him that you are tough, that you know the law, and that you will persevere no matter what. It is to your advantage to make him afraid of you. Yet sometimes you need his cooperation, so you must know when to be nice to him and when to apply pressure. (I use "him" when referring to the opposing attorney because, in litigation, usually your opponent is male. If you are a woman, the difficulties of dealing with him are multiplied because even before he meets you, he may have decided that you are either a pushover or a bitch, and that whichever you are, you are not a good lawyer.)

You need to convince the judges before whom you appear that you know the law, that there is a good reason behind every statement you make, and that you would never ever mislead them. You must convince juries that you are credible and that your client deserves their verdict.

There is always room to grow. There are always ways you could have handled a case better, which is one of the reasons you are never bored.

ROBERT FLEMING

Elder Law

It seemed to me that most of the students in my law school class were unsure of their ultimate goals. I was different. I knew with absolute certainty why I was in law school, what I would do with my degree and my professional future. As it happened, I was wrong.

Although my plans drifted from environmental law to the more prosaic water and mining law practice, I knew that I would want to utilize my undergraduate degree (chemistry) and my scientific orientation. Two years out of law school I had learned the hard truth: a new lawyer has little control over what cases or clients might appear. There was a softer truth as well: I surprised myself when I found that I enjoyed working with individual clients, and particularly those with mental or physical limitations.

In one regard, my law school predictions were correct. I doubted that I would "fit in" in a corporate or large firm practice, and the passage of time has proven that my doubts were well founded. I have practiced alone, with a single associate, in partnerships of up to four lawyers and in government settings. Each arrangement has had its attractions.

One other thing I correctly predicted in law school was that I would not be drawn to a litigation-based practice. An office practice filled with appointments with real clients is very rewarding and professionally satisfying.

Our firm practices "elder law." We prepare estate plans, advise clients about long-term care costs, and counsel family members on end-of-life issues. The common thread is that our clients tend to be elderly or disabled, or to be the children or parents of elderly or disabled individuals.

Recently I went through an extraordinary personal experience related to the law practice. A young woman had been a long-time client. I had handled the proceeds of a personal injury settlement while she was a minor, and she left the money in trust with our firm after reaching her majority. She was physically disabled and had a shortened life expectancy, but she exhibited personal strength. A few years ago she decided to name me as her agent for health care decisions—not because she distrusted her family, but because she wanted to remove her mother from the agony of making the ultimate decision.

When I received the call from the hospital, I expected to be told that she had become non-communicative. Instead she remained articulate, and was demanding the removal of the breathing machine which kept her alive. Her father objected, hoping for a miracle. Her mother agreed with her decision, but was in agony. Her siblings represented several different views on how she should proceed. Her physician was sure that if he could get her through her current treatment, she could live several more years—though, he acknowledged, she would never be weaned from the breathing machines.

At her bedside I asked her how she felt about the decision. She clearly mouthed the words "I'm tired– let me go." I went to a room filled with the well-intentioned individuals in her life, each of whom was grappling with her wishes in a different way, and argued for her personal autonomy.

The legal principle was never at issue. She was competent, and had the absolute right to direct the removal of the treatment, and the hospital staff knew it without having to hear it from me. I left the hospital with the certain knowledge that by the time of my arrival at the office she would have died—and she did. In a strict sense, I did not practice law that day—but I accomplished something terribly important to me personally, and my faith in the law and the practice of law was reinforced.

Law school was at least an adequate preparation for the legal aspects of the practice of law. It did not, however, prepare us for the medical, social work, financial, personal or emotional components of the practice. It may be that those components are more easily learned in the on-the-job training of the real world. Still, it would have been nice to have some sense of the application of legal principles to real people's lives.

THERESA GABALDON

Large Firm; Law Teaching

My sister, who is a romance novelist, has the best job in the world. This is largely because she has self-defined it to involve working at night, getting up very late, and eating chocolates for breakfast.

I, a law professor, have the second best job in the world; if eating chocolates were a necessary part of the job description, it would clearly rival my sister's. As it is, I have enormous flexibility about what I do and, within reasonable bounds, when I do it. The highlights, and only strictly scheduled events of the week are, of course, classroom appearances. I currently teach to an average class size of around 120 students; put a microphone in my hand and I become Oprah Winfrey. Coming up with different ways to cover the material is part of the fun, and if I choose to play a game of "Jeopardy" with corporate law topics, none of my teaching colleagues will object (at least not to my face.) My students are good-natured and appreciate whatever effort is expended in their behalf.

Performing scholarly research and writing is another important part of my task, and it is here that the possibilities for marching to one's own drumbeat are most unlimited. I choose my own topics for inquiry, and simply work on them until I have said what I have to say. My most productive "thinking" time starts at 4:00 a.m. and I try to take advantage of it. This may lead to a lull later in the day, but a quick trip to aerobics class recharges my batteries.

Although the description thus far may suggest that the law professor leads a life that is somewhat distanced from others, this is only true if he or she decrees it. If you display any disposition to listen, as well as to impart, students will be by to chat about a truly breath-taking assortment of subjects. Your colleagues can, if you choose, be your sounding boards, your confidantes, your matchmakers, and, every now and then, your bowling partners.

My immediately prior incarnation was as a partner in a large law firm. As such, I had the third best job in the world. In all honesty, flexibility was not one of the things that commended it. Rather, it was the technical challenge—present also in law teaching—and the sense of command. Frankly, the money wasn't bad, either; in ten years of teaching I have yet to achieve my salary in my last year of practice.

I specialized in corporate and securities law, and these are the areas that have carried over into my teaching and my scholarship. It was, at the time, something of a "glamour" practice. The deals were huge, the pace was fast, and the travel arrangements were luxurious. The pressure, however, was intense, and I can remember the feeling in my chest as I realized that a deadline was approaching and that the legal judgment being brought to bear on a multi-million dollar deal was mine. I have no regrets about having lived that life or about having left it, simply because I have found something I like more.

Because I have truly enjoyed both of my law-related professions, I have to believe that there is something about the law that has "worked" for me. I know that it has not, and does not, "work" for everybody. I enjoy the solving-the-maze aspects and the challenges of communicating my solutions to others. I suspect, however, that I lack the passion for justice, fairness, etc., that motivates some—and that's probably just as well for a corporate lawyer. In fact, from my observations, it is passion of this sort, combined with some type of corporate law-practice, that frequently leads to dissatisfaction with the law. There is fulfillment in serving particular clients well, in teaching, and in being an upstanding citizen and contributing member of society, but it will still leave some people feeling that there should be something more.

DAN COOPER

Criminal Defense

The most satisfying part of being a criminal defense lawyer is representing people who are despised by the public, the press and the prosecutors. Most cases remain obscure and create no reaction. On occasion, however, a defendant comes along who stirs the conscience of the community into moral outrage. It is defending this person that makes me proud to be a lawyer.

I recently represented a man who, along with his wife, was charged with child abuse. The facts were grisly. When I first met my client I was somewhat taken aback by his absolute and total lack of guilt. I try not to prejudge my cases. I was, however, aware when I received this case that the evidence was overwhelming against my client. I was perplexed at his total lack of emotion. Throughout the duration of the case he remained stoic in the face of constant hostility. The prosecutor called my client "a monster." The newspapers covered the case extensively and without objectivity. Even some close friends of mine asked how I could represent this man. The trial lasted nearly two weeks and, although I could not honestly say that I had fun, it was an experience I would not trade. The victim in the case, a nine-year-old girl, was found hog-tied in a motel room. She weighed thirty-two pounds and had been beaten. She had a chipped front tooth, bruises on her face and at least twenty scars on the top of her head which, the State alleged, came from a blunt object. A psychiatrist testified that she had never seen a worse case of psychological and emotional child abuse. A pediatrician testified that the child had been systematically starved for at least four years. A radiologist testified that the child's growth would, in all likelihood, be permanently stunted. And the most damaging witness of all was the little girl—tiny, charming, precocious. She broke down in tears as she turned to look at her mother and stepfather. My client stared at her impassively.

Against the advice of some very skilled trial lawyers, I put my client on the stand. The other lawyers felt that my client's testimony would only enrage an already upset jury. But I wanted the jury to see how narrow and rigid was my client's view of the world. His testimony was stilted, rigid, unsmiling and, I felt, demonstrated a myopic, inadequate personality perfectly capable of being unaware that his nine-year-old stepdaughter had been systematically starved and abused. Certainly his testimony would not prove his innocence. But there was an outside chance that the jury would convict of the lesser, non-intentional child abuse charge if they felt my client was rigid, myopic and pathetic. It was a slim chance in an unpopular, highly publicized case. My closing argument to the jury was emotional. I had convinced myself, if no one else, that the lesser offense would be the appropriate verdict. That the jury convicted my client of the greater offense has not changed my mind. But perhaps my feelings today about that child abuse case typify the nature of this job. I am proud that, in the face of overwhelming adverse publicity, against insurmountable evidence, while not able to convince a jury of my client's innocence, that jury knew that the defendant had a lawyer who fought for him.

RANDY STEVENS

Prosecutor

It took just a little more than a year after my graduation from law school for me to realize that private practice wasn't for me—at least not at that time in my life. I wanted more variety, more action, more excitement. I also wanted to be handling cases that had greater significance than just importance to the client. Having watched several excellent trial attorneys perform in court, I knew that courtroom practice was something I had to try, but I also realized it would take years to get any meaningful experience if I stayed in private practice. Telling the people I worked with that I'd be back in a year or two, I left and joined the local prosecutor's office. That was fourteen years ago.

From my perspective, the *total* experience available in prosecution cannot be duplicated elsewhere, especially for an attorney in the first four or five years. It isn't just the legal experience; it is the broader awareness of life, people and society, awareness of aspects of our society that most of us never dreamed existed. While at the same time, prosecution is an accelerated course in all aspects of trial practice.

Prosecution is the perfect opportunity for you to find out if you really want to be a trial attorney. Almost every young attorney experiences some degree of trial resistance—a hesitancy to try a case in front of a jury. There is a fear of making mistakes, of embarrassing oneself, of "freezing up" and not knowing what to do next. In a busy prosecutor's office, this resistance is usually overcome simply because there isn't time to dwell upon it. A heavy caseload doesn't allow for it. It isn't unusual for new prosecutors to find themselves trying several cases a week. If they begin to enjoy what they are doing, and are comfortable in court, it is only a matter of time before they want to begin trying more complicated and more serious cases. But not all attorneys experience this. After six months to a year, and sometimes even sooner, some realize that they aren't enjoying courtroom work, that they don't like the pressure and the demands of trial work, something no one can really know before they've given it a try. Most prosecutor's offices expect this to happen with a percentage of the young attorneys they hire.

It is usually during the fourth and fifth years when trial skills begin to reach a plateau, which means the attorney can try any type of criminal case with a high level of competency. Most trial attorneys will agree: if a person can competently prosecute a lengthy, difficult criminal case, that person can probably try almost any type of civil case. Law firms recruit heavily from prosecuting offices.

Most attorneys who prosecute do so for five to ten years, then they move on to something else. Looking back, asking myself why I've stayed so long in prosecution, the answer really isn't that hard to determine: I've thoroughly enjoyed myself. I've actually looked forward to going to work each morning. The constant flow of different types of cases, the interchange with victims and witnesses; working with every level of law enforcement: all go together to constitute a level of excitement that makes the job more than just enjoyable. It's experiencing life three or four times more than the average person. Along with this is the additional feeling that in some small way, you are doing something positive for society.

ZELDA B. HARRIS

Representing Victims of Domestic Violence

The most amazing part is that people trust you with their most intimate, painful and difficult secrets. I remember the first time that someone, other than my family and friends, put their trust in me. The weight of that experience was overwhelming. As a young attorney practicing poverty law I frequently violated the age old principle of "never take your work home." But to me, it was more than work, it was livelihoods, homes, children, safety and dignity. I must admit that I also engaged in quite a bit of social work practice by helping clients move from one home to the next, purchasing groceries, holiday gifts for children, the endless rides to and from court and the occasional cash that I could spare. The only thing I would trade is the fifty pounds of stress, oddly and strategically located on my hips, that I gained trying to "cure" my client's poverty.

I am a witness to the truth of violence, violence survived by victims of domestic abuse. I am in debt to the scores of clients who have risked their personal safety, privacy and the unknown to reveal the horrors of their lives to me. To the attorney considering embarking on this venture, I'd like to outline some of the very harsh realities of this practice, but also let you know that the benefits are life changing and shape your humanity.

I have stood witness with "Karen T." when her daughter, still nursing, was physically removed from her breast by court security officers when I lost the temporary custody hearing. I also remember the day when the three of us stood strong before the same juvenile court judge, who had to publicly and openly admit that Lisa should be returned to the nurture and protection of Karen.

I am a witness for a 22 year-old woman, "Tammy E.," who was raped by her father for seven years, disbelieved by her mother and sisters, removed from her home, abused by two partners, yet was able to bear two beautiful, healthy children only to have them taken from her by the state in their best interests. My photo album today still holds the picture of the day that Tammy's third daughter that was successfully, openly and with Tammy's consent adopted by a loving family that would never erase the reality of Tammy from the child's life.

I bore witness to a mother addicted to drugs, "Deborah P.," beat her addiction, stay clean, gain housing, employment and custody of her children, only to be found dead in her apartment, stabbed to death by a never-caught killer. My heart will not forget the warm embrace that I received from Deborah's children the last time I saw them in court; they knew and I knew that Deborah loved them.

A lawyer is a witness, but not a passive witness. We have voice and power. We can give credibility to the indignities that our clients have suffered. And, more than that, we have an absolute obligation to demand that the legal system, with all of its insensitivity and unfairness, listen and act.

You will not win every case or argument. But if you pursue each case with rigor and integrity, then you have earned the privilege to hold your client's trust. That is an absolute victory.

HECTOR CAMPOY

Judge of Juvenile Court

Never in my wildest dreams did I envision myself becoming a Juvenile Court Judge. In my mind's eye, before, during and for many years after law school, I was going to become the consummate trial lawyer. One day however, the Presiding Judge of our Juvenile Court invited me to become a part time judicial officer at our Juvenile Court. It took me very little time before the process enraptured me.

While issues of public safety and the safety of children are always foremost in our consideration, Juvenile Court Judges are constantly monitoring the development of relationships. When we take a child into our legal custody through a child abuse action, we hope to provide services to parents in order to rehabilitate the family and reconstitute it—in the event that those efforts fail we attempt to develop new, permanent relationships for these children through adoptions or other permanent legal arrangement. When we take a child into our fold through a delinquency process, we again aim to provide services and a corrective action plan, if you will, to rehabilitate children's behaviors.

Having done this for in excess of 18 years, I can honestly state that I am still surprised at the response of children and parents in our venue. Children, very many times, overcome incredible obstacles in order to correct the direction of their lives. This is wonderful to witness. Parents on the other hand, all too often, fail to seize the opportunity that the relationship with their child brings to them. This is not so wonderful.

The work is gut wrenching. The future of children and the future of families, in the face of societal pressures and trends, can provide some joy and exhilaration–it can also provide some extremely sobering moments.

All in all, our review of relationships at Juvenile Court is much more stimulating than how other courts review transactional events. Other courts determine whether a crime was committed, whether a person ran a red light or whether a contract was breached. These occurrences relate to events that in turn prescribe a remedy or response. The subject matter at Juvenile Court focuses on relationships that are dynamic and unpredictable.

RITA A. MEISER

Large Firm

I write as a person whose initial perception envisioned a happier legal life in a small firm, and who has been pleasantly surprised at where I have ended up. My primary orientation in becoming an attorney was to maximize my involvement with people. The areas of law in which I am mostly involved reflect this goal. Mostly I practice hospital law. This is one of those areas that you do not know exists when you are in law school. It encompasses: removing from a hospital staff a physician who does not perform at the proper standard of care; determining what procedures must be followed when a physician decides to remove life support, and working through the administrative procedures necessary to have a hospital add a department or beds. The work appeals to me because it involves effecting positive, tangible change in a way that is often lacking in the practice of law.

My second area of practice is employment discrimination, primarily from a defense perspective. This work is intriguing. I learn the business operations of the client, as well as meet and work with people involved in the world of business. It has not been my experience that practice from the defense posture necessarily mandates advocacy of personally offensive legal positions. Business people are generally fairly practical. If they recognize that a policy or practice is unlawful and will cause them continuing economic harm, they are generally receptive to changing it. The lawyer plays a role in advancing this recognition.

Finally, I represent two adoption agencies on a pro bono basis. The gratifications are obvious and the ability to participate in this type of activity is often a luxury less easily available in a small firm.

A large firm offers a new lawyer diversity, not only in terms of the type of legal practice offered, but in the people themselves. I initially perceived this to be an advantage of a small firm, but I now find it to be one of the greatest attributes of a large firm. I assumed that I would have closer personal relationships and find the working atmosphere more pleasant and intimate in a small firm. I now believe that a large law firm incorporates numerous types of personalities, and its size permits this diversification not to generate conflict. To the extent one specializes, the pool of working relationships narrows, thereby promoting the more intimate working relationships.

There are advantages and disadvantages to large firm practice, and what those factors are is the function of the given firm. The emphasis upon time commitments, responsibility, and client contact are all variables which must be assessed in evaluating the personality of any firm. In my particular firm, client responsibility and contact came quickly; however, this is not true in every large firm. If you are considering work in a large firm, interview carefully, particularly for second year clerkships, and try to select the firm which you think has the personality with which you are most compatible. Use your second year clerkship at that firm not only to verify whether your perceptions were correct, but to develop your ability to analyze the makeup of other firms, so that if you interview at another firm, you will more quickly be able to assess whether it's for you.

MARGARET McINTYRE

Representing Workers

When I went to law school I knew I wanted to practice public interest law. Many think that to do so one must work for federally funded legal services program or for a non-profit agency. I now know that you can also represent low income clients in private practice and still make a living. I have been doing so for five years.

Most of my clients have been fired from their jobs for discriminatory reasons, although some of them are still employed and are being subjected to a hostile work environment, such as sexual harassment or harassment based on another discriminatory motive. Others have been denied wages or benefits owed to them by their employers.

Some of those who come to see me may not have legal claims and some may have arguable claims, but weak evidence. For those it is better to accept early that the law cannot redress all wrongs, rather than go through the painful process of litigation, only to have the case dismissed for insufficient evidence. It can be very difficult to persuade some people of that, but it's my job as a lawyer to give them the best advice I can, not to tell them what they want to hear. Others are visibly relieved when I tell them that I don't think they have a case, and they realize that they can just put their losses behind them and move on.

Listen to a client's goals. Some want to feel vindicated, to hear a jury say that their employer violated the law. Others are willing to settle for money, whether to compensate them for lost wages, or to soften the hurt of whatever humiliation they have suffered. Most people want something in between, and are unsure about their goals until they learn the strength of their case and what will be involved in pursuing their goals, in terms of time, expense and the psychological toll litigation will take on themselves and their family. For each client, the answers to those questions are different. But in every case, I need to know a potential client's goals, because I must believe I can accomplish those goals before I offer representation.

One of the hardest goals to accomplish for employees is to get them back to the jobs they have lost. This is difficult to achieve because in these cases the emotions run high, and relationships have become strained. Some clients don't even want to go back to a bad situation. But when they do want to go back, and you help make it happen, that is tremendously rewarding.

Most cases settle before going to trial, usually for close to what the person lost in wages and benefits, although some will recover payment for emotional distress damages as well. Sometimes a client is able achieve other goals apart from a monetary settlement. For example, an employer may agree to undergo anti-harassment training, or agree to adopt comprehensive medical leave policies. Such agreements will give a client the sense of accomplishing something beyond his or her own case, and that brings a great deal of satisfaction.

One of my biggest challenges as a sole practitioner is figuring out a fair price to charge my clients for my services. Fortunately, the civil rights statutes provide for fee shifting, meaning that if an employee prevails in his or her claim against her employer, the employer must pay the plaintiff's attorney's fees. Even so, with each client, I must figure out whether to charge by the hour (at my regular or reduced rate), charge on a contingency basis, where my fee is a third of the employee's recovery, or charge some combination of the two, where I charge a reduced hourly rate and also a small percentage of any recovery. The right fee arrangement will depend on the economic value of the case, the client's ability to pay and the forum where the case is being litigated, i.e. at an administrative agency or in court. In a lawsuit, expenses alone can run from $2,000 to $5,000, depending on how many witnesses must be deposed. The financial decisions involved in commencing a lawsuit are difficult, but when the risks are shared by the attorney and the client, all decisions in the case are made with great care. In the long run, that's the best strategy for maintaining a successful practice.

If you are thinking of going it alone, know where to get help. It's important to link up with other lawyers through bar associations and other professional groups. I have learned a great deal about employment law through activities and seminars sponsored by the National Employment Lawyers Association. In addition, I remain connected to my law school, CUNY, the City University of New York. It has created the Community Legal Resource Network (CLRN), which provides technical and research support to alumni in small or solo practices who are trying to keep legal services affordable. For more information about the Community Legal Resource Network, contact www.lawschoolconsortium.net.

RICHARD DAVIS

Mid–Size Firm

I arrive in my office at 7:30 a.m. I look at my calendar and realize that I have to travel to a hospital which our firm represents to meet with the Administrator and Risk Manager. Others will be present. A few days ago a 20–day-old premature baby died at the hospital while on a ventilator. The original account suggests that the machine malfunctioned, preventing the baby from breathing normally.

Immediately after the accident, the Director of the Medical Lab at the hospital wanted to test the ventilator. I advised a delay long enough to notify each of the interested parties and to give them an opportunity to be present. The manufacturer of the ventilator and the parents of the baby were notified.

The test is scheduled to begin at 9:00, but I get there early. This will allow me to become familiar with the machine and interview the hospital's personnel who were on duty when the incident occurred. Arriving at 8:15, I talk to the respiratory technician, the nurse on duty and the medical lab technician who will do the testing. By 8:45 I have a general idea of how the machine works, of the suspected problem and of what happened the day in question. I also learn that the hospital coffee gets old after the second cup.

The first person to arrive for the meeting is an investigator from the County Medical Examiner's Office. The family asked that office to be present and to determine the cause of the baby's death. We exchange pleasantries. I am a little anxious and apprehensive because I really do not know what the tests will reveal. My hidden hope is that the tests will prove my client blameless.

The manufacturer is sending someone from its national headquarters in Texas. It is now 9:00, and we receive a call advising us that the manufacturer's rep will be late. The small talk and anxiousness continue. At 9:30, the manufacturer's representative arrives. There is an immediate disagreement over the tests that should be run and who should run them. After discussion, ground rules are laid and pictures are taken to verify and preserve settings on dowels and pressure gauges. Each test is run carefully and meticulously. The pressure gauge is saved for last because it is the suspected culprit. It proves faulty.

Further tests are necessary to determine why the system failed but that necessitates a breakdown of the unit. Moreover, the necessary equipment is not available. The manufacturer's representative wants to take the machine back to the factory for further testing. I disagree. I feel that the machine should be stored in a place where no one can get to it without my knowledge and prior approval. Besides, there should be no destructive testing without giving every interested party an opportunity to be present along with an expert. I suggest that since the Medical Examiner's Office is involved, it should store the machine at its facility. The Medical Examiner's investigator nixes that idea but recommends that it be placed in the Police Department's storage room. We agree and the police are called.

When I arrive in my office around 3:30, I find thirteen telephone messages, most of which require a return call. I learn that two cases were settled and a person with a 2:30 appointment showed up and left after waiting about one-half hour. My secretary says that she was very angry.

I dictate a memo to the file concerning the test because I am certain that a lawsuit will be filed. I sort through the telephone messages and mail so I can arrange them according to some priority.

At 4:30 I receive a telephone call from a friend who is being investigated by the FBI. He wants my advice. I make an appointment for the next day. Next I receive a call from a representative of Farmers Insurance Group. He has a question concerning the value of a case and what should be paid to settle it. I recommend a figure. I answer a few letters and review tomorrow's schedule. I realize that I have a deposition scheduled at the same time that I set the appointment for my friend. I call him back but there is no answer. My calendar indicates that I have a trial next week and there are some things that I must do to be ready for it. I make a list. It is now 6:10 and it is dark outside. There is still a lot of work to be done but it will have to wait until tomorrow.

LESLIE COHEN

Disability Law

When I decided to go to law school, it was always to become a "peoples" lawyer. I always wanted to fight for individuals' civil rights. However, when I went to law school, I perceived that fight to involve struggling against racism and sexism, and encroachments on first amendment rights. At that time, little did I know that 12 years later I would actually be fighting discrimination, but for a different group of people—one of the last groups to gain civil rights in our society—persons with serious disabilities or mental illness.

For the last three years, I have been working for a public interest law firm which is the recipient of several federal grants to represent persons with disabilities to be free from abuse and neglect, free from discrimination and to promote access to adequate services and programs. No day is a typical day, but any day could include part of the following:

I discuss with an advocate on how to approach a school district's failure to provide a child with traumatic brain injury appropriate services. Under the federal Individuals with Disabilities Education Act, all school districts are required to provide children with special needs a free and appropriate education including any related services they may need. Should we request a hearing to get the school district to pay for the services of a cognitive trainer to help the child? We decide to submit our expert's report and let the school district respond.

I next speak with an attorney in our office about a pending Americans with Disabilities Act case. Her client, who is deaf, has not been provided interpreter services during required training and in-service meetings at his job. The client is frustrated and feels he can't learn how to do his job better or advance because he is not receiving the technical assistance other workers are. We are in negotiations with the employer and discuss whether providing the client with interpreter services in the future will be enough, or should he receive remedial training and/or compensation for being denied an interpreter for so long.

I receive a phone call that a former client, who had been inappropriately institutionalized at the state hospital for many years. Now he might be returned. Evidently, through lack of appropriate care at a local mental health agency, the client has deteriorated and is in need of hospitalization. I dash off a letter to the local mental health agency telling them of the situation and demanding that they stabilize our client's care so that he can be returned to his community placement.

I then rush off to a meeting of persons discussing proposed legislative changes to the criminal rules concerning the competency to stand trial law. I am concerned that proposed changes may result in incarceration of individuals with mental disability for long periods of time unnecessarily and in contravention of constitutional principles.

There are just a few of the issues I will address on any given day. Representing persons with disabilities involves important civil rights issues. As our jurisprudence begins to address the rights of persons in the United States who have been previously ignored, such as persons with disabilities, gays and lesbians, immigrants, and children, there should be lots of exciting opportunities available for law students to enter public interest law.

MIKE CHIORAZZI

Law Librarian/Legal Information Specialist

To quote a famous 20th century philosopher poet, "Lately it occurs to me, what a long, strange trip it's been."

I entered law school with no real idea exactly what an attorney did, let alone what kind of law I would like to practice. Then, one day in my first year, a light bulb went on. I was being trained in this newfangled thing called Westlaw. I had, what was for me, a profound insight—this computer stuff

is going to be big! That was the extent of my vision.
I never claimed to be particularly deep.

Talking with law school librarians, I found that
several of them had law degrees. As I learned more
about what they did, an idea took hold; after law
school I would go to library school. At worst, I could
delay adulthood for a year; at best, I could find a
career. My decision was not well received by my
family. They had hoped for another F. Lee Bailey
Jr.; they were getting Marian the Librarian.

What do law librarians do? Work in law firms,
corporations, legislative libraries, administrative
agencies, court libraries, law book publishing hous-
es and law school libraries. The field also offers
opportunities to specialize, in areas such as foreign,
comparative and international law, collection development (what to buy to meet an institution's
needs), special collections (rare books), and web
design. There are more law librarians out there
than you might think—the American Association of
Law Libraries boasts over 5000 members.

I work in an academic setting and have found the
work always interesting, varied and challenging.
Starting as a reference librarian, I assisted and
trained library patrons in the use of library materials. One moment it might be members of the public
researching their own legal problems (from barking
dogs to Living Wills), the next a professor interested
in a comprehensive listing of 19th century contract
treatises. I also taught a class on computer assisted
legal research.

Best of all, I get to work for and with law students—an eager and intelligent group, and always interesting.

More and more law firms are hiring librarians to supervise their information technology infrastructure and to provide highly specialized expertise in in a wide array of areas of practice (some examples: complex litigation, securities law, environmental law, government contracts and intellectual property).

With the Internet becoming increasing more important, the demand for librarians, and their knowledge of cutting edge technologies, will surely increase. What the Internet needs is a good librarian.

Beginning law school, I never in my wildest dreams imagined a career as a law librarian. It's not for everyone, but since I have thoroughly enjoyed the long, strange trip I've never looked back.And, after a while, even my family came to agree that I made a great decision.

WILLIAM C. CANBY, JR.

Federal Appeals Judge

My work cycle is monthly, not daily. One week a month I travel to another city to hear appellate arguments. The other three weeks I am home in chambers dealing with the results of those arguments.

An Argument Day. I arrive at the courthouse where I am supplied with a desk. I have read the briefs for today's arguments during the past week, and now review bench memos prepared by my law clerks. The bench memos summarize the facts and analyze the legal issues.

After half an hour I leave for the robing room, where I meet the other two judges assigned to hear cases with me that day. We enter the courtroom and the presiding judge calls the calendar. The first case is a criminal appeal. Was there probable cause for the search that revealed the cocaine? That determination is highly factual, and all three of us ask questions about the evidence presented at the suppression hearing.

The next case came from the National Labor Relations Board. Was there substantial evidence to support the Board's determination that a union steward was fired for union activity? He had been guilty of some unrelated discipline infractions. When there are mixed motives for firing, what is the test to determine whether the firing was permissible?

We continue through the calendar, hearing either 15 or 30 minute arguments per side in each case. I find that I am on edge during the arguments, both because I find arguments exciting and because I don't want to miss what is said or pass up the opportunity to inject my own questions. We continue through the calendar, without stopping to rule or recess. We hear an admiralty case (man overboard), a diversity case (breach of contract), and an antitrust case (vertical conspiracy).

We return to the robing room to discuss the cases. Because I have least seniority, I give my views first. Some cases are quickly disposed of; the search was legal and the conviction can be affirmed in a short memorandum. We disagree about the antitrust case; that one will take a long time, require an opinion, and I may dissent. The presiding judge makes the writing assignments and we all go to lunch. As I relax I am reminded that arguments are the most satisfying but tiring part of my job. I will spend the rest of the afternoon dictating notes of this morning's cases and getting ready for tomorrow's calendar.

A Day in Chambers. I begin by going through the morning mail, good and bad. Some are memos from other judges concurring in opinions I have drafted and circulated, almost invariably with minor suggestions or corrections. One memo from another judge suggests that one of my proposed opinions is seriously off track. I will have to go back through the opinion, read the cases the other judge cites, and either make changes or risk his dissent. Next I review two proposed opinions by judges in cases where I was a member of the panel; they were heard six weeks ago. I assign each to one of my three law clerks for review. Each will come back to me with a memorandum commenting on the draft.

I next work on the pile of proposed opinions that have come back from my clerks with such memoranda. I go through each opinion, read a case or two if crucial, and check my notes from argument against the opinion. I review my clerks' comments.

I then draft a memorandum to the other judge, perhaps concurring, including suggestions for change and noting possible problems.

I meet with my secretary and law clerks together to go over the work in the office. How many opinions are in the mill, and how late they are? Clerks are making initial drafts of almost all of them; I am working on one or two from scratch. We review assignments of bench memos for next month's arguments, and set deadlines for them.

Finally, I get to work on an opinion I am writing: Indian law. I have been working on it off and on for six weeks, and find it difficult and challenging. Ideas for it keep coming up when I am doing other things, and I use some of them. Soon I will float it to my colleagues; eventually it will come down, I hope the way I want it to. *The result matters to a lot of people.* Sometimes it is hard to see that fact behind all the paper in the office, but it comes to the surface every so often. And that makes all the matter to me.

BARBARA SATTLER

Criminal Defense, Solo Practice

Growing up in the 50's, I used to watch Perry Mason and think about how great it must be to be a criminal defense attorney. At the time it was only a dream because I didn't know any lawyers, no one in my family had ever graduated from college, and all the lawyers I saw on TV were men. By the mid–70's the world had changed considerably. After living through the 60's and earning a BA and MA, I found myself working as a counselor in a state agency feeling extremely frustrated because my efforts to help people seemed fruitless due to bureaucracy and regulations.

At the old age of 29, I revived the long-dormant idea to going to law school. Now fifteen years later, after trying over a hundred cases including murder, terrorism, and dog abuse, I am a sole-practitioner doing criminal defense, and trying to raise a child. To my surprise I often do more counseling than legal work and still butt my head against a system that seems unresponsive, hostile and unconcerned with individual justice. Often my most valuable service to a client is listening or hand-holding, rather than giving legal services.

With all its frustrations, I wouldn't give up criminal defense or private practice.

Criminal defense work is fast-paced and exhilarating. People ask me all the time, "How can you represent those people and sleep at night?" Although sometimes the people I represent are stupid, uneducated, and may have committed a heinous act, the system is so badly skewed, to punish and to expedite, that the majority of the time the punishment so outweighs the crime that representation is easy. Someone once said a criminal defense lawyer sees "bad" people at their best; a divorce lawyer sees "good" people at their worst. What is difficult for me is dealing with prosecutors who seem more concerned with statistics, and judges who seem more concerned with expediting their calendar than with finding what justice is, or trying to solve a real social problem.

At the end of a trial which didn't go well, I may question my performance (perhaps I could have been better, but I never question that my client deserves my best).

On a typical day, before going to the office, I have to figure out with my husband who will take and pick up our son at daycare and arrange for his other daily activities. Because I run a business (and employ a full-time secretary, part-time attorney, and other support staff), often many hours in the day are filled with administrative matters such as paying bills, deciding what books and supplies are needed or can be put off, fighting with the IRS, and my version of billable hours. These are problems neither law school nor my five years as a public defender ever prepared me for.

I usually handle around twenty active cases (not including inactive appeals or cases which are in other stages of waiting) which typically include DUI's, drug cases, child molestation and rape, domestic violence, and murder. On a typical day I talk to clients (this is where the counseling comes in), write motions, write letters begging for, or explaining, why a certain deal or plea bargain should be given, go to court hearings, interview witnesses, do research and speak with other lawyers, probation officers, or police officers. Sometimes I don't have time to eat lunch or make a personal call.

I will never forget the first time I head the words "not guilty," nor the first time I heard "not guilty," in a murder case. I still feel a thrill seeing my name in print or my picture on TV (at least on a good hair day) and, of course, winning a case. However, over time what has provided the most satisfaction and pride is receiving cards from clients who are writing to thank me, not because of the result (which sometimes is not good), but because they know I fought hard, did my best, and, most importantly, cared.

JANE ANON

Holiday Letter from Second–Year Associate in Large Firm

Dear Friends & Family:

I am writing you my First Annual Holiday Letter. I apologize that it is emailed to you and not in a letter but I haven't had time to buy a) cards b) stamps or c) to address envelopes. Frankly I'm not sure where my address book is. It may well be buried underneath a pile of laundry. Or leftover take-out. Considering how rarely I am home, you would think my apartment would be cleaner, but quite the opposite: I tend to think when I do have time off, I deserve to spend it resting, not tidying.

This has been a year of ups and downs for the family. I should point out that the family consists of me, my five plants, my possible rodent problem (see take-out containers, supra), and all the motions I have given birth to this year. The motion family has been a mixed bag. Back at the beginning of the year I was able to really nurture them and they turned into fine upstanding citizens with a command of the facts, attention to deal, and real persuasive skills. They were winners. But then, I don't know, people wanted me to write more and more of them, and their gestation periods grew very short. Now people seem to want me to write a motion in about a day, or perhaps six hours. All I can say is they're just asking for crack babies.

I know what you're thinking, that this is a pretty pathetic holiday letter. It doesn't have any PEO-PLE in it, you're saying. Why is she talking about her motions like they are her children? Let me explain. You see, here at the Firm, we learn you don't need to have people in your life to be happy! In fact, the people you deal with—opposing counsel—make you want to have even less contact with people, unless it's contact between them and the grille of your car. The only people you need in your life are those on your Team. If you have others in your life, they might not understand why you need to work on Christmas Day. And your birthday. For example, the Firm fed-exed work to me at my parents' house the day after Thanksgiving last year. Perhaps Fed Ex doesn't deliver on Thanksgiving itself.

Nevertheless, this year I learned a great deal. I made three court appearances, took two depositions, and wrote seven hundred motions. I have learned that Receiving a Fax is almost always a bad thing. I have learned that if you manage to stay awake past 3am or so, you get a second wind and feel like you've slept. I have learned that it is better to work on Sunday because you are less distracted. I have learned that if you stop exercising altogether you don't get fat right away but one day you wonder what happened to your butt.

And I learned that while practicing for a big firm can sometimes be very hard, it can also be great. Winning is great. I have written some motions that have had big impacts, and the partners here are very good about giving credit where credit is due. It is a fantastic feeling to know that your work and ideas and writing and research convinced a judge to rule for you. It is good to work with people who are extremely smart; I am learning a lot from them and feel like my writing has improved immensely. I like having responsibility and figuring out hard-to-solve problems. I like having clients that people have heard of. On the other hand, I worry I should be using my law degree to help people more, not corporations. I know there are pro bono opportunities, but I never seem to have enough time. Overall, I enjoy the intellectual challenge of the work and think my cases pose interesting challenges.

And I learned that my friends and family are pretty patient with me, even though I never see them. I keep promising I'll call soon. When things slow down. Soon, I promise. Right after I finish this motion.

ANDY SILVERMAN

Legal Aid

It is 9 a.m. I arrived at work awhile ago. The waiting room is filling up and it is my day to be "on."

Being "on" in the legal services parlance signifies your day to do intake interviews. It is the first time the client talks to a lawyer. Such days generally amount to 10 to 15 of these encounters ... the real guts of a legal services practice. I know it is a day that I will get no other work done but seeing clients.

The phone rings ... it is the intake worker informing me that my first client is ready. I am now officially "on" and the stream of clients may go on all day, one right after another.

A young woman with a three-year-old tagging along walks into my office. After the introductions, I go for the extra legal pad and colored pens I always have ready and hand them to the child. I know that if the interview is going to be at all meaningful I have to keep the child happy and busy.

The woman tells me that she is two months behind in rent and the landlord has sent her an eviction notice. She has been out-of-work for the past four months and her ex-husband who she cannot find has not paid child support for the past year. Her problems sound overwhelming. Where do I start? Is there anything legally I can do?

Well, being a lawyer, my initial reaction is to think of legal remedies, the law school approach to the problem. Is there a violation of the landlord-tenant law? Is the eviction notice proper? Will she have any defenses to a possible unlawful detainer action? I start going down this road and quickly realize she can no longer afford this apartment and all she wants is time to find suitable but cheaper housing for her and her child. A phone call to the landlord from me, the lawyer, might do it. She tried the day before and failed. I call and the landlord reluctantly agrees. And another call to a friend in the public housing office helps her cut through the bureaucratic maze to find new housing. She leaves a bit relieved.

Before my next client I think about whether I am a lawyer or a social worker. Did my last client need a lawyer? Or did I do for her just what a corporate attorney does for the corporation president: identify the true problem and find the easiest and fastest way to resolve it. Well, it does not matter, I helped someone and that's all that really counts.

No more time to reflect, the next client is standing at the door. He is a man in his 50's who works part-time as a laborer. He had purchased an insurance policy because of a newspaper advertisement that had made generous promises. But when he became ill, the company said his claim was not covered. Sounds like a legal problem and one that another lawyer in the office may be interested in pursuing. She has handled similar problems and is looking for "the" case to litigate. This may be the one. I get the facts and tell the client we will be in contact. I will talk to the other lawyer tomorrow when I am "off" intake.

Legal problems keep flowing in all day. Food stamp cutoffs, car repossessions, housing foreclosures, there is no end. They have one common ingredient: a person in trouble that needs help. That personal side of legal services keeps me going. It is frustrating; it is gratifying; it is being a legal services attorney.

At the end of the day an older woman walks into my office as my final intake of the day. She does not speak English well but gets across that her son is in the county jail. My first reaction is that she has a criminal problem which legal aid lawyers do not handle. In my tired state I think that I may be able to get rid of this problem quickly. But I hear her out and become fascinated. I remain after closing hours talking to her about her son's complaints about the conditions in the jail. I have heard about that "awful jail" for years but now may have a real, live client that wants to do something about it. She tells me that her son and others in the jail would like to talk to a lawyer about such a suit. I promise her I will see her son tomorrow. It all seems worth it.

JAMIE RATNER

Government Attorney

When I was in law school, I did not have any definitive plan for what I was going to do when I got out. I ended up taking a job with the Transportation Section of the Antitrust Division of the U.S. Department of Justice. I did not have a lifelong dream to prosecute, and in fact philosophically I was not inclined to be a prosecutor. But the job was wonderful. It gave me an opportunity to see from the inside how the U.S. government behaves, it gave me a chance to live and work in Washington, D.C. (which is a fascinating place to live for awhile, although not necessarily a place to ultimately settle down), and it gave me a chance to practice law in a setting where the client was only good analysis and the right thing to do.

Practicing law for the government is a unique thing, but in many ways I consider it the only way to practice law. Money is not the issue: getting it right is the issue. If you think something should be done, you do something. If you think something should not be pursued, you recommend dropping it. Sure, it is a little hard on your stomach lining when you are asked to cross-examine a well-known economist during an airline merger hearing at the Civil Aeronautics Board before you have found out whether you passed the bar. True, you spend a lot of nights at the office when a merger of the Southern Pacific and Santa Fe Railroads is dropped in your lap and you and another lawyer are told that the two of you are the two people in the country responsible for making sure that the railroad industry in the western United States remains competitive.

But one great thing about practicing law for the government is that very early on, you get responsibility and great work. If you accept that responsibility and do your work properly, you can accomplish a lot. Your job makes you the adult in charge. You investigate and prosecute price fixers who are taking money from ordinary consumers. You make sure mergers don't give a firm so much power that there will be significant harm to the economy. You help to develop coherent policies concerning deregulation of the airline industry. You write Senators explaining the economic and legal implications of proposed legislation and you may even help negotiate treaties.

I will never forget the people. Most of us, non-lawyer and lawyer alike, were there because they liked the work and cared about it, and we were all in it together rather than competitors for some mythical status on some hierarchy. Usually we worked in staffs of two or three. We traveled together, investigated together, threw frisbees down the hall shattering everyone's name plates, jointly wrote briefs and memos and stuck our own brand of humor in the footnotes, played softball, fought with the front office and opposing counsel, and spent a lot of time in that strange state which is relaxation and intensity and humor and frustration all combined in the same space at the same time. Some of my colleagues even married each other. Some of the smartest, most capable, and funniest people I have met in my life I had the opportunity to work with at Justice, and some of them remain my closest friends.

I don't want to lie to you—while I treasured my time in Washington, working for the government in Washington, D.C. can also drive you to the brink. The tourist traffic around the White House gets on your nerves when you are running a grand jury at the federal courthouse and you are a little late. Or you may not have the same political bent as the people in charge. Political appointees who do not have much of a clue can be your supervisors. (What you learn to do in such a situation is to explain everything fully in an effective and persuasive way; I used to feel confident that if I had managed to explain the matter to some of the people in our front office, persuading a commission of experts or a judge would be quite easy by comparison.)

Practicing law for the government offers a large reward. It isn't monetary; it is something more lasting. You can get training, you can get experience, you can make it a career if you want, you can get things done, and you have an opportunity to accomplish things that improve the quality of life for others in the world, which is what being a lawyer is really all about.

BILL BOYD

Law Professor

It's just after noon. The bluebooks will be delivered shortly. I wonder how the students have done. Was the exam too difficult? Too easy? Was it fair? If not, it wasn't for lack of effort.

I don't look forward to grading exams. Not many of us do. As the Dean is fond of quipping, "Exam grading is what we get paid for. The rest is fun." In any event, most of us worry about the grading. We know the process is far from scientific. The goal is to reduce the margin for error—to design a test that measures a student's command of the subject matter as comprehensively as time permits. This is no modest goal.

The exam today is in bankruptcy. Bankruptcy is a two-hour course. Frankly, that is not enough time to cover such a complicated body of substantive law and procedure. But this can be said about most courses. Perhaps I tried to cover too much. I continually ask myself what it is that students need to know so they can begin to deal intelligently with the range of bankruptcy issues they are likely to confront in practice. Realistically, how many of them will have to worry about the role of a 1111(b)(2) election in a "cram down" of a Chapter 11 plan? But then, can any self-respecting course in bankruptcy not expose students to such mystifying concepts?

It's a difficult line to draw. A well-conceived course is one that accommodates the realities of the limits of time and the needs of most students with the crush of information contained in most areas of the law.

Most of us strive to make our exams reflect this accommodation. The exam should test what we have judged to be important. Obviously, it isn't feasible or necessary to test for everything we cover. But a fair cross-section of the material should be implicated. The trick is to weigh the questions commensurately with the time and attention given the particular point or points in class.

Contrary to what students are inclined to believe, the exam isn't intended to "do in" a certain percentage of students. There are no "traps" aimed at tripping up the unwary. Nothing would please us more if all the students did well. After all, their level of performance reflects upon the quality of our teaching.

We are sensitive to the imperfections in the examination process. We labor hard to compensate. We look for clues that reinforce what the "raw scores" suggest is a good, or a bad, performance. We tend to resolve doubts in a student's favor. It isn't unusual for a teacher to overlook an important omission, or even significant mistake, and to assign an A or B grade to an exam that otherwise is exceptionally good. In such cases we attribute the omission or error to test design or exam pressure.

We don't want students to do poorly. Poor performances present perhaps the greatest difficulty. What accounts for the poor performance? Was it the test? Most of us reread the "bad" exams. We don't want to "ding" a student. We examine carefully for "clues." Is there a problem with completeness? Does it appear that the student seriously misallocated his or her time? Is the deficiency in the depth or accuracy of analysis? Has the student missed or mistreated even the most fundamental of issues? Is the performance truly unsatisfactory.

Well, here they are. Let's see how they've done. Hmm. OK. Not bad. What? You didn't learn that in my class. Oh, that's better. What explains the earlier blunder? Hey, this is not bad at all. Good point. I hadn't thought about it quite that way myself. Whoops. You can't mean that. Did you misread the question? I see what you did. You were assuming the creditor was only partially secured. Too bad. But the analysis is correct given your assumption. Let's see now. You were clearly wrong on the conversion issue. And you misread one part of the question. But you've hit most of the major points. Some interesting analysis. Very respectable blue-book.

DEBORAH BERNINI

Judge—Trial Court

I have only been on the bench for six months, so I begin each morning by asking myself, "Is this the morning I will succumb to 'Black Robe Disease'?" I spent a good deal of my fourteen years as a litigator criticizing the boneheaded, biased, and cowardly decisions of the judges I appeared before. I had no trouble challenging their authority. Now I feel as if I have stepped through the Looking Glass.

I am amazed at how difficult it can be to "do the right thing" and how unclear the answers often are. I often feel like a first year law student, wanting to yell at the professor, "So what's the damn answer?" Evidentiary rulings are easy, as are most legal rulings. It is the questions of fact that make me pause. Decisions regarding credibility, intent, sincerity, remorse, motivation, fear, and anger are what make the courtroom one of my favorite places to be, but are also what make this job so difficult. I realize that decisiveness is one of the most appreciated qualities in a judge, but I am less quick to judge other human beings in my formal role as judge, than I ever have been in my personal life.

My biggest problem is bad lawyers. I do not mean inexperienced, but rather those who are unprepared, ignorant of the law, or some combination of the two. I have lost my patience with three lawyers in my brief tenure, and all three were criminal defense lawyers whose unpreparedness resulted in costly prices paid by their clients. Having spent most of my lawyer years as a public defender, I struggle with my desire to interrupt or intervene when a defense lawyer appears to be blowing it. Perhaps I am simply not aware of what the lawyer's tactics; perhaps my "help" is not welcome. But there are times when I know major mistakes are being made. If I feel that an accused's rights are going down the toilet, I get involved. No lawyer's ego, theory of the case, or reputation is more important to me than the right of a Defendant to get a fair trial.

I wish that lawyers talked less and said more. I cannot believe how many attorneys can talk for over thirty minutes before they tell you why they are there and what they want. I also now understand why judges fall asleep during trials. I have actually drawn blood digging my nails into the palms of my hands in an attempt to appear alert while trial lawyers waxed eloquent to a jury. Everyone in the courtroom appreciates a lawyer who can get to the point: the clerk, the court reporter, the judge, and especially the jury.

Get to the point and watch your reputation. A trial lawyer's reputation is everything. It means more than ability or talent. The best reputation is that you are honest, you quote the law correctly, and you don't play disclosure games with your opponents. Judges talk among themselves and messing up with one judge will quickly be held against you by others. That doesn't mean that you should never challenge a judge. But pick your fights carefully, find some law that backs you up, and always start with the comment: "With all due respect, your honor." It will at least give you limited immunity for any carefully disguised insults you plan.

I have the greatest job in the world. I get to spend my days in the courtroom, my favorite place to be. My goal is to see that justice is done, and sometimes I see that goal reached. I get to work hard, meet interesting people, watch talented lawyers practice their craft (sometimes), and explain to the public how important our system of justice is—and at the end of each day I go home without the worries and burdens of the trial attorney who constantly wonders if some issue was missed, if some deadline was forgotten.

I hope I always remember how hard it is to be a trial attorney. Maybe I don't have to succumb to the Disease.

PAUL BENNETT

Representing Children

I represent children in Juvenile Court who have been removed from their homes by Child Protective

Services. Their parents may have been neglectful, abusive, or too indisposed to care for them. Many parents have a drug or alcohol problem. Some have mental health problems. Some just need a little help to get through bad times. When the children cannot safely stay with their parents, they become wards of the Court. The Court then makes many significant decisions affecting their lives: where they live, with whom, how often they see their parents, when they can return safely home.

When I am asked what I do when I represent children, I am reminded of two lines from the Cat Stevens' song, *Father and Son*. In the first line, the Father says to his son: "You're still young, that's your fault, there's so much you have to learn." In the other, the Son replies: "It's always been the same old story. From the moment that I could talk, I was ordered to listen."

The adults in the child welfare system often exhibit a point of view like that of the Father. "What do they know? They are just kids!" And there is some truth to that. Kids have a remarkable capacity to behave like children. They can be stubborn, irrational, impulsive, self-destructive, succumb to peer acceptance, and think only of themselves. Sometimes. (What is the old adage? One teenager, one brain. Two teenagers, half a brain. Three teenagers, no brain.)

On the other hand, sometimes children can have remarkable insights into their situations, their own behaviors and even their parents' behaviors. Kids can know a whole lot more than we think they know. They have important things to say and the adults in the system need to hear what they have to say. So, on behalf of the child in the song, our job is to get others to listen (and I mean really listen) to what these children have to say.

To get others to listen to our child-clients, we have to understand them ourselves. So we spend time with them and listen to what is going on in their lives. Sometimes we are all business. Sometimes we just hang out. But in all cases, we try to pay attention and build trust. We let them know that we work for them—not the other way around. We give them our best advice to help them to make good choices. But they are their choices, not ours. So, in the end, we have to be careful to express their voices, not ours.

It is not always easy. It can be frustrating to figure out what a child is really saying. Sometimes what a child wants makes no sense or is even dangerous. It can be frustrating when we are not effective in getting others to pay attention–especially when a child has something very meaningful to offer. Sometimes, it can be frustrating because the situation is bigger than any of us and all of the choices are second best.

But when it works, when we do our job well, it can be tremendously rewarding to represent a child. We know that we can make a difference in a child's life in a very positive way when we persuade a Judge or a child protective worker to see the situation through the child's perspective. At the very least, we can make the adults in the system pay attention. When we are more effective, we can help the adult decision-makers to make better decisions because they have heard the child's point of view. At our very best, we can help a child weather a most difficult time in their lives.

CHARLES ARES

Law Professor

Teaching law is hard work. I've been at it a long time and keeping up with movements in the law and getting prepared for class seem to take me about as long now as when I started.

But there is another way in which law teaching is hard. The longer I'm in the academic world the more I worry about just what it is that we teach our students. I don't mean "the law" and "the legal method"—we do that better and better all the time. I mean what we teach, mostly implicitly, about the role lawyers are supposed to play. We teach students from the very outset, as we should, that they are to be highly skilled partisans, that they are to be analytical and very skeptical of factual and legal propositions. They learn under our prodding to state the case as strongly in their clients' favor as the credulity of their audience will permit. They may, in fact, learn not only that truth takes many elusive forms but that sometimes it doesn't really exist. Only zealous representation of our client really counts.

I wonder how many students think that the "legal method" involves lying, or at least "massaging" the truth. Many of us who have been in the profession a while don't realize that we may, at least unconsciously, convey the wrong message to neophytes. One of the most heart warming and yet depressing statements I've heard from a law student was recently uttered at the end of my course in Professional Responsibility. On the way out of the classroom, this good and conscientious student said, "I had almost decided I didn't want to be a lawyer because I don't want to lie for people. But now that I've learned we're not supposed to lie for clients, I feel a lot better."

Good people can be good lawyers. It isn't easy, but then preserving one's integrity never is.

INDEX

References are to Pages

449

†